Social Work in Practice

SOCIAL WORK IN PRACTICE

Fourth NASW Symposium

Selected papers / Fourth NASW Professional Symposium on Social Work / October 22-25, 1975, Hollywood-by-the-Sea, Florida

Editors, BERNARD ROSS and S. K. KHINDUKA

NATIONAL ASSOCIATION OF SOCIAL WORKERS

1425 H STREET NW

WASHINGTON, D.C. 20005

Designed by Jeanette Portelli

Copyright © 1976 by the National Association of Social Workers, Inc.
All rights reserved
International Standard Book No.: 0–87101–073–9
Library of Congress Catalog Card No.: 76–39587
NASW Publication No.: CBO–073–C
Printed in U.S.A.

 3

Contents

Editors' Preface

There is a temptation to think of social work as something "good" which those who believe in it should defend while it is making its way in a world which is to some extent hostile to it, or to think of social work as "bad," a palliative in place of justice to the poor, a confused, sentimental, time-and-money-wasting activity which we somehow have to tolerate. Both conceptions are static, failing to take into account that social work is dynamically one with the society of today. It is neither good nor bad; it is fact, to be studied like any other fact in a changing scene.[1]

So wrote Bertha Capen Reynolds, a great social work pioneer. Her point of view is both thought-provoking and pertinent. This publication, growing out of the Fourth Professional Symposium of the National Association of Social Workers, has undertaken to present material covering a spectrum of issues and practice relevant to the profession today. The articles that follow are best not judged as "good" or "bad" but should been seen, as Bertha Reynolds urged, as a slice of current social work thought and practice to be studied in the context of past history and future hopes.

Consistent with the ethos of social work, the title of this book reflects high expectations, but the reasonable reader will realize that the selection of articles was limited by the nature of the papers presented at the symposium. The specific selection was dependent on the good judgment of the members of the Symposium Book Committee: William G. Bell, Walter Dean, and Jessie P. Dowling, and of the coeditors, S. K. Khinduka and Bernard Ross. (The order of the listing of the editors, incidentally, was not the product of reason, but of chance—the flip of a coin.)

That this book has come into being is a result of the persistence, energy, and professional competence of Beatrice Saunders, director of the Department of Publications of NASW. The editors want to express respect, affection, and thanks to her and to our colleagues who constituted the Symposium Book Committee. We hope the authors represented here, as well as readers, will find this volume stimulating and relevant. They

---

[1] Bertha C. Reynolds, *Learning and Teaching in the Practice of Social Work* (New York: Farrar & Rinehart, 1942), pp. 3–4.

may see in this selection of articles evidence of disparate assumptions, inconsistencies, unaccountable conclusions, and untidy thinking and practice; we hope they will also see dedication, feeling and concern, speculative and creative thinking, innovative and skilled practice, and first-rate spirit and leadership. In our judgment, this book illustrates all of the above; it reflects our time and life just as social work reflects our time and life.

—BERNARD ROSS
September 1976 S. K. KHINDUKA

PROFESSIONAL SYMPOSIUM PLANNING COMMITTEE

ELAINE ROTHENBERG, MSS (Chairperson) Dean, School of Social Work, Virginia Commonwealth University, Richmond, Virginia

IRWIN S. BAHL, MA, Social Worker, Callier Hearing and Speech Center, Dallas, Texas

WILLIAM G. BELL, PH.D., Associate Professor, Department of Urban and Regional Planning, Florida State University, Tallahassee, Florida

PAULINE R. COGGS, MA, Assistant Professor, Department of Social Work, University of Wisconsin-Extension, Milwaukee, Wisconsin

JAMES GOODMAN, PH.D., School of Social Work, University of Minnesota, Minneapolis, Minnesota

S. K. KHINDUKA, PH.D., Professor of Social Work, George Warren Brown School of Social Work, Washington University, St. Louis, Missouri

J. JULIAN RIVERA, MSW, Assistant Professor, School of Social Work, Adelphi University, Garden City, New York

BERNARD ROSS, PH.D., Dean, Graduate School of Social Work and Social Research, Bryn Mawr College, Bryn Mawr, Pennsylvania

SUE WHEAT, MSW, Coordinator, School Mental Health Programs, Adams County Mental Health Center, Commerce City, Colorado

Contributors

Positions at the time of the symposium (October 1975)

BUDD BELL, MA, Legislative Chairperson, Florida Chapter of the National Association of Social Workers, Tallahassee, Florida

WILLIAM G. BELL, PH.D., Associate Professor, Department of Urban and Regional Planning, Florida State University, Tallahassee, Florida

JANE BIERDEMAN, MSW, Chief Social Worker, Social Service Department, Fulton State Hospital, Fulton, Missouri

MARTIN BLOOM, PH.D., Professor, George Warren Brown School of Social Work, Washington University, St. Louis, Missouri

BARBARA S. BROCKWAY, PH.D., Assistant Professor, School of Social Work and Department of Family Medicine and Practice, University of Wisconsin-Madison, Wisconsin

WILLIAM BUTTERFIELD, PH.D., Assistant Dean, George Warren Brown School of Social Work, Washington University, St. Louis, Missouri

JOHN M. DALEY, DSW, Associate Professor, Graduate School of Social Work, University of Texas at Arlington, Arlington, Texas

DONALD T. DICKSON, JD, PH.D., Associate Professor, Graduate School of Social Work, Rutgers University, New Brunswick, New Jersey

LAURA EPSTEIN, MA, Associate Professor, School of Social Service Administration, University of Chicago, Chicago, Illinois

KATHLEEN FITZGIBBONS, MSSW, Behavioral Social Worker, South Lake Clinic, Minnetonka, Minnesota

EILEEN D. GAMBRILL, PH.D., Associate Professor, School of Social Welfare, University of California, Berkeley, California

MITCHELL I. GINSBERG, MA, Dean, School of Social Work, Columbia University, New York, New York

BRADLEY GOOGINS, MSW, Assistant Professor, Community Organization/Social Planning, Graduate School of Social Work, Boston College, Chestnut Hill, Massachusetts

SHIMON S. GOTTSCHALK, PH.D., Associate Professor, School of Social Work, Florida State University, Tallahassee, Florida

ADRIENNE AHLGREN HAEUSER, MSSW, Assistant Professor, School of Social Welfare, University of Wisconsin-Milwaukee, and Center for Social Service, University of Wisconsin-Extension, Milwaukee, Wisconsin

CAROL HOLTON, MSW, Assistant Professor, University of Wisconsin-Extension, Center for Social Service, Milwaukee, Wisconsin

BETTY S. JOHNSON, MSW, Associate Professor, Center for Social Service, University of Wisconsin-Extension, Milwaukee, Wisconsin

PAUL K. H. KIM, DSW, Assistant Professor, College of Social Professions, University of Kentucky, Lexington, Kentucky

HAROLD LEWIS, DSW, Dean, School of Social Work, Hunter College, City University of New York, New York, New York

CAROL H. MEYER, DSW, Professor of Social Work, School of Social Work, Columbia University, New York, New York

MARJORIE D. MOSKOL, MSSS, Executive Director, Professional Services for Women, Inc., and Assistant Project Director, Rhode Island Consortium for Continuing Education in Social Welfare, Rhode Island College, Providence, Rhode Island

WILLIAM K. MOTLONG, MSW, Clinical Director, Bremen Township Committee on Youth, Oak Forest, Illinois

DOLORES G. NORTON, PH.D., Associate Professor, Graduate School of Social Work and Social Research, Bryn Mawr College, Bryn Mawr, Pennsylvania

ROBERT M. RYAN, DSW, Associate Professor, College of Social Work, Ohio State University, Columbus, Ohio

ROSEMARY C. SARRI, PH.D., Professor of Social Work, School of Social Work, University of Michigan, Ann Arbor, Michigan

MICHAEL B. SCHWARTZ, DSW, Associate Professor, Division of Child Psychiatry, Department of Psychiatry, School of Medicine, Southern Illinois University, and Psychotherapist, Private Practice, Springfield, Illinois

ARAMINTA SMITH, MSW, Assistant Professor of Social Work, School of Social Work, University of Missouri, Columbia, Missouri

BARBARA BRYANT SOLOMON, DSW, Professor, School of Social Work, University of Southern California, Los Angeles, California

LEONARD SZYMCZAK, MSW, Family Therapist, Bremen Township Committee on Youth, Oak Forest, Illinois

EMANUEL TROPP, MSSW, Professor, School of Social Work, Virginia Commonwealth University, Richmond, Virginia

JOYCE S. WANDO, MSW, Staff Development Coordinator, State of Florida, Division of Health and Rehabilitative Services, Jacksonville, Florida

KENNARD W. WELLONS, DSW, Associate Professor, College of Social Professions, University of Kentucky, Lexington, Kentucky

JUDITH WERKING, MSSW, Counselor and Clinical Instructor in Primary Care, School of Medicine, University of Wisconsin-Madison, Wisconsin

Part I:

Theory and

Practice

The Structure of
Professional Skill

HAROLD LEWIS

Dictionary definitions of "skill" are as helpful to an understanding of the
social work profession's application of this concept as are false teeth to a
mummy. The craftsmanship evident in their manufacture and their ability to withstand the ravages of time can be admired, but those definitions
serve no practical purpose. Unfortunately, the definitions that appear in
the professional literature are only slightly more useful. They all start
with an awareness of the complexity of the concept when applied to
actions demanding full concentration.[1] But they somehow contrive to separate knowledge, or value, or style dimensions from the skill that contains them, thus reducing skill to a technique. The result of these separa-
tions and uneven emphases is to locate theory or purpose or both outside
skill.[2]

Skill is directly observable in the act; it is not the actor or the product.
Moreover, its essentials must be understood in concert with each other.[3]
When reference is made to "knowledge and skill," or "knowledge, values,
and skill," which is frequently the case in the literature, support is given
to the misleading notion that skill itself does not encompass knowledge
and values. One unfortunate by-product of this erroneous view has been
the prevalence of a belief that the cognitive and emotive are separable
in the act and in the actors. Some writers have gone so far as to argue
that different "types" inhabit the profession: the researchers, scientific
types who do the thinking, and the artists, imaginative types who do the
feeling.[4] Such misleading formulations are costly to the profession. They
retard the development of sound education for practice.

There is consensus among those who write about skill that skill is
informed and therefore knowledge-based and that skill is manifest in action requiring the implementation of a method or procedure. There is
less agreement that skill is intentioned and therefore value-laden and
that it is idiosyncratic, bearing the attraction of institutional and individual styles. In the author's view, knowledge, action, intentions and

values, and style are essential dimensions of skill that need to be understood jointly. In the discussion that follows, these dimensions are considered in detail to provide a substantive view of the content of skill and a framework for judging degrees of skill.

KNOWLEDGE

Uninformed practice is usually recognized by the nonsystematic, unpredictable behavior that characterizes its performance. Chance plays the major role in accounting for the results achieved. Sustained effort is justified by faith and fate, with fact and fiction indistinguishable in the practitioner's report on what does or does not work and why. If you ask a worker what led him to do what he did and he cites intuition, insight, and the sign of the zodiac as reasons, you have cause for concern. Theory and reasoned association between the known and the expected are alien to him. Unlike the skilled practitioner who will entertain a hypothesis even when uncertain as to its truth, the uninformed worker entertains none, often accepting logically indefensible propositions as truths. For the unskilled worker, certainty often represents his right to be wrong at the top of his voice.

It is not necessary for practitioners to be equally knowing to assure a useful practice. The casework supervisor and the case aide, for example, may do equally well in helping a client complete an application for homemaker services. If both follow the rules that assure appropriate action in a well-defined request for help, a systematic and predictable behavior should follow. Agency manuals often provide a set of rules that define a technical level of practice, and every novice appreciates the support such manuals provide during their induction into a service program. In time, these rules help generate a habituated behavior in the worker who applies them because they can be followed with minimal need for personal judgment. For this reason, technologies that are the residuals of considerable skillful practice require little professional judgment and therefore minimal skill in their application. It is unnecessary for a practitioner to be professionally informed when behavior is prescribed. In such a circumstance, the decision to use the technology, not the application of the technique itself, demands a professionally skilled activity. Knowing how to use the phone and knowing when to use it both involve judgments, but of a different order. Knowing what to say in response to a distress phone call in a suicide prevention center involves certain judgments, which differ from the kind of judgment needed in answering inquiries about available agency services.

Similarly, four levels of intellectual demand in complex judgments can be differentiated. At the simplest level, as when a program aide assigns children to seats in the day care center bus, a rule can be followed with a minimal requirement for worker judgment. At the next level, to choose among rules—as when assigning work loads to professional staff—relevant propositions that anticipate consequences must inform the choice. At the third level, when the task requires a choice among propositions— as when allocating limited resources to competing programs—it helps to have some understanding of the theory or theories that can sequence these propositions and their related programs in some priority order. Finally, if the need is to choose among theories—as when psychodynamic, behavioral, and existential modes of helping are proposed as the methods of choice for an agency's practice—an understanding of what is known and not explained by a particular theory, as well as what is known and explained by alternative theories, is essential. In brief, degrees of complexity in judgment can be determined by the type of intellectual effort required.

The intellectual work can be differentiated further if the reasoning that such work entails is considered. For example, when routine activities are required—as when a worker identifies, describes, and classifies a range of evidence that meets the legal definition of neglect—the task calls for an enumeration of alternatives from which choices will be made. This expectation asks the worker to list what can be ascertained, including all known possibilities. When no clear routine is evident and propositions are required to inform the activities, the worker is expected to order the alternatives on some scale of priority.

In the neglect situation, the worker is required to order the range of alternative actions that could be considered likely to provide protection for the child and assist the family in its efforts to alter the neglectful behavior. This task requires the worker to conceive of appropriate criteria for ordering choices, to weight the criteria on the basis of available evidences and to sequence alternatives, to recognize and take into account the intercorrelations that influence the sequencing of alternatives, and finally, to anticipate over time the probable changes in priorities that would follow their implementation. In addition to identification, description, and classification, the worker must have a grasp of typologies, knowledge of the alternatives for intervention, and an ability to scale the mix of both the typologies of conditions deemed neglectful and the type of intervention deemed appropriate. Thus far, he will have identified neglect and will have classified the neglect into, possibly, three major categories— physical, emotional, and supervisory.

The worker may also have classified alternatives for action to protect the child to include counseling, along with one of the following: (1) providing a homemaker, (2) removing the child to the custody of a competent relative, (3) placing the child in a temporary shelter, or (4) remanding the child to the custody of the court to assure appropriate supervision. Weighting the areas of neglect and the alternative care arrangements, the worker may feel that alternative four is the only one likely to effect a change in the child's situation. But if that alternative is not possible, alternatives two, three, and one, in that order, should be pursued. Finally, having chosen the order, the worker must decide to act on the alternatives in the order specified. In addition to a rationale explaining how the particular intervention will yield the desired result, this decision will require, for example, knowledge of the status of the court calendar, the attitude of the sitting judge, and the alternatives available to the court—all the elements which influence the chances that the court will support a judgment of neglect requiring removal.

The worker's decision to act is informed by judgments, but more is required. He must believe that the judgments he has made have produced the basis for a decision. He must conclude that the moment for decision has arrived because all possible explanations of observed evidence have been considered and closure on choices is timely and appropriate. Obviously, such a decision cannot be made without relating action to the wider setting of the practice.

Other factors in addition to intellectual factors contribute to the difficulties encountered in specific situations requiring judgment. For example, incomplete information, the mood and temper of the person judging, and the environment in which the judgment is made all contribute to difficulty in arriving at sound judgments. But it is essential that difficulty in making judgments not be confused with the intrinsic complexity of the judgment. It is possible for both the simplest and the most complex judgment to encounter similar difficulties. Nevertheless, the level of practice skill will be judged in part by the cognitive ability required, under normal conditions, to properly inform the practice.

ACTION

Technique is the aspect of skill basic to its action dimension. Technique involves the worker in an orderly procedure designed to accomplish a desired aim. Knowing "what" and "where" may orient the worker to the tasks, but without mastery of the "how" of implementation, the performance will not come off. Like the electronics theorist who cannot repair his own hi-fi set, the scholar who knows all about helping and theories of helping may be more able to receive help than to give it.

Sets of techniques are sometimes constituted as methods. Methods acculturate the practitioner to the profession and its practice in a pervasive and fundamental way. In their technical attributes, methods transmit to the action the accumulated and tested wisdom of the past. Every technical tool has years of experience, experiment, discovery, and intervention invested in it. To the novice, who may be totally unaware of this investment, an agency admission form may bring a level of method sophistication he could hardly achieve so rapidly and accurately from any other learning opportunity.

It is this power of the technical in method that makes techniques most attractive to those who seek facile solutions to difficult problems in uncertain situations. For example, the checklist syndrome, the listing and totaling of problems as a magic substitute for diagnosis, has developed in recent years. The professional skill associated with action in uncertain situations, however, is not to be found in such a technique. A skilled professional must master techniques, but in addition must be competent in methods that use these techniques and in the design of a program of intervention utilizing appropriate methods.

Tools useful for technical work take many forms: physical, mental, emotional, or combinations of the three. They may be as ordinary as a checklist or a registration card or as complex as a computer, a calculus, or a high level of self-awareness. It is not the form of a tool and the difficulty in its use that marks the person who uses it as a professional: Action skills are evident in the judgments entailed in the design and appropriate application of the technique that utilizes the tools.

A practice that is deficient in technical tools is more dependent on professional judgments than a practice not so deficient. The advent of drugs and complex instrumentation in diagnostic and treatment procedures has generated a number of technical specialties in medicine, which has opened up to nonmedical personnel a number of tasks formerly seen as the doctor's alone. Far fewer technical advances have been achieved in social work. As more is known about the administrative, relational, and learning elements in the helping methods used by the profession, social workers may expect that important technologies will develop; technicians will perform many of the tasks currently calling for professional decisions and their informed judgments.

INTENTIONS AND VALUES

The intentional character of skill is evident in what is favored or disfavored in its application. When a worker engages in some sensible action, the effort seeks the realization of something worthwhile or the avoidance of something undesirable. The child, for example, is removed from a threatening home situation to provide a more caring milieu and to avoid the dangers to which he would otherwise be exposed. The problem is that the worker's intentions may be subscribed to without ever appearing in the product resulting from the effort expended. Substitute care or an institution, for example, may prove more damaging than the child's own home. In social work practice, the ability to avoid this separation of intent and result is an important measure of professional skill.

A skilled practitioner would therefore be one whose practice evidences behaviors that assure the presence of value-informed intentions in the service he provides. Such a practitioner knows and can communicate the ethical imperatives that guide intentions. He can enumerate the oughts, shoulds, musts, and shalls that circumscribe the permissible limits of innovation and creativity in seeking to realize the hoped-for consequences of his effort. In addition, this worker evidences the ability to imagine and apply unique and original responses to a request for service; he will explore the "possible" contained within the constraints of the ethical.

It is necessary to assume that recipients of service bring their own intentions to their contacts with workers. Part of professional skill is evident in the worker's capacity for incorporating the recipient's expectation into the definition of intention that guides his practice. When the resource and sanction for service are institutional, a similar requirement holds for the organization's expectations. Obviously the worker's tasks in seeking to assure the presence of value-informed intentions in the service he provides will vary in complexity. These variations can serve as a value-related measure of the degree of skill involved in practice.

At the simplest level, when the worker follows rule-governed directives, no value component would seem to be involved. For example, instructions to clear with the social service exchange; to ask for the names of other agencies or professional persons helping with the need identified; or to note all sources of support, financial or otherwise, that the client now depends on do not carry any clear intention other than to gather information. What is overlooked in such activities is the commanding, in addition to the directing, nature of the rule. You shall, must, will, do these things is implicit in each instruction. When the practitioner seeks the justification for the command, it is not found in the if–then propositions that inform the directives. Rather, the justification will be located in an ethical imperative related to some fundamental value that underpins the goals of the service.

Thus, at the more complex level, when principles of practice combine a theory-based proposition with an ethically justified commendation, the judgment required of workers is more difficult. (Commendation refers to the oughts, shalls, musts, and shoulds that appear in principles intended to guide a practice, mandating behavior in accord with the propositional content of the principle.) The instructions cited as examples in the preceding paragraph could be viewed as suggesting the principle that efforts on the client's behalf should be coordinated to maximize the benefits that can be provided. Certainly, each of the instructions, if followed, could potentially assist in such coordination. In fact, many other rule-type directives could be cited and followed to meet the intention imbedded in this principle. On the other hand, the same set of instructions could be viewed as fulfilling a different intention: that clients must not be encouraged to exploit limited available resources unfairly if the worker fails to determine whether duplication of services is involved.

It is not possible to determine which of the intentions, if not both, are being implemented in the worker's behavior without identifying the relevant ethical guideline. Thus, if the value sought is justice and the ethical imperative is based on a Rawlsian view of fairness, the worker knows that unequal advantage in the provision of service can be justified only if such advantage raises the expectations and resources available for the most disadvantaged clients. Based on this ethic, the shoulds, musts, and shalls would support efforts to achieve coordination so as to maximize what is available, particularly for those least able to manage the agency service network on their own; this would thereby avoid inequities generated by the service system itself.

The ways an ethic may be implemented are limited only by resource and imagination. The more skilled worker draws on both in formulating practice principles that incorporate an ethical imperative. He will follow these principles to assure adherence to the intentions prescribed by the ethic. Practice sometimes generates value dilemmas for which there are no ethical prescriptions. In such instances, considerable axiological skill is required to develop an adequate ethical framework.

What laws are to science, limiting ethical prescriptions are to values in that they orient the worker to the essentials which delineate the values in application; ethical prescriptions cannot be violated without departing in practice from the values that are used to justify the goals of the worker's actions. The ability to formulate such prescriptions, to apply them appropriately in the development of practice principles, and to follow their guidelines in the provision of service all entail skill, but of a decreasing level of complexity.

STYLE

The style element of skill will be evident in the performance and the product of the professional activity. Adept or inept, adroit or awkward, deft or clumsy, the so-called style of the practitioner will be characterized by its attractions, not the values and knowledge that inform it. The beauty or lack of beauty of the product, its simplicity, coherence, clarity, precision, balance, and harmony will call attention to the practitioner's style, not the product's rightness or goodness. Inevitably, it is style that transmits the warmth and color of the human involvement in the helping process. Those who mistake style for all of skill, who fail to appreciate the values, knowledge, and actions that in fact constitute its essence, reduce the skill of the practitioner to an intuitive art.

The first observation to be made about style is also the most crucial. The task that requires limited skill and the one which requires considerable skill may both be performed attractively and reveal beauty in their products. The degree of skill required does not vary in accordance with the style with which it is carried out (i.e., style, unlike the other dimensions of skill, cannot be used as a measure of degree of skill). Those who, in their confusion, think otherwise will subject their clients to great risks. Helping an unwed mother decide to relinquish or keep her child will require considerable skill, even if the process is ill devised and lacking in refinement; helping the mother choose a maternity wardrobe within the limits of her means will require less skill, even if done with unusual grace and sophistication. The judgments entailed in each of these tasks need not be informed to the same degree, the ethical and cognitive issues are of a different order; and the choice of actions to be taken make qualitatively different demands of the practitioner.

The second observation to be made about style concerns the need to discipline its idiosyncratic elements. Having to manage agency and professional style and the elements of style that shape the activities of the service recipient, the worker must exercise considerable control over his personal style without losing its unique and enhancing attributes.

Style, like all the elements of skill, changes over time. Many influences, including natural maturation processes, act to alter a practitioner's style. Still, those attributes that are unique to a particular style will most likely continue to be manifest in the idiosyncratic thread that marks the work of its creator. This quality of style, that is, its consistency in evolving the imagery by which it is identified even as the elements from which it is formed change, makes the style recognizable at different times and in varying contexts.

There are limits to the variations in style that can be tolerated in any one setting; some styles are particularly appropriate in one form of practice and highly inappropriate in another. Postmortem reviews that seek to establish reasons why some well-informed, principled, and methodologically proficient person could not make it in an organization highlight this problematic aspect of style. Of all the attributes of skill, style alone asserts the individuality of the practitioner in an unmistakable, not easily compromised fashion. It is relatively easy to mask unprincipled, uninformed, and untrained behavior. A profession that wishes to cultivate its innovators must address the question: How can the widest range of distinctive styles be tolerated, while curtailing the excesses of individual styles that are destructive of goals and purposes?

Finally, it is important to face up to the fact that differing styles may not be congenial. An "analytic" can sometimes drive a "gestalt" up the wall, and an "uptight" can ulcerate someone who "hangs loose." A profession will recognize the need to provide opportunities for conflicting types to operate in environments that favor their development so as to maximize their contributions and minimize their mutually induced traumas. On the other hand, it would be tragic for a profession to be identified with one type to the exclusion of all others. All types of styles are to be found among consumers and providers of service. To avoid unnecessary strains in the delivery of a service, the possibility must be provided for choices that would bring workers' and clients' complementary styles together.

DEGREES OF SKILL

With the four dimensions of skill as a framework, it is possible to differentiate among the preprofessional (technician), professional (master), and advanced professional (expert) levels of skill. When the worker is expected to operate from fairly well-established rules—following directives and commands, adhering to agency style, and utilizing tested techniques and tools of practice—the expectation is preprofessional. When the worker is expected to operate from principles whose justifications are to be found in value-related commendations and theory-based propositions—adhering to professional as well as agency styles and utilizing various methods of intervention—the judgments required are professional. When the worker is expected to consider alternative theoretical formulations and conflicting ethical imperatives—adhering to personal as well as professional and agency styles—and to design a program of action utilizing diverse methods as appropriate, the expectation is for advanced professional skill. Naturally, any one worker may evidence skill at varying levels in each of the four dimensions and may, over time, develop increased skill in each of these dimensions. The framework, however, focuses on what is to be done, not who does it, in defining levels of skill (see Figure 1).

Fig. 1. Diagrammatic Evaluation of Degrees of Skill

Degree of Skill	Dimensions of Skill			
	Knowledge	Action	Values	Style
Advanced professional (expert)	Theories	Design	Ethical imperatives	Personal, professional, and agency
Professional (master)	Propositions	Method	Commendations	Professional and agency
Preprofessional (technician)	Directives	Technique/ tool	Commands	Agency

Finally, it should be stressed that skill in professional practice is not free of the societal and cultural constraints that affect client and worker alike. Class, race, sex, and cultural differences necessarily influence the choice of what is to be valued, what is to be believed, what is acceptable style, and what action is to be taken. Social workers should, for practical reasons, be open to a catholic view of skill lest the profession be justifiably denoted as parochial, class-bound, racist, and sexist in its practice.

NOTES

1. For a discussion of actions that demand full concentration, *see* Arthur Koestler, *The Act of Creation* (New York: Dell Publishing Co., Laurel Edition, 1967), pp. 550–555.

2. For examples of definitions and applications of the concept of skill, *see* Werner W. Boehm, *Objectives of the Social Work Curriculum of the Future,* "Curriculum Study," Vol. 1 (New York: Council on Social Work Education, 1959) ; Ernest Hollis and Alice Taylor, *Social Work Education in the United States* (New York: Columbia University Press, 1951), pp. 220–225; Ruth R. Middleman and Gale Goldberg, *Social Service Delivery: A Structural Approach to Social Work Practice* (New York: Columbia University Press, 1974), pp. 83–89; Helen V.

Phillips, *Essentials of Social Group Work Skill* (New York: Associated Press, 1957); Bertha Capen Reynolds, *Learning and Teaching in the Practice of Social Work* (New York: Russell & Russell, 1965), pp. 51–53; and Charlotte Towle, *The Learner in Education for the Professions* (Chicago: University of Chicago Press, 1954), pp. 248–250.

3. Michael Polanyi, *Personal Knowledge* (Chicago: University of Chicago Press, 1958).

4. Margaret Blenkner, "Obstacles to Evaluative Research in Casework," *Social Casework*, 31 (February 1950), p. 56.

The Challenge of
Quality for
Practice Theory

EMANUEL TROPP

A pressure has been building up within the social work profession for a long time and has finally boiled over, having been sidetracked, postponed, or compromised for many years. That pressure is the demand for raising the level of quality of professional skill. All these years, the National Association of Social Workers (NASW) has stated its commitment to this mission, and it has made a number of efforts in this direction. The most notable of these was the 1962 Princeton Conference called "Building Social Work Knowledge," which contributed a great deal of thought but raised so many questions that the outlook seemed overwhelming.[1] In the late 1960s and early 1970s, larger societal issues created counterpressures that served to further delay the unfinished business.

But the lid has blown off and the quality issue is now the hot, burning core of the most significant discussions in the profession. It can no longer be talked away because it comes so strongly from the ranks of those who practice. This inescapable push has also been recognized clearly in statements by leaders of the two major professional bodies, NASW and the Council on Social Work Education. One of the first warning signals was flashed in 1968 by Briar, when he said, "If we preserve our commitment to the generic ideal . . . our graduates would learn less and less about more and more and we would graduate generic dilettantes, who can dabble superficially in everything and work deeply and expertly in nothing."[2] In 1974 the *Report to the Task Force on Structure and Quality in Social Work Education*, written by Ripple, brought the issue to a head by noting that a repeated theme heard during its deliberations was that MSWs "know *about* a great many things, but they don't know how *to do*, to practice" and that "it is clear that most, if not all of the options proposed are directed toward improving the quality of social work education."[3]

The cry for quality is not simply a complaint about the level of competence of graduates; that would indeed be an underestimation. It is nothing less than the unfinished business of the entire profession—of *all* who practice social work today. If social workers do not know clearly just what the quality standards are for experienced professionals, we surely cannot have any standards to apply at the beginning level of competence.

It is possible that, for some, the hope for quality is a yearning for the "good old days," when everyone practiced by the same set of ground rules. Reid and Shyne had something to say about those good old days in their classic study of casework practice: "Although we may have some general notions of the characteristics of interpersonal treatment, systematic knowledge of its specific ingredients . . . is sorely lacking." [4] In a 1970 survey of all casework theories, Simon confirmed this view with the simple statement that "it might be said that there is only rudimentary treatment theory in social casework." [5]

If the concern is not validly seen as a return to the past, is it a hope for some futuristic orientation, what we have come to call "innovation"? Social workers have had a plentiful supply of this commodity, but it still does not seem to meet that gnawing concern for quality. We have chased innovations like fireflies, as if for some magical answers. This has, in fact, been an escape route from the much harder central task: to identify the solid core of what we *do* know and then elaborate on it in ever increasing refinement. Although some practice theorists have been contributing in significant ways to the necessary work on this agenda, the work has only just begun.

If the concern for quality is not seen as a yearning for a return to the past or a search for magical new answers, then what is it? The balance of this paper is addressed to this question; it is discussed in three stages: (1) the quality goals sought, (2) the obstacles, and (3) the approaches needed to attain the goals.

QUALITY GOALS SOUGHT

The concern for increased quality starts from a conviction of the need for more competent use of skill with those who need social work services. That is why social workers are in business. So, the term "quality" turns simply and definitively into "competence." The demand for quality is a demand on the practitioner to achieve a coherent, understandable, and explainable rationale and skill for enabling people to more effectively carry out interpersonal tasks. It is also a demand on the profession for educational and certification processes that designate the conditions under which it can be said that someone has achieved the ability to perform in this manner.

On the subject of training for the scientific professions, Arrowsmith says that skills must be taught with "emphasis on thoroughness, precision and accuracy." [6] "Thoroughness" has a solid ring to it; it means to know and to do something by some recognizable standard of completeness. "Precision" means the ability to make calculations by some standard of refinement. "Accuracy" means the ability to identify the matters requiring professional appraisal and action by some standard of objective fact. If social workers can agree to these broadly based but not unrealistic guidelines for competence, the next step is to look at their significance for the profession.

Three questions can be posed as the key tests of quality, or competence: "What do we *know*?" "What can we *do*?" "How well can we *explain* their relation?" Inherent in this package of three seemingly simple questions is that social workers do need some clearly stated intended results, that they can use their special knowledge selectively and apply skill appropriately and competently, and that they can explain the connective processes in clearly understandable language.

The need for competence requires a firming up and organization of the knowledge social workers already have about interpersonal behavior, about the specific approaches for using this knowledge to enhance interpersonal functioning, and about the different ways methodology is developed in relation to various social systems (e.g., one-to-one relationship, family group, peer group, and community group). As we solidify our knowledge, we move from pure art, which cannot be questioned as to "how you get from one point to another," to an artistic science—so that we can indeed answer reasonable questions.

OBSTACLES

Bartlett told us why we were not yet there when she noted the "anti-intellectual attitude that has existed and remains strong in social work," which is reflected in the opposition to any attempt to "break into pieces" the focus of a problem for fear we would lose the whole person. She said that we found our earliest security in one cluster of theory, borrowed from psychoanalysis; then recognized its limitations; and later swung widely in the other direction to draw from social science theories—again from outside our knowledge. She stated, "Social workers have tended to identify with psychiatrists, social scientists or others, rather than to move their own knowledge fully over into social work's own area of practice." [7]

Although social workers have made some progress since Princeton, we have mostly continued to avoid the hard tasks. In grasping for the easy lures of whatever is "the newest game in town," we have opted for a catch-as-catch-can eclecticism—a little piece of behaviorism here, some gestalt therapy there, some transactional analysis here, ad infinitum. We have been called a profession constantly in search of panaceas.[8] We do not trust ourselves much. All this continues to turn us away from our internal knowledge organization.

The educational rebel, Kozol, identifies this phenomenon as the instinct for nonstop locomotion. "It is very, very attractive to keep moving around. It is extremely hard to stay in one place and follow through on one thing." [9] Drucker says that the "normal human reaction is to evade the priority decision, by doing a little bit of everything." [10] And one of the most classic pieces of avoidance has been for social workers to use the concept of the "whole" as a means of not having to look at the parts. Piaget states that gestalt psychologists made a useful contribution, but "by viewing the whole as prior to its elements . . . they simplified the problem to such an extent as to risk bypassing all the central questions— questions about the nature of the whole's laws of composition." [11]

NEEDED APPROACHES

The remaining discussion, by following the questions raised at the Princeton conference, and by mapping the essential steps needed today, points to an approach to developing practice theory that can become a base for a fortified, competent, and accountable use of social work skills. To be able to answer the questions posed as key tests of quality (What do we know? What can we do? How well can we explain their relation?), it is necessary to come to grips with a series of tasks identified as (1) simplification, (2) specification, (3) schematization, (4) systematization, and (5) specialization.

Simplification

The first task in the process of making sense out of a mass of seemingly unrelated data is to locate *identifiable components*. This means engaging in a process of elimination to reduce some segment of knowledge to its essential parts. But a great deal of social workers' difficulty has stemmed from the insistence on finding complications. By continually insisting that human relations are so complex that we cannot—even dare not—look at their components, we create a mystique and thus effectively block any effort at analysis.

Simplification is the first step in the ordering of knowledge. Observe that contemporary biochemistry has focused on the human cell as the basic source of information about total body functioning; strategies of prevention and treatment are being developed from this nuclear source. Major life processes can be observed in the individual cell.[12] Through this new concentration on cellular biology, analysts are learning how the body mobilizes its own resources to help itself. What a tremendous gain it would be for social workers if, by a similar examination of the smallest units of our work and an identification of their components, we could describe simply how people can and do help themselves and what we, therefore, need to do to facilitate this process. In fact, we already know these things; but we have not accomplished the task of simplification in order to begin the process of organizing our knowledge.

As we delve into the interior of the "social cell" to examine just what happens in one person's *effective* performance in a single relationship with another, we will be able to build on the resulting findings to analyze interpersonal relationships as they occur in varying and more complex role arrangements. We will know what fundamentals contribute to optimum interpersonal functioning, along what dimensions these routes to effectiveness occur, and what ways of interacting aid or hinder it. Because of a heavy dependence on psychiatry, social work has developed a greater interest in nonfunctional behavior than in behavior that is optimum. This has severely limited social workers' range of vision. If we can grasp the simplest essentials of how people interact optimally in their daily lives, we can use that as a base for perceiving, evaluating, and intervening in the interactions that occur in one-to-one, family group, peer group, community group, and administrative counseling.

Every piece of a practitioner's work needs to be stripped to its essentials: Who are the players? What are their roles? What do they do? When one player does such-and-such, how is this likely to affect another player? We must be able to see the components clearly to know just what we are dealing with. This process of simplification is not simpleminded; rather, it is the necessary precursor for the more complex work ahead. As in the relationship between anatomy and physiology, we need to see the individual components as entities in their own right before we can see how they affect each other. When social workers act to simplify, we lay the ground for the important deductive potential. The components become symbolized through *conceptual* terms, which, when connected with each other in some action process, create *principles*. The principles describe how the parts function and are, therefore, guides to action.

The moment we obtain two principles that make contact with each other, we have a clear deductive opportunity; that is, if this is so and if that is so, then something else must also be so. This logical deduction is the rewarding culmination of that careful reduction to essentials. Deductive reasoning offers social work an infinite resource to cultivate for the multiple elaborations it needs to organize its knowledge.

Specification

It is implicit in the first step, reduction to essentials, that those essentials needed to be specified. Although conceptually a successor to simplification, the process of specifying may occur simultaneously; but it is analytically necessary to examine it separately. Specification is an identification of what each component is, and it is accomplished by designating, defining, and differentiating. To designate something is to give it a conceptual name that represents its meaning; to define it is to explain that meaning in both descriptive and connective terms; to differentiate it is to separate it from other components by indicating what makes it different. For instance, in qualitative analysis in chemistry, the identification process might include the naming of the elements in a given portion of food; but to include the definition of sodium, for example, might seem silly because any chemist can quickly define it. But social workers, unlike chemists, have hardly begun to define their "elements." We must ask ourselves why we have to much trouble agreeing on the mere description of our own landscape even though, when faced with the most farfetched, not clearly defined ideas from non-social work sources, we buy them unquestioningly!

If we can specify what the components of a single knowledge cell are, we are then in a position to begin to connect those components. Social work literature is filled with talk about the difficulty of dealing with elements separately because of their interrelatedness, as though it were already known just which elements were being interrelated. This is just another avoidance ploy, which has an advanced and sophisticated ring, but that is its mortal weakness: the literature just does not state the meanings of the parts that are so easily subsumed within any interrelationship.

Schematization

After reducing our mass of knowledge to its essentials and specifying what they are, it is necessary to connect them in some design that describes reality and is rationally explainable. This connective process is neither a mechanistic nor a mystical procedure; it is a type of interlocking, which takes note of new elements that are introduced as those identified are reunited.

One type of schematization is a system of classification. Social work theory has contained a number of classification efforts, which have categorized various elements by some criteria of similarity. Classification is, however, only the first step in schematization. The larger task involves creating a connecting map of both the components and the classification groupings so that the relationship of each component and each grouping to each of the others takes on an orderly and illuminated meaning. This undertaking involves the placing of elements into a working juxtaposition with each other, on simple levels at first and then in more complex patterns. Schematization is a patterning process that serves to shed light on the relationship of the parts to the whole. As even lower-level essentials are schematized, the very act produces what may appear to be a complexity of a forbidding order.

To illustrate how this process can be accomplished, a schema that could be developed as a basis for simultaneously grasping the parts and the whole of the nature of social functioning will be used as an example.[13] After careful examination of the literature, with a continuing check against reality as it is experienced, it becomes evident that there are two essential (and commonplace) dimensions to social functioning: the social and the psychological. Further, just about all the writings reduce the psychological dimension to triads that sound strikingly similar, such as thinking-feeling-doing or ideas-emotions-actions. On the basis of a more specifically defined version of these combinations, a more refined triad takes shape, namely, cognition-valuation-action.

As for the social dimension, at first it seems to consist only of self and other. But it becomes clear that there is a third entity, created by the merger of self and several others into a collective unit, which might be called "society" (or any miniature replica thereof). Thus there now is a social triad of self, other, and society, within which the basic patterns are easily seen to be self-to-self, self-to-other, and self-to-society.

Then, placing these two patterns against each other (i.e., vertical against horizontal), a three-by-three screen illuminates nine areas within which all social interactions fall; for example, one of these areas is "valuation of self." After that, it is not at all difficult to fill in these nine sections with the many interpersonal behaviors identified in the literature and now organized in an understandable manner—the totality of which is the arena of social work, namely, social functioning.

Systematization

To seek to place in a scientific order of logical progression a systematization of both social interaction and professional facilitation of social interaction may sound like more than a human relations profession can offer. It can do so, however, and for the sake of claiming competence, it must. This does not imply a push-button kind of design because it recognizes the many unknowns and unpredictables in human affairs; but it does accept the proposition that although social workers can reasonably ask to be relieved of the requirement for certainty, they can no longer avoid the criterion of probability. And so, having identified, defined, and patterned the moving parts, the next step is to produce some *sequential* ordering of the professional tasks needed to facilitate effective social interaction.

Although the many-faceted nature of human relations and the counseling process is too intricate to devise a system whereby an XYZ button needs to be pushed in an XYZ situation, this cannot absolve social workers of the necessity of locating some middle ground; otherwise we are left with nothing beyond the older pattern of playing it by ear. That middle ground is the spelling out of all the guiding principles we now know, as they describe (1) what is *likely* to happen to people as a result of certain interactions in their lives and (2) what is likely to happen to them as a result of certain enabling acts by a social worker.

Once all the operational principles (specifically, the principles within each interaction system) have been formulated and schematized, what will look like an intricate set of crisscrossed guides and cross-referenced qualifiers will result. This is where the art enters the picture, as it does in all professions. Social workers will need to know these principles with such thoroughness, accuracy, and precision that, when we face each new situation, we first undertake an elimination process to rule out those principles that are *not* applicable and then an identification process to determine which principles *must* be considered. As we balance and counterbalance our own directives that flow from our cross-referenced principles, we must make judgments about where to place the emphasis at one time and where at another—*and* in what order. This is quite different from a mechanistic approach, which is the job of a technician who literally follows a manual. It is a quality imperative of the highest order, one that requires the systematic and simultaneous application of a combination of guiding principles selected on the basis of a truly professional judgment.

When we arrive at this point, we can speak of a coherent rationale for an applied social science, of a significant degree of quality and competence. If this seems remote, let it be said that a great many social workers *already do these things*. The problem is that they have not explicated sufficiently what they do and why in a systematic way. In this sense, we have not yet moved much beyond an awareness of our unfinished business, and much of the blockage is tied in strongly to the final task: specialization.

Specialization

This last consideration is both the necessary precondition and the natural culmination of all the preceding tasks. The present clamor for specialization arises primarily from a desire for greater competence in something specific. It is only as social workers see our way clear to specialization that we become more receptive to the needs to simplify, specify, schematize, and systematize because a demand to be able to do all these tasks in relation to *every* modality would scare any sensible person. Indeed, it will be a substantial accomplishment to perform all these tasks in a *specialty within a specialty* (i.e., a specialization by function in addition to a specialization by field of practice). If this idea of specialization sounds extreme to those ears still attuned to the generic theme, attention must be drawn to the fact that it is nothing more than what the profession has already moved into doing this past year.

What has happened to the thinking around specialization that has turned the social work profession increasingly in this direction, just when it thought it was going the other way, and why has this happened? The *Report to the Task Force on Structure and Quality in Social Work Education* states that "the critical issue seen by most people . . . is not whether the objectives of the master's program is preparation of a generalist or a specialist but a series of questions within the assumption of specialization." [14] This statement should not come as a surprise to those who practice because the recommendation of the NASW Council on Social Work in Mental Health and Psychiatric Services reported, in early 1974, that ". . . there was a need for specialization in general and . . . for specialization by method or function. . . ." [15] So, the cry is strong and clear from the ranks of practice: a specialization by function in addition to a specialization by field of practice—a specialty within a specialty. This does not imply a return to a total separation of all kinds of practice. It simply means that while all social workers should be able to make some contributions in various modalities, "some" is a long way from the thoroughness, accuracy, and precision required of a competent specialist.

In early 1975 it was reported that the NASW Board of Directors had agreed to test the specialization model developed by the NASW Practice and Knowledge Division, which was a model of specialization "by method with subspecializations in each determined by field." [16] What a fantastic turnaround this has been from what we assumed as gospel truth for so many years! In the early 1950s, schools of social work decreed that it was no longer necessary to train practitioners by field of practice. By the mid-1960s, this assumption was being seriously questioned and, by 1975, it had been overwhelmingly rejected. Similarly, the trend toward the elimination of separate methods began to take hold in graduate schools in the early 1960s; now it is being said that this too was a move in the wrong direction. If it took twenty years to rediscover the values of specificity in fields of practice, it is fairly safe to predict that by 1980 social workers will be returning en masse to specificity in method. That movement has already begun.

This dual reversal might give cause for concern if it were not so firmly buttressed by other professions. In a Faculty Senate report to Columbia University, deBary said, "The trend toward specialization . . . reflects not only social changes but the vast expansion of knowledge and the individual's difficulty in coping with it. There seems to be no way of achieving a sense of mastery or individual competence except by cutting out for one's self some manageable segment of the whole." [17] If this is generally true today, the need for greater specificity is one that would apply also to the preparation of social workers on the undergraduate level.

CONCLUSION

The call for specialization is a realistic way to bring to a close a discussion of five tasks that have been presented as the central challenges to quality in the development of practice theory in social work. It is realistic because it is either already a fact or something that most professionals are now aiming to make a reality. It is realistic because it connects with our current condition in such a way as to make the other demands seem, at their easiest, connected—and, at their most difficult, more evidently necessary. It even makes those demands more achievable because it realistically restricts their scope to one modality at a time.

But it would be foolhardy to regard the challenges to quality as either easy to accomplish or as leading to some blissful new state. While these challenges neither promise a rose garden nor ask for blood and tears, they do require sweat; but they carry an intended message of hope that the hard work will be accomplishable and well worth the effort. This appeal is intended to convey both a belief that social work cannot go on much longer without facing the five tasks and a faith that it will be able to rise successfully to meet them. When the profession does so, all who call themselves social workers will gain a long-needed *self-confirmation*, with which they can confidently face the many challenges to confirmation that are coming with increased frequency from others outside the profession.

NOTES

1. *Building Social Work Knowledge* (New York: National Association of Social Workers, 1964).

2. Scott Briar, "Flexibility and Specialization in Social Work Education," *Social Work Education Reporter*, 16 (December 1968), p. 46.

3. Lilian Ripple, *Report to the Task Force on Structure and Quality in Social Work Education* (New York: Council on Social Work Education, 1974), pp. 38, 66.

4. William J. Reid and Ann W. Shyne, *Brief and Extended Casework* (New York: Columbia University Press, 1969), p. 15.

5. Bernece K. Simon, "Social Casework Theory: An Overview," in Robert W. Roberts and Robert H. Nee, eds., *Theories of Social Casework* (Chicago: University of Chicago Press, 1970), p. 378.

6. William Arrowsmith, "The Shame of the Graduate Schools," *Harpers Magazine*, 232 (March 1966), p. 52.

7. Harriett M. Bartlett, *The Common Base of Social Work Practice* (New York: National Association of Social Workers, 1970), pp. 37–38, 71–72.

8. Stanley J. Brody, "Maximum Participation of the Poor: Another Holy Grail?" *Social Work*, 15 (January 1970), p. 68.

9. Jonathan Kozol, "Moving on to Nowhere," *New York Times*, March 24, 1972, p. 39.

10. Peter Drucker, *The Age of Discontinuity* (New York: Harper & Row, 1969), p. 195.

11. Jean Piaget, *Structuralism* (New York: Basic Books, 1970), p. 8.

12. Gene Bylinsky, "Upjohn Puts the Cell's Own Messengers to Work," *Fortune*, 85 (June 1972), p. 152.

13. For a detailed approach, *see* Emanuel Tropp, *A Humanistic Foundation for Group Work Practice* (2d ed., New York: Selected Academic Readings, 1972), pp. 31–45.

14. Ripple, op. cit., p. 35.

15. *NASW News*, 19 (February 1974), p. 2.

16. *NASW News*, 20 (January 1975), pp. 1, 3.

17. Wm. Theodore deBary, "A Program of General and Continuing Education in the Humanities," *Columbia Reports* (April 1973), p. 3.

Quality and Accountability in the Service Structure

CAROL H. MEYER

During these times of economic disaster, political retreat, and social regression, social workers remain on the side of justice while those who govern the country care little which side we are on—if indeed they care at all about justice. How then can one discuss accountability when the social work profession itself is accountable to such an uncertain mandate? It is equally difficult to consider the expectation of quality service in an atmosphere where the essential tools of our trade, social services, are gradually being eroded. Thus accountability, but for what, and quality, but with what supports, are the dilemmas.

To some extent social workers have had to live with similar dilemmas in response to uncertain mandates throughout this century. For example, we have tried to be accountable to clients, but there have never been sufficient or always appropriate services to offer.[1] But today, because people are more open in their demands and because expectations for services are greater as the conditions of daily living worsen, the task before social workers seems to have overtaken our competence. Perhaps the only option is to advance headlong into the dysfunctional environment. Accountability suggests that there is no hiding place; that the overwhelming problems around us are exactly the arena of social work activity. Quality means that whatever we do we have to do well. This is a tall order, but the alternative of retreat is not available.

There comes a time when the only way out of a continuing crisis is to think about it. Obviously, there are uncounted ways to think about the quandary posed by the twin expectations of accountability and quality. The author has chosen to organize the present analysis along three dimensions: (1) the *purposes* of social work, (2) the value of imposing a *coherent view* upon what we do, and (3) affirmation of the ongoing demand for *professional autonomy*.

THE NATURE OF ACCOUNTABILITY

First, some thoughts about accountability itself. Accountability has many definitions. The dictionary says it has to do with responsibility and the ability to be counted on, but of course the dictionary does not explain how to achieve that desirable state. In Washington, for almost eight years, presidents and their aides have conceived of accountability in its most narrow context: as loyalty, not to a public constituency, but to a political power elite. This kind of accountability should prove that the term has no intrinsic value; it can be attached to low as well as to high social purposes. On another level, accountability to oneself seems to be a mark of today's culture. Encounter, meditation, mind-altering drugs, and the retreat to "I," whatever the derivation, seem to be withdrawal responses in an alienated, fragmented society. Thus accountability to oneself and not to others can exist; it can contain no social purpose at all.

Social workers are as vulnerable as everyone else to readings of accountability as misplaced loyalty or self-promotion. Today's world appears to be decreasingly supportive of high moral or social purpose. Blatant discrimination against class, race, sex, and age appears so undisguised that those on the bottom, no less than those on the top—all scratching for survival—seem to be saying, "I'm all right Jack." It was mind-blowing to hear the previous secretary of the Department of Health, Education, and Welfare say that too much of the gross national product is invested in people programs; to hear the secretary of the Treasury Department suggest that fiscal support of New York City should be as punitive as possible; and to know that an unelected president vetoed a child nutrition bill. Everyone suffers greatly from the shock, grief, and ineptitude that derive from extended moral deprivation in government.

Can social workers escape this depravity? Can we confront social restraints with action rather than paralysis? Being part of this put-down society, can we affirm what we think social accountability is and proceed to meet its requirements? In our role as social critics, we will not become rich or famous; as experts in the social services, we will not become popular. Perhaps to be accountable is to be none of these things. But there are many of us who have made a choice to seek accountability in the sense of social responsibility.

THE PURPOSES OF SOCIAL WORK

Ideally, a socially responsive profession should be able to demonstrate that through the passage of time, its purposes have changed as society and scientific thinking have changed.[2] The uneven development of social work in this regard should not be depressing, though, when compared to the progress of, for example, the delivery of health care services. Nevertheless, in social agencies it is still common to observe intake policies that were constructed to serve clients or address problems that no longer exist. It is exceedingly hard for institutions and professions to keep up with the pace of social change.

The social upheaval in the 1960s threw a scare into social work, and the consequences of that scare are interesting. The once impermeable purposes of social work practice, especially the casework core, seemed to fly apart. Whereas once there appeared to be fairly general agreement about purposes, today we are experiencing a kind of crisis of coherence wherein multiple practice models are each addressing different purposes.[3] As gleaned from the literature, iconoclastic practices, and the disparate educational goals of schools of social work, social work today seems to be whatever one says it is. Like a hot potato, the issue of social work purposes is tossed from agency to agency, school to school, writer to writer, practitioner to practitioner. Does one vote on professional purpose? It is time to come to grips with this issue because one thing is sure: Society will lose patience with a profession that claims as its purpose that everyone does his own thing.

Two competing themes in social workers' assumptions of purpose seem to exist. One kind of practice seeks to be immediately responsive to all the complexities in society, reaching for threads that have come apart from the weave of the social fabric. The other kind of practice seeks to carve out a manageable piece with which to work in the hope of coping by defining narrow goals. The first theme is overwhelming, and the second is underwhelming. This tendency toward polarization has been characteristic of the professional pendulum swing between focus on the person and focus on the environment since before social workers were organized as a profession. It is our way of continually living out the dilemma of cause and function, assuming, perhaps erroneously, that they are antithetical professional purposes.[4]

The reason definition of purpose is so important in a discussion of accountability and quality in relationship to service structures is that *form*, the way services are organized to meet ideal goals, and *function*, the way practice is done, are intimately related. The way services and access to them are arranged, the way manpower is utilized differentially, the nature of supervision, the size of caseloads, the sources of funding— all these administrative concerns actually determine the expected outcomes of social work. In the same way, practice theory serves the purposes social workers hold. So if we aim to change society through practice means, our theory must offer wide-ranging options. On the other hand, if we aim to change the person, we select a theory that offers narrower psychological parameters and tend to brush away environmental strain as obfuscation. In psychotherapeutic practice, for example, the selection of certain types of clients, highest educational levels of social workers, smallest size of caseloads, private sources of funding, and even continuity of intensive supervision all have specific consequences. But psychotherapeutic practice appears to allow for some assurance of quality service because it draws narrower and apparently more comprehensible boundaries. Are its purposes sufficiently comprehensive, however, to include clients and problems not suited to psychotherapy, and thus is it also a socially accountable mode?

Social workers have to be wary of holding their purposes and social accountability hostage to quality because quality itself is a relative concept. For example, if intake were reduced to the most helpable clients, if only the most experienced and skilled practitioners were selected, and if narrow and clearly achievable goals were defined, the result might indeed be a high quality of practice. But to what end, for what purposes, and accountable to what forces in society? The example is familiar, and through it social workers confront the granddaddy of all issues. Is it possible to have social accountability along a broad range of social concerns and still maintain standards of quality?

The other theme of practice, the one that reaches toward broad purposes—such as social change—is hazardous if those purposes are beyond professional competence. Just as quality practice without social accountability would be an empty gesture, so also would rhetorical claims of accountability without the promise of quality. There is a great deal of activity today in the realm of the "human services," self-help groups, sociopolitical neighborhood experiments, and so on. Social workers need to be associated with these endeavors and with larger political enterprises, but it is difficult to discern the practice methodology that would be called on. A problem with professional boundaries does exist. On the one hand, social workers are pulled by the "fifth profession" (those elements of all helping professions engaged in psychotherapy) and, on the other hand, by the catchall "human services." When it comes to undefined, proliferating programs in large-scale social, economic, and political change, it seems unlikely that they will be affected significantly through social work practitioners' carefully honed practice skills.

A professional purpose that would join competence with social vision, quality with accountability, needs to be affirmed. If social workers could agree on a central purpose as being to support people in the pursuit of their unique and real life tasks, they might achieve that long sought for balance between cause and function, between person and environment, between accountability and quality. Even Mary Richmond tried, although in vain, to reach such accommodations.[5]

As far as service structures are concerned, the following would be involved: the invention and delivery of social services at the time and place needed to support family life; the creative use of psychosocial supports, including therapeutic encounters to enable people to cope with dysfunctional environments; and newly developed methodological avenues to modify those environments. In shifting attention from the polarized psychological and social constructs to the psychosocial "interface," where person and environment must seek a mutual adaptation, we will be performing a professional task done by no others; we will also be catching up with advanced professional disciplines which recognize that, in this era, people work in medicine and in mental health is environmental work as well.[6]

An Illustration

The ideas just discussed relating to the purpose of a practice approach focusing on the interface need to be illustrated. To begin with, from an agency's point of view, an identifiable constituency—whether a problem group, an age group, a status group, or a geographic group—is served. Through whatever structure or institution—be it a hospital, a mental health catchment area, or a family agency—the identified client constituency would be potential consumers of the services offered. Because case-related goals would be client goals, little screening out at intake on the grounds of workability, class, race, or other such classifications would take place. The search for the favored client model would be given up in favor of only one model: whoever needs the service offered. If the agency's 10-year-old clients are knife-wielding street kids, practitioners are not going to search for bed wetters. If child abuse is a serious problem in the community, practitioners are not going to save their caseloads for overprotective mothers. Such a broad service net is going to demand the skills of social workers along the whole range of the educational continuum, as well as other professional disciplines and such associative personnel as foster parents, homemakers, and indigenous case-finders.

Social workers' engagement with the real problems of their clients will turn up environmental deficits and opportunities seldom confronted before, just as it will turn up some groups of clients never served before. Different from a traditional psychosocial approach in casework, where focus on the person-in-his-environment tended to serve clients with less and less environmental strain, in a selective fashion, this approach structures the practitioners' perspective to the client (all clients) in his field.

Throughout the helping process, the person and the environment are locked into a dual focus. This aim of achieving a mutually adaptable balance between the person and his environment requires a supporting practice theory. An ecological, or ecosystems, perspective is concerned with the interconnectedness of variables, both psychological and social. New and challenging events are occurring in practice—all of which will have to be intertwined with the design of services in the agency or service structure.[7]

For example, the notion of a social work "case" would be different, and it would have to follow that work loads, manpower arrangements, and general agency policies would have to reflect that redefinition. The case might be an individual, a dyad, a family, a group, or a community. Furthermore, that case would be comprised of people who are transactionally related to their schools, jobs, houses, neighborhoods, hospitals, courts, agencies, families, and idea systems (environmental concerns). To complicate the nature of the "case" even more, they would be characterized individually by their culture, ethnicity, race, religion, peer group, personality structure, and geographic location. Finally, given the transactional nature of life and therefore of cases, the units of attention would include, variously, teachers, landlords, family members, employers, social workers, doctors, nurses, neighbors, and all others who belong in the client's unique field, or ecology.

Assuming that each case would contain its unique thumbprint, the essential practice task would be to make an individualizing assessment of the client's situation, a definition of his problem that is different from all others. Then, through a continuing, mutual process of definition and decision-making by the client and worker together, multiple interventions would occur. Imbalance, maladaptations, gaps in services, inhibited coping or cognitive capacities, miscommunications, and cross-purposes in the client's life could be realized through work with any or all of the people constituting the unit of attention, or the case. The client's ecology is the total, significant milieu of which he is a part; the systems conception helps practitioners locate and relate the salient variables in the case: thus the term "ecosystems."

Because of the complex dimensions of a case, the concerns involved could take practitioners from the client's self-image to the way the agency structures its services. Interventions could reach into the social fabric as well as to relationships and organizations. All are part of the client's world and thus part of the practitioner's concern. Thus the author has attempted to bring together the apparent disparities in purpose that are suggested by a psychotherapeutic and a social change approach. The demands of such a practice would require a sense of coherence to put it all together.

THE IMPOSITION OF COHERENCE

In the last analysis, the way quality practice is expressed is through skill. One of the major problems for social workers, however, is that skills cannot easily be matched to the uncontrollable forces going on at all times in our cases. Despite the temptation to contain these forces so as to manage them, simplification of complexity does not really work out either. When we oversimplify, we go back to the risk of losing accountability by doing the least possible for the least number or we risk quality by distort-ing the problem. Whatever craftsmanship we develop as we enter the ecology of a client's life will depend a great deal on the range and depth of our *knowledge* and the facility with which we can conceptualize and impose coherence upon our work. Even to approach the degree of co-herence necessary, we have to take into account *quantity* as an aspect of ac-countability and, ultimately, of quality. Rethinking our purposes will in-evitably push us to new, imaginative uses of *policy* as an aspect of prac-tice. Coherence means reversing the telescope and looking through a broad rather than a narrow lens.

Quantity

Why is *quantity* a key issue? Why do we have to account for numbers in any magnitude? And if we do, what will we sacrifice? There is a rising demand for services from the middle class as well as from increasingly vocal poor and minority groups. The rapidly growing aged population, families in need of social supports, and people whose psychosocial needs will surface with the advent of a national health program are but some of the groups who will seek social services in increasing numbers. Can social workers bear to live with this popularity? To the degree that we can de-liver, we will be accountable.

And why are numbers related at all to quality? From an ecosystems perspective, a case would be distorted through overlooking the connected-ness of factors in a particular situation, or through treating some phe-nomena in isolation when they are in reality group phenomena and more amenable to noncase methods. Once we comprehend cases in their eco-logical dimensions, it is difficult to avoid the demand of quantity ser-vices because, for example, when the client's problem is housing, his case will bring to light other tenants' cases; as another example, when the cli-ent is a child experiencing difficulty in a school, that child's case will un-earth other children's cases in that school.

How quantity can be woven into quality service can be demonstrated by a simple case illustration. A 13-year-old unwed mother who comes to a clinic can be helped in an individualistic way, but she can also be viewed as an example of the clinic's caseload or catchment area for which it has assumed responsibility. Are there ten more children who are 13, pregnant, and have similar concerns? If so, should they be a group? Will a simple survey of this small collection of children indicate that they need a special educational program because their school has suspended them? If there are five hundred such children, what then? Is this the time to engage the community in developing a network of self-help and professional services? Although the single case is unique, it can also be part of a class of cases. Can practitioners hold themselves accountable if they believe their caseloads bear no relationship to their colleagues' caseloads, or to other children in the community not yet touched by the agency's service? Knowledge of the epidemiology of a problem may be the best prescription for correcting tunnel vision. Finding many more children in the same situation as that 13-year-old might even lead to a redefinition of the problem.

Policy

The creative use of *policy* is another way to achieve coherence in our work. When variables in cases are complex, it seems irrational to expect practitioners to cope with social problems by using interviewing skills, for example, that are not commensurate with the task. Social workers are used to viewing policies as the governors of practice, but when problem situations are complicated, it is often expeditious to use policies creatively as tools of practice.

An all too typical child welfare problem, separation, can be used as an example. Traditionally, practitioners have placed children in foster care away from their natural parents to where the foster parents live. The assumption probably was based on the historical explanation that the child's welfare would be improved by moving him from a poverty to a nonpoverty area. One of the consequences has been the child's suffering from the impact of separation, no matter how "bad" or how "sick" his mother or father was. Social workers' response was to talk with, console, "work through," and in all possible ways try to assuage the sorrow and guilt felt by the child. As we have come to learn about filial and maternal deprivation, we have begun to include natural parents in our ministrations for the sake of both child and parents.[8]

A creative twist in agency policy could save children and families from psychological damage and agencies from endless expenditures as they send practitioners with their teaspoons to empty the ocean. Would it not be logical to consider locating foster homes in the same locations as natural parents' homes? Children could remain in the same schools, not fret about differences in family names and be confused about whose children they are, and stay connected with their own identities. Separation would then be a physical reality to be tested and not a psychic death. Because foster care is a temporary placement, perhaps children could go home on weekends or at least for shorter visits.[9] Thus they would be helped to understand their parents' difficulties and still enjoy the physical and emotional protection of foster parents. Closing the gaps among the actors in the child placement maze is a professional task of real merit; no longer would practitioners have to concentrate on the effects of separation, which itself has been a creation of agency policy. Creative new policies in foster care would move the social worker from excessive reliance on the personal encounter with the child in helping him with his sorrow to the real, and more complex, problem arena where child, natural parents, foster parents, and agency meet.

Opportunities exist in every service program to bend the client's environment through policy shift. Practitioners need only to get a coherent perspective on their caseloads. It will also be essential for social workers to gain specialized knowledge about the field of practice in which they are involved. Social work has expanded its knowledge boundaries as far as methodology, settings, problems, and responsibilities are concerned, but coherence will be served best through comprehensive field specialization. Service structures would be able to capture all the essential variables and, as in the foster placement example, would be more apt to see options for new and for multiple interventions.

SOCIAL WORKERS AND AUTONOMY

The complexity of the work to be done, the avowed goals of social accountability and quality services, and the commitment to deliver depend on solid professional practice. And today staffing is one more complexity to be faced by social service structures. The mix of social work man and woman power covers the entire educational continuum from AA, BA, BSW, and MSW to Ph.D. and DSW. Because of the kind of work encompassed, the mix also includes volunteers, indigenous people, community groups, people in associated disciplines, and so on. The work a social worker does inevitably engages him with people from other disciplines and with other social workers, who have varying strengths and capacities. The task is to differentiate, to keep them all straight as to who is to do what. Differentially prepared social workers are not alike in the work they do, and differential work roles and tasks and differential career opportunities have yet to be hammered out.[10]

Social service structures, like hospitals, are both employers and institutions in which professionals and technicians practice. The line between freedom and control often becomes shadowy because accountability always beckons the administrator. Beyond the matter of clear job definition is the thorny issue of autonomy and how much of it social workers should enjoy. Perhaps the answer is that practitioners should have as much autonomy as warranted by their preparation and competence for the job they do.

But there is more to say about autonomy. Given a structure of services and as clear a job mandate as possible, autonomy can derive only from a person's inner sense of responsibility. A practitioner cannot be talked or rewarded into responsible work; it has to be possible for him to choose autonomy freely. Accountable and quality service in social work programs, in the final analysis, hinges on what staff members do in the course of their independent work. A staff that is kept under tight administrative control will exchange a sense of accountability for obedience—and they are not the same thing. The complexity of the tasks facing practitioners will require creativity, flexibility, and autonomy. It is not closer supervision that is needed; rather, staff development opportunities and programs of intellectual enrichment and professional exchange and participation are required. Social work practitioners are not the enemies of agencies; they are the expression of agency policies and programs. The accountability of the profession will be evaluated on the basis of the quality of the work done, and we are all in it together. The larger the scope of our work, the greater the comprehension and rigor that must be brought to it. It is not common sense but knowledge, not a debate about breadth or depth but an affirmation of coherence and competence that will strengthen us.

Ours is an imperfect society, and social work is part of that society. It seems remarkable that this profession continues to enjoy anniversary celebrations which are testimony to our professional survival. We take time to change, sometimes generations of time. And just when it appears that all is hopeless, we take up new challenges and try again. Is it our self-effacement or our courage that sustains us? In each new era, whether one of social progress or regression, we hang in there. And that is the real meaning of accountability.

NOTES

1. For a recent example of several studies that trace the "uncertain mandate" in social welfare and social work, *see* Walter Trattner, *From Poor Law to Welfare State* (New York: Free Press, 1974).

2. For an exposition of the way developments in social work (casework) theories and in science have not kept pace, *see* Carel B. Germain, "Casework and Science: A Historical Encounter," in Robert W. Roberts and Robert H. Nee, eds., *Theories of Social Casework* (Chicago: University of Chicago Press, 1970).

3. For examples of varied approaches (although applicable mostly to casework), *see* Francis J. Turner, *Social Work Treatment* (New York: Free Press, 1974); Alan Pincus and Anne Minahan, *Social Work Practice: Model and Method* (Itasca, Ill.: F. E. Peacock Publishers, 1973); Carol H. Meyer, *Social Work Practice: The Changing Landscape* (New York: Free Press, 1976); and Howard Goldstein, *Social Work Practice: A Unitary Approach* (Chapel Hill: University of North Carolina, 1973).

4. *See* Porter R. Lee, "Social Work: Cause and Function," in *Proceedings of the National Conference of Social Work, 1929* (Chicago: University of Chicago Press, 1930). Lee identifies the dual qualities of idealism (cause) and efficiency (function) as integral elements of social work, although there have been periods of polarization when social reform and scientific method have been pursued separately.

5. *What Is Social Case Work?* (New York: Russell Sage Foundation, 1922). In this attempt at definition, Richmond elaborates on work with man in his life-space, including the primary use of environmental supports. *See also* Carol H. Meyer, "Purposes and Boundaries—Social Casework 50 Years Later," *Social Casework*, 54 (May 1973), pp. 268–275.

6. *See* William E. Gordon, "Basic Constructs for an Integrative and Generative Conception of Social Work," in Gordon A. Hearn, ed., *The General Systems Approach: Contributions toward an Holistic Conception of Social Work* (New York: Council on Social Work Education, 1969).

7. *See* Carel B. Germain, "An Ecological Perspective in Casework Practice," *Social Casework*, 54 (June 1973), pp. 323–330; and Ann Hartman, "To Think about the Unthinkable," *Social Casework*, 51 (October 1970), pp. 467–474. The Germain article attempts to define an ecological perspective, and the Hartman article comments on the necessity for a systems conception to account for the multiplicity of variables in cases. Together, the approach can be called an ecosystems approach.

8. *See* Shirley Jenkins and Elaine Norman, *Filial Deprivation* (New York: Columbia University Press, 1972). This is a study of the effects on parents of the placement of their children. Literature on maternal deprivation is more well known, but filial deprivation was first studied formally in this book.

9. *Child Welfare*, a journal of the Child Welfare League of America, reports regularly on varying forms and varying temporal periods for child placement.

10. *See NASW Standards for Social Work Personnel Practices*, NASW Policy Statements, No. 2 (rev. ed.; Washington, D.C.: National Association of Social Workers, 1975).

The State of Society

MITCHELL I. GINSBERG

Emphasis on social work skills and competence is an absolutely essential focus today because people in need require the best in professional practice. Technical competence that is recognizable and accepted by the community is the foundation of the social work profession. Social workers cannot permit their necessary involvement in social and political issues to dull their concern for technical competence. Sometimes it seems easier to focus on the broader issues, but even in that arena, technical competence is essential in influencing social policy issues. The right to exert influence must be earned; no one will concede it because of good intentions. Likewise, effective practice never results solely from good intentions or worthy goals. This profession is not likely to be popular, but in any case to be respected for competence is more important.

Because social work is carried on in the context of societal forces and conditions, political, social, and economic factors affect all that we do. Social work skills and social policy development are directly interrelated; no division or dichotomy can exist between the two, and discussions about which is more important are fruitless. Also, there is no basis for a crusade for either ideology, and any effort to bring about ideological unity should be opposed. The profession must have room for a variety of ideologies within the context of a commitment to services for people.

POSITIVE TRENDS AND DEVELOPMENTS

In this paper, some of the current trends and developments in society that affect social work practice will be addressed. Although pessimism and concern are warranted, there are some positive trends and developments. For example, the campaign for equal rights has made important, albeit insufficient, progress for some individuals and groups. The sexual revolution has had positive consequences for personal liberty, and the Women's Liberation Movement has been a constructive force.

Professional and management roles for those who have been kept out have started to open up. At the same time, there has been a beginning, even if reluctant, recognition that consumers and clients must have some voice in the programs which affect them. Despite the profession's value system, there has been too little involvement of consumers in social work. Social workers have tended to view such involvement more as a "fad" or "cause" than a recognized process. Unfortunately, there is something of a backlash against this approach at this time. There has also been more awareness of the importance of racial and ethnic factors in the provision of services.

Knowledge and information available to social workers have increased and, it is hoped, they have a somewhat more realistic understanding of what they know and do not know, and what they can and cannot do. The problem has not been *lack* of knowledge; rather, practitioners have not made effective use of the knowledge they already have.

Above all, this nation has been able to survive the almost incredible political shocks that have taken place in the last few years. This alone is of overriding importance.

ECONOMIC CONDITIONS

Despite these pluses, there is good reason, based on objective evidence, to be pessimistic about current trends and developments. The economic situation has been and continues to be disastrous for the people and programs with which social workers are involved. Inflation has had its impact on everybody, but there is no question that poor people have been hurt the most. The consequences are much more severe for certain groups—for minorities, the aged, those on fixed incomes, welfare recipients, and so on.

The recent recession has had an even more serious and lasting impact than inflation because it tends to hit hardest at low-income groups. Minorities and women are generally the first to lose their jobs, having been the last to be hired. All too little attention has been paid by social workers and everyone else to the disastrous consequences of the loss of a job or to the inability to obtain one. Unemployment means much more than just the absence of money.

Unfortunately, social workers' orientation and training have tended to emphasize subjective and individualistic factors instead of more objective ones, such as no money, no jobs, and poor housing. It is especially difficult to understand and accept unemployment, knowing that much of it is a result of deliberate national policy. Presumably, to reduce inflation, no action has been taken by the Administration on unemployment; but obviously, that objective has not been achieved to any significant extent. Even though the recession has substantially increased the number of people who live below the poverty level, there has been a frustrating lack of indignation and outrage at this policy. As Garfinkel and Plotnick state in "Poverty, Unemployment and the Current Recession," "To the extent that recession in general, and this recession in particular, are justified on the basis of curing inflation, at least from the point of view of the poor, the medicine is worse than the disease." [1]

A recent paper prepared for a Social Policy Committee meeting of the American Public Welfare Association concludes:

> In sum, the costs of unemployment include losses in federal revenue, a worsening of income distribution, increases in the number of persons in poverty and in the poverty gap, decreases in production, and significant social costs such as the retardation of family formation, increases in illegitimate activities, and deepening of race and class divisions.[2]

Attitudes of the Administration

Let us look closely at the attitudes and actions of the Administration. President Gerald Ford has made a number of speeches about the need to cut back on expenditures for social welfare. He and his colleagues have defined these expenditures as a major cause of inflation. Ford has repeatedly expressed his concern for the need for higher expenditures for the Defense Department as a result of inflation; but that has not been matched by a similar concern as to the impact of inflation on social programs.

The president has also made a number of speeches in which he expresses great concern for business and supports additional aid for companies and corporations. He has attacked some members of Congress who, he said, would prefer to devote more government support to redistributing some of the American wealth to aid the socially deprived.[3] Whatever it means, Ford has pledged to get government "out of your business, out of your life, out of your pockets, and out of your hair." He has said that it is not government's business to help change income distribution in the country. The question is, Whose business is it if not the government's? What Ford really means is that he continues to support a situation whereby 1 percent of the population has substantially more income and resources than the bottom 20 percent of the population.

Vice-President Nelson Rockefeller, too, has made speeches about the dangers of bureaucracy and high government spending, especially in the form of welfare programs. He has repeatedly expressed his dedication to states' rights and states' responsibility, and we know all too well what that can mean.

In his farewell speech as retiring secretary of the U.S. Department of Health, Education, and Welfare, Caspar Weinberger emphasized "the growing danger of an all-pervasive federal government." As an illustration, he said, "This shift in federal spending has transformed the task of aiding life's victims from a private concern to a public obligation." [4] That statement represents a clear-cut difference in philosophy between Weinberger and the Administration on the one hand and the social work profession's point of view on the other. Yes, it is a private concern; but it is also a public obligation.

One cannot help but be impressed by the repeated concern about business expressed by the leadership of the present Administration. Would that a similar concern were expressed for social welfare programs! Obviously, business is highly important in this country, and there is no value in or basis for simply attacking business as such. But business should at least be held to the same standards as everyone else. There is little or no evidence of this. Not too long ago, for example, the people of this country heard about the payment of bribes, or "kickbacks," by Lockheed Aircraft and other companies, which was defined as common industrial and business practice. What was overlooked was that, if such expenditures are defined as kickbacks rather than bribes, they might become tax deductible. For such purposes might Americans' tax money be used— but not for programs for poor people!

The people of this country have also been hearing about illegal political payments of all types, as well as cheating and fraud in grain sales and deliveries—the list goes on and on. Note the public attention and concern about such actions in comparison with the attention given to welfare fraud. Recently Lewis Engman, chairman of the Federal Trade Commission, said: "Our airlines, our truckers, our railroads, our electronic media and countless others are on the dole. We get irate about welfare fraud but our system of hidden regulatory subsidies makes welfare fraud look like petty larceny." [5] That was not the statement of a social worker, but of a leading figure in the Administration!

The Administration's general stance is reflected also in its attitudes toward cities and social problems. Not so long ago the president announced that the "urban crisis was over." That indeed was news to most of us who live and/or work in the cities. At the same time, he was willing to help such companies as Lockheed, Penn Central Transportation Company, and Franklin National Bank—although it would be hard to define these as models of management efficiency.

It would be a mistake, however, to think that these attitudes are confined to the president, to this Administration, or to any one political party. The reality is that many congressmen reflect similar points of view. There are differences on some issues, but Congress has failed to provide significant alternatives in most areas of social work concern. Many of our expectations for this Congress have simply not been fulfilled. At this point it is difficult to find many major voices in either political party with points of view significantly different from that of the Administration. One cannot overlook the actions of recently elected governors in such states as Massachusetts and California, where it is indeed hard to distinguish between the actions of "liberal Democrats" and their conservative Republican predecessors. Even in New York State and New York City, the Democrats have moved much more toward fiscal conservatism: "The Democratic shift toward fiscal conservatism is so pronounced that differences with the traditionally conservative Republican party [in the state and the city] are becoming increasingly blurred." [6]

The reality is that most of these attitudes have widespread public and political support. Many political figures are responding to what they believe are the attitudes of most people. To support this contention, one need only ask social workers in Massachusetts and California about the public support for their governors' actions. The attacks on welfare programs and on social work have been heavy, and there have been recent attacks on welfare recipients. The victims are again being defined as the cause of the problem.

New York City

Many of these attitudes and trends are illustrated by recent developments in New York City. New York City is not the whole country, of course, but what happens there is usually the forerunner of what will happen elsewhere. The city has been faced with an overwhelming fiscal crisis, and only reluctantly and in grudging fashion has the president been willing to provide any help.

Much of the blame for New York City's difficulties has been attributed to welfare costs and other social programs. Obviously, these programs are expensive. But what are the city's choices? The city has made mistakes, but the problems it faces are not unique to it. The truth has been and is that many poor people live in New York City, and it is to the city's credit that it has made some effort to do something for them. As Jimmy Breslin wrote in a column in the *Boston Globe* on August 11, 1975, "Our city has perhaps been too compassionate, but for that I shall ever be proud to say that I live here."

Recently, Secretary of the Treasury William Simon compared New York City's welfare costs with those of other cities, using this comparison to suggest that New York was spending too much.[7] But his comparison was meaningless because he compared New York with other cities that carry neither financial nor other administrative responsibilities for welfare programs. Chicago is a good example. It has a welfare population proportionately almost the same as that of New York City, but it spends nothing for welfare—the state carries most of the burden, with some contribution from the county. Compare that with New York City, which is required to contribute almost a billion dollars a year for welfare and Medicaid. Chicago is widely praised for balancing its budget. Without having to pay for welfare, Medicaid, and other services, it becomes easy indeed to balance a city's budget!

Social workers must accept the reality of these factors and these forces and the impact on what they do. Likewise, they must reject the point of view that they should not or cannot do anything about them. Obviously, doing something will not be easy, and their role is indeed limited.

SOCIAL POLICY ISSUES

Social work has a special stake in social policy issues simply because it is the kind of profession it is. Social policy also affects all the services social workers offer and is an area in which many social workers practice. It is part of the responsibility of all social workers—including clinical social workers, private practitioners, and agency workers—to recognize and accept their responsibility to identify and promote appropriate social change. Private practice has value and is important, but no social worker should seek private practice as a refuge from carrying his appropriate responsibilities as a social worker.

It is essential that social workers become more knowledgeable and sophisticated about economic and political factors, which requires much more knowledge of the political process than is usually required of social workers. An excellent illustration of the way the political process works is contained in an article by Elizabeth Drew titled "The Energy Bazaar." [8] She hows how many conflicting interests over a particular issue can result in paralysis and an inability to do anything. She indicates the different forces and factors that operate and how they cause individuals and groups to act differently than expected, and she points out that the first objective of all politicians is to be reelected. Understanding these and other facts can help social workers avoid disappointment and disillusionment and function much more effectively.

Yet social workers must recognize that there is often a need for trade-offs. Most important, social welfare issues pose conflicting dilemmas and difficulties. For example, most of us would prefer increased cash payments to food stamps; but if the former is not feasible, should we really oppose the latter? There may indeed be a strong rationale at times for a refusal to compromise, but this can result in little or no impact on how issues are resolved.

There is also a need for social workers to understand better such matters as budgets and tax policies and their impact on programs for people. The federal budget is the single most important government document, but how much of it do social workers understand? How many recognize that the only group to be affected negatively by the 1974–75 tax proposals of the president would be people with the lowest incomes? That group would wind up paying more taxes, and every other group in the country would pay less.

Obviously there are limits on what each person can be knowledgeable about, and policymakers will not necessarily pay attention to social workers even if they have information and know the facts. But one can be absolutely sure that without the information they certainly will not listen! Social workers also have to be aware that political and policy decisions are often made without regard to research findings, even when available. Although frustrating, this realization is no excuse for not continuing the efforts.

Social workers need to develop knowledge and understanding that reduces the danger of rhetoric and unachievable goals and helps to distinguish between the "oughts" and the "is's." Otherwise, they will either retreat into narrow clinical preoccupations in the worst sense or become cynically disengaged opportunists. Both are unacceptable; the only alternative is to continue the struggle to be better informed and to have at least some impact on policy decisions.

All this has specific and direct relevance to social work education. It is essential that more emphasis be placed on the teaching of such subjects as political science, government, and politics. It is interesting that preparation for social work emphasizes psychology, sociology, and similar subjects instead of these.

Accountability

Much is being said and written today on the issue of accountability, and it is indeed one that social workers have to face. It is a crucial issue in current practice, and more and more accountability is being demanded of us. Certainly we need to be more accountable. But a legitimate question is, Accountable to whom and for what? We must be aware that different interests, which may often be in conflict, are involved. Thus being accountable in welfare means one has to be responsible to welfare recipients, taxpayers, political leaders, staff members, and so on. It would be hard to make the case that there are not likely to be differing viewpoints among them.

Another part of the accountability issue is the difficulty in developing and using appropriate measurement instruments. To do that, social workers need to be clearer about their objectives and be able to break them down into small, more manageable elements. Also, more emphasis must be given to consumer response to services—an element that has not received much attention, but is an important part of accountability. At the same time, social workers should not oversell their capacity or knowledge about what they can and cannot do, and they must constantly work to improve their abilities.

The profession has been increasingly interested in such aspects of professionalism as licensing and peer review. These can be constructive aspects of accountability, but are not ends in themselves.

What is crucial in our programs is the people involved. Too often social workers seem to be so busy being accountable that they do not see clients or give any service. Some recent reports indicate that workers in some public welfare agencies are spending a maximum of four hours a week actually seeing clients because they are so busy with forms and with being accountable. Considerably more attention and emphasis has to be focused on the dilemmas involved in accountability to the agency, to the consumer, to the profession, and to each other. Experience in this profession, and in other professions as well, demonstrates that accountability solely to a profession and its membership is not enough.

Administration of Programs

Certainly there is need for more effective organization and for better management of social programs, and sufficient attention has not been given to the use of new managerial knowledge, techniques, and hardware. But it must be remembered that although automation and computers have important roles, they certainly provide no panaceas. They themselves are value-free, but they can be used in ways that are destructive to people. The challenge is to make them effective tools. Social workers need to speak up much more strongly on management and organizational issues. Too often social workers accept the widely held notion that they cannot be good administrators, even though there is little evidence to support such a view. Knowledge and competence in the programs involved are significant plus factors rather than handicaps in regard to management.

At the same time, considerable evidence points to the fact that many businesses are less than efficiently administered. There is no justification for poor management on the part of social welfare; but just imagine the public uproar if social workers did as poorly as some businesses, institutions, and governmental departments. This is not an excuse for being inefficient and ineffective, but it is important to keep in mind that social workers are administering and operating programs in one of the most difficult areas of human endeavor. Better administration is essential, but it must be made clear that major social problems will not be solved by better management alone.

Social Services

The current debate about possible changes in Title XX of the Social Security Act social service program gives us the opportunity to emphasize the need for clearer definitions of service roles and for testing different approaches to social services. Title XX should not be oversold. It is a useful piece of legislation; but thus far it has not provided any additional money, and inflation indeed means that the same amount of money results in less service.

Some people have been pushing to reopen the old debate on the concept of the separation of services from income maintenance. As a concept, it was oversold in the first place by many of us, but there is little or no value in opening up another major debate on the issue. Not much service has been offered under either system. The question is, how can we insure that the right kind of services are provided for people and that the appropriate workers are responsible for seeing that the necessary services are delivered?

Employment

The importance of focusing on employment and the meaning of work much more than in the past needs reemphasizing. Not only has too little emphasis been given to this important issue, but social workers have also given the impression that they are not too interested in it. Early in 1975 at a national conference on full employment, George Meany, president of the AFL-CIO, indicated that employment was the crucial issue for him and his membership. But he went on to say that, unfortunately, social workers do not seem much concerned about it. Work is a crucial issue for people and is an area in which social workers can make a contribution. In addition, unions and industry do offer significant potential for an expansion of service programs and employment opportunities for social workers.

Collaboration

There is also the need to work cooperatively and in collaboration with other professionals and disciplines. Social workers have an opportunity to provide leadership in helping to coordinate and, if possible, integrate human services. This will not be easy, but if we do not take on this assignment, others will do it for us.

SUMMARY AND CONCLUSIONS

Many important issues—health insurance, welfare reform, social security, juvenile and criminal justice, and so on—have not been dealt with in this paper. The health field, including national health insurance and health maintenance organizations, will offer significant opportunities for service if the appropriate legislation is adopted and if social workers are involved and have something to offer. Also, such important issues as changing family patterns, sex roles, attitudes toward racial and ethnic issues, attitudes toward work, and lack of confidence in government and the professions (including social work) have not been dealt with.

Instead, the intent of this paper has been to make clear what the social and political climates are and what their inevitable effects will be on the social work profession. Also, some areas that call for new and expanded efforts have been suggested. Performance is essential in itself and is a way of making a meaningful contribution to social problems. But, as individuals and as a profession, we have been overly preoccupied with organizational and internal issues.

The importance of focusing on professional competence should be reemphasized. In the days to come, an important if not radical question may well be how to change the professional rigidities and the ideological biases that handicap us in our practice. This means we must concentrate on how we deliver services, who our clients are, and how we can make more democratic the relationships between worker and client.

Social workers have much to offer in helping to meet the needs of people in the context of the social concerns discussed in this paper. Although we are often attacked as "do-gooders," we have reason to be proud of this description. But, as a friend has suggested, the description is especially meaningful when we are also "good-doers." Doing good in itself is not significant unless we are also good at what we are doing.

NOTES

1. *Public Welfare*, 33 (Summer 1975), pp. 10–17.

2. American Public Welfare Association Social Policy Committee, "Problems of Unemployment and Underemployment." Unpublished paper, Washington, D.C., 1976.

3. *New York Times*, August 26, 1975.

4. From a speech titled "A View of the Federal Government," given on July 21, 1975, before the Commonwealth Club of San Francisco.

5. "Consumer Is Paying Plenty" *U.S. News and World Report*, November 4, 1974, pp. 81–82.

6. *New York Times*, September 14, 1975.

7. Correspondence with the author, September 8, 1975, and July 31, 1975.

8. *New Yorker*, July 21, 1975, pp. 35–72.

The Future of Social Work Skill

BARBARA BRYANT SOLOMON

As the last quarter of the twentieth century begins, futurism is neither science fiction nor dramatic form. It is, rather, a societal force of great power that has generated its own disciples and its own discipline. Futurism is also a serious field of inquiry wherein future probabilities are determined through the use of sophisticated mathematical tools. Despite the significance of probability in gaining a perspective on the future of the society or the future of the social work profession, there is at least one certainty: The future will bring change.

The intellectual challenge represented by the complexities involved in identifying, predicting, and even controlling change has intrigued a host of social critics, including Alvin Toffler, Phillip Slater, Theodore Roszak, Margaret Mead, Nicholas Rescher, and Charles Reich.[1] Their writings evoke a surreal image of giant fortune cookies labeled "future shock," "ecospasm," "counterculture," "co-figurative society," "post-welfare society," and "Consciousness III." The collective message seems to be "break open your fortune cookie and find the conceptual map to the future." Social work, as part of the institutional structure of American society, has conceived of itself as an instrumentality of change on behalf of its client systems. But, our fortune cookies have so far not provided any clear vision of social work's future.

If there is continuity between present and future, it could be expected that our future will continue to reflect an intense commitment to the development of professional skills. It is not surprising, given the complexity of our professional goals, that social work practice entails a diversity of skills—such as organizational tinkering, behavior modification, program evaluation, assertive training, community development, sex discrimination counseling, advocacy, and affective education. These and other skills are practiced in settings as diverse as ghetto courts, industrial organizations, police stations, migrant labor camps, new towns, and doctors' offices, as well as in the traditional settings. This remarkable diversity could suggest that there is no clear direction, no guidance system that can give social workers a lock on the future. Consideration of a certain aspect of the Mariner spaceflights might help to dispel that notion, however.

On a cold night in February 1973, Mariner IV pushed off from earth for a fly-by rendezvous with the planet Mars. The spacecraft was designed to maintain a specific orientation in space that would permit it to point heat shields at the sun, antennae at Earth, and cameras and other instruments at Martian points of interest. Under normal circumstances, this orientation is maintained by fixing a tracking device on board the spacecraft onto certain stars visible along its orbit. Unfortunately, the separation of Mariner IV from the restraints that had protected it during launching dislodged sunlit particles of dust which drifted in front of its star tracker and lured the spacecraft from its proper orientation. But space scientists on the Mariner project were not trained merely to carry out a specific set of technical maneuvers that, if ineffective, would leave them at the mercy of chance. These scientists knew how to apply knowledge from physics, astronomy, mathematics, and engineering to the solution of the problem posed—*even though that problem was not one which any of their teachers had ever anticipated!*

By the time Mariner VI began its journey a year later, the problem had already been solved. When the sunlit dust particles again drifted in front of the star tracker, instructions now held in the computer put into operation an intricate set of maneuvers that would reestablish proper orientation. The crucial information was not born in the comptuer; it developed out of the creative application of knowledge in the minds of men—knowledge gained through the unbeatable combination of education and experience.[2]

It is the position of this paper that the future of social work skill lies inevitably in the partnership of social work education with social work practice or, more specifically, in the ability of social work education to prepare practitioners who can develop and apply the multiple skills needed to solve a wide range of problems—even unanticipated and rare problems. As Kadushin suggests, however, our batting average in the game of professional practice may need to be far less than a thousand to prove our worth.[3] At the same time, our strikeouts should be based on the inadequacy of information needed to link theoretical perspectives to action strategies, or even on the inadequacy or incompleteness of theory, and *not* on the unexpectedness or infrequency of the problem presented.

The remainder of this paper addresses the following issues: (1) social work education's relative commitment to the university and to the profession, (2) the challenge to social work education to teach the integration of theory and practice, and (3) the relative commitment of the social work profession to practice involving microsystems and macrosystems. The tensions produced within the profession by these issues can be creative or destructive, depending on social workers' capacity to manage them successfully.

THE UNIVERSITY AND THE PROFESSION

The consensus in the profession is that the source of the knowledge base for practice is in professional education. In fact, it is the commitment to a scientific base for practice that provides primary justification for social work education to be located within the university system. Ben-David, in his discussion of the professional school in higher education, makes the point that a body of systematic knowledge which goes beyond the traditional skills of different occupations has to exist. If such knowledge does not exist, there is no reason to teach the professional skills in a university; they would be better acquired in actual practice.[4] Universities have placed top priority on building systematic knowledge, that is, theory-building. Social work educators in the university, therefore, are often subject to the same research and publication demands as their colleagues in comparative literature, political science, or geology. But social work educators must serve two masters: the university and the profession. Furthermore, many social work professionals perceive the criteria used by the university to identify competence in faculty (e.g., a doctorate) as not necessarily identifying professional competence.[5] These professionals—staff of social agencies, social work practitioners in host settings, private social work practitioners, and those involved in the administration of the National Association of Social Workers—are much more likely to define faculty competence in terms of effectiveness in developing in students those skills that are directly applicable to the client population they will encounter after graduation.

   Not all the pressures felt by social work educators come from within the profession. There is certainly not total agreement among academicians about the legitimacy of professional education in general within the framework of the university. The positions range along a broad continuum. At one extreme is Mayhew, who contends that the rationale for a professional school within the university not only can be provided but that the rationale does not depend on the professional school's commitment to "a search for truth." From his point of view, "the professions can draw support only from the American tradition of service to the community." [6] At the other extreme is Wolff, who decries the presence of professional schools in the university and suggests that "all professional schools . . . should be driven out of the university and forced to set themselves up as independent institutes." [7] His major reason for adopting this radical point of view is the same accountability to the community that Mayhew found commendable and as providing greater justification than the search for truth. Wolff, however, feels that a professional school in a university inevitably has divided loyalties—to the community and to the university. But the university ought to have total commitment to its goals from all its constituent parts.

The degree to which social work education's dual perspective is a case of divided loyalties can certainly be questioned; it appears more likely that a complementary alliance exists. Social work educators in university settings have been among the strongest supporters of the accountability of education to professional practice.[8] At the same time, that graduate schools of social work do not encourage their faculties to keep current with the concerns, demands, or realities of practice is not a wholly unwarranted criticism. But creative proposals have been made that promise to intensify the concurrent involvement of educators with practice and practitioners with education.[9] The field component of social work education has always been a significant one, and from the standpoint of number of hours involved, the field component could be considered *the* most significant one. In fact, professional disciplines that do not have a tradition of field experience in their curricula (e.g., public administration) have studied and adopted the field component of social work curricula as models for their own professional education.

Yet the question of whether graduate schools of social work emphasize theory and theory-building to the detriment of practice is, perhaps, a wrong concern. The need to integrate theory and practice is a widely accepted goal of professional social work. The greatest obstacle to achieving that integration is a basic distortion in the very conceptualization of theory and practice as separate entities. Social workers do, in fact, have theories of human behavior and theories of practice. The challenge is to integrate the theories of behavior, or behavioral science theory, into theories of practice.

INTEGRATING THEORY AND PRACTICE

The development of effective practice theory depends on the effective translation of behavioral science theory into an action system for problem-solving. Generations of students in social work have been confronted with a veritable thicket of behavioral science theories—psychoanalytic theory, learning theory, personality theory, general systems theory, and so on. On the other hand, they have also been exposed to another thicket of practice theories, or intervention models—behavior modification, gestalt therapy, transactional analysis, or crisis intervention. But, the bridging concepts and principles have been far too few and much too vague. What is required, then, is a more effective methodology or methodologies for connecting behavioral science theory with theories of practice. Stated another way, what is needed is a more effective technology for the integration of general theories of human behavior with specific theories of practice.

The unevenness of social work education in providing an opportunity system for students to integrate behavioral science theory and practice theory has led to a variety of outcomes. Some graduates have been exposed to an integration process, but usually in regard to a narrow theoretical perspective; there are still those among us who remember with admiration and gratification the skill of the great orthodox teachers out of the psychoanalytic, Rankian, or even Rogerian traditions. Many other students have not been exposed to a specific technology for integration, although such integration was almost always identified as a value and as a goal. Some of these students were able to make the necessary linkages after entering practice. Of course, social work educators point out that graduate education can only provide a beginning level of knowledge and skill, which the practitioner builds on throughout his professional life. This process is surely enhanced if one has mastered the skill of integrating behavioral science and practice theories. Furthermore, there are far too many students who learn considerable theoretical jargon but remain essentially atheoretical, intuitive, and often idiosyncratic in their practice.

Perhaps the most useful advances in the teaching of social work practice have come with the emergence, in the professional literature, of conceptualizations of practice that do not depend on specific theories of personality or interpersonal behavior. Argyris has been concerned with "intervention theory and method," but with primary emphasis on intervention with complex organizations—business firms, governmental bureaus, city governments, labor unions, or universities.[10] On the other hand, Bloom described such a methodology with specific focus on social work and its target systems. In *The Paradox of Helping,* Bloom states: "The practice form equivalent to the scientific method wears many guises and can be found in all the helping professions." [11] He then proceeds to demonstrate that in specific but different practice theories—task-centered casework, behavior modification, problem-solving casework—there is a single set of events and these events follow the steps in the scientific method: (1) an orientation toward problem-solving, (2) problem definition and formulation, (3) generation of alternatives regarding probable causal system, (4) decision-making, (5) implementation, (6) verification, and (7) termination and continuity of effect.

One might well question why it is useful to climb up the abstraction ladder to a more general theory of practice. Is it not true that identifiable skills are more likely to be derived from more specific theories of practice? A response to these questions can best be couched in a parallelism. If my daughter wished to learn to sew (or, in the spirit of contemporary unisex, my son), she could learn something useful by watching a demonstration which could insure that she could sew at least one garment. If she were taught to sew by a pattern, however, she would be able to sew as many different garments as there are patterns. But perhaps the greatest lesson of all would be for her to also learn to make patterns; then she would be limited only by her creativity and ingenuity. Bloom's model of scientific practice is, then, "a pattern for patterns" that is subject to a variety of ideological interpretations. Most importantly, if this general theory of practice were taught as part of the core content of the social work curriculum, it would provide a solid base upon which specialized practice strategies and continuing education could readily be constructed.

THE MICROSYSTEM—MACROSYSTEM ISSUE

A pervasive theme in the Twentieth Anniversary Symposium of the National Association of Social Workers was the inseparability of microsystem and macrosystem objectives. But several symposium papers referred to the intraprofessional tension regarding the relative emphasis to be given to microlevel and macrolevel practice in social work education. The issue conjures up memories of the upheavals, torments, and rhetoric of the 1960s that left many of us in social work education deeply wounded. That rhetoric defined us as hopelessly irrelevant, even disoriented from our "real" goals as a profession. We were told that we were ignoring the fact that most of those who need social work services present problems which stem from the dysfunctional operations of an oppressive society, while we offer only to tinker with the rational adaptations made to deal with that oppression.[12]

Ironically, the message most frequently heard in the 1970s has been exactly the reverse. Social work education is now accused of abandoning that area of practice in which it has been most effective, that is, direct service to clients. It is said that educators have given too much attention to the larger social system and its problems: institutional racism or the ascendancy to power over people's lives of more and more remote bureaucracies, whether embedded within the hierarchy of centralized government or within the interlocking boards of multinational corporations. It is now suggested that these systemic problems are impervious to the skills educators actually possess; further, that by giving these problems an inordinate emphasis in the curriculum, educators have limited the opportunities for students to develop potentially more powerful skills in the direct service area.

The issue of the relative emphasis to be given microlevel and macrolevel strategies of intervention in social work education is not easy to resolve; cogent arguments are made in support of a variety of positions. There is certainly evidence that spokesmen for the profession, including social work educators, refuse to adopt an either-or position and maintain a commitment to practice at the individual level and the system level. A report of the Carnegie Commission on Higher Education confirms the presence of this commitment to a dual perspective. But it indicates that, upon examination, it is apparent that clinical concerns far outweigh system concerns:

> At this stage in its development, social work education continues to have a very large commitment to clinical types of practice . . . The majority of social work students are still being trained for individualized direct service to the clientele who come to the attention of social agencies. Only a minority, even at the graduate level, are being trained specifically for positions as the organizers and managers of those services.[13]

When the professional currents of the 1960s and early 1970s are considered as a whole, the shifting emphasis given to microlevel and macrolevel concerns is consistent with the shifting orientation of the total society toward its poor and minority populations. In that sense, social work is an expression of society's values and priorities. Macrosystem problems —for example, poverty and dysfunctional systems of criminal justice, health, and education—are experienced most intensely and with the most destructive consequences by the poor and minority populations. Thus social work's retreat from macrolevel concerns would be as reactionary and regressive as the social and economic policies of the Nixon-Ford administrations, which social workers have attacked so vigorously. Social workers undoubtedly have strong feelings of impotence and frustration when they consider the lack of success they have had as a profession in dealing with macrolevel problems. These feelings should energize social work's search for more effective strategies. Furthermore, there should be a continuing concern, among more than a small proportion of the nonminority members in the professional organizations, for collective action against the dysfunctional and oppressive political and economic systems that, in the long run, impinge negatively on all people.

Evidence exists that close attention to the development of behavioral science theories which explain macrosystem behavior can in fact lead to more effective strategies of macrolevel intervention. Boulding's scholarly analysis of social protest activities in the 1960s demonstrates the connection between theories of behavior and theories of intervention. On the basis of his analysis, he was able to develop several hypotheses regarding the relationship between the nature of the protest and its outcome. One hypothesis is his suggestion that "the form of the protest should be closely related to the object of the protest." [14] For example, the sit-in demonstrations were extremely effective because the form utilized by the demonstrators was observably connected to their goal. Boulding also suggests that social protest is most successful when it serves to crystallize feelings or attitudes that are already present in a majority of the population. And there were strong feelings among the American public in support of the right of all Americans to have equal access to public accommodations. Boulding's hypotheses are related directly to social work's concern for developing strategies to deal effectively with macrosystems.

During the halcyon days of the Great Society programs in the 1960s, minority-group spokesmen expressed their belief in the right to self-determination by demanding the right to control the service delivery systems in their communities. Furthermore, they suggested that liberal, white social workers give paramount attention to those problems endemic to white communities which are at the source of so many of the problems experienced in minority communities. Thus, from the perspective gained by Boulding's analysis of protest activities, the position taken by those minority spokesmen can be viewed as something more than empty, militant rhetoric. Instead, it was congruent with the notion that there must be a change in the attitudes held by the majority before any protest aimed at crystallizing attitudes not currently held by that majority can be implemented effectively.

Yet professional social workers (and other helping professionals) have made relatively few systematic efforts aimed at dealing with macrolevel change. It may very well mean that when the economy again expands and the gap between haves and have-nots again becomes intolerable, the resulting urban unrest may again release a flood of dollars into social programming in poor and minority communities. If so, the real success of the last wave of urban welfare programs may then become apparent: the creation of a level of political and social awareness that will lead to the closing of those communities to social workers and others who merely ride in on the crest of federal dollars to dispense services—which may be ineffective or irrelevant—and ride out again when federal dollars subside.

It should be clear that the need to manage the relative emphasis of microlevel and macrolevel concerns in social work education and practice must be given top priority in the immediate and long-range future. The Carnegie Commission report suggests that effective management might well entail maximum development of both rather than the selection of either as the dominant concern of the profession:

> . . . the field of social work education, taken as an entity, has attempted to meet various demands and to avoid a monolithic choice. This is the in-

evitable tendency of any organized field of activity that is concerned with problems of domain. To make a choice at the present time among the various demands would mean a delimitation of the areas in which the social work profession might have a claim to render service.[15]

THE CHALLENGE AHEAD

The ability to confront tough problems with a combination of objectivity, optimism, and energy is perhaps the most remarkable skill that social work professionals have mastered. Moreover, we have little patience with doomsday theories that contain no escape hatches toward which professional activity can be directed. Thus the discussions and analyses of the critical issues facing the professions are intense and scholarly, but—above all—shot through with hope. So it is that the emphasis in this paper has been on basic trust in the partnership of social work education and social work practice to resolve or at least constructively manage those critical issues.

More important, perhaps, the future of the profession is not really in the year 2000. It is today. Furthermore, today will all too quickly become part of the history of our next twenty years as a profession. We are not short on challenges; we are not wanting for issues and controversies; we are not oblivious to our vulnerabilities and shortcomings. We also have, however, intelligence and professional skills—real and potential—for making the next twenty years the most productive and exciting yet experienced.

NOTES

1. See Alvin Toffler, *Future Shock* (New York: Random House, 1970), and *The Ecospasm Report* (New York: Bantam Books, 1975); Phillip Slater, *Earthwalk* (Garden City, N.Y.: Doubleday, Anchor Books, 1974); Theodore Roszak, *The Making of a Counterculture* (Garden City, N.Y.: Doubleday, Anchor Books, 1969); Margaret Mead, *Culture and Commitment* (New York: Doubleday, 1970); Nicholas Rescher, *Welfare: The Social Issues in Philosophical Perspective* (Pittsburgh: University of Pittsburgh Press, 1972); and Charles Reich, *The Greening of America* (New York: Random House, 1970).

2. An excellent nontechnical discussion of the Mariner space program is available in a report of the National Aeronautics and Space Administration, *Five Months at Sea* (undated).

3. Alfred Kadushin, "The Challenge of Accountability from the Perspective of a Nonpractitioner." Paper presented before the NASW Twentieth Anniversary Professional Symposium, Hollywood-by-the-Sea, Fla., October 1975.

4. Joseph Ben-David, *Trends in American Higher Education* (Chicago: University of Chicago Press, 1972), p. 92.

5. *See* Delwin Anderson, "Practice and Education: A Commentary," *Social Work* (November 1974), pp. 651–653.

6. Lewis Mayhew, *Changing Practices in Education for the Profession*, Southern Regional Education Board Monograph No. 17 (Atlanta, Ga.: Southern Regional Education Board, 1971).

7. Robert Paul Wolff, *The Ideal of the University* (Boston: Beacon Press, 1969), pp. 12–13.

8. *See* William C. Brennan, "The Practitioner as Theoretician," *Journal of Education for Social Work* 9 (Spring 1973), pp. 5–12; and Arnold Gurin and David Williams, "Social Work Education," in Everett Hughes et al., eds., *Education for the Professions of Medicine, Law, Theology and Social Welfare* (New York: McGraw-Hill Book Co., 1973), pp. 230–232.

9. *See* John L. Erlich and Jesse F. McClure, "The Grassroots Ivory Tower," *Social Work* 19 (November 1974), p. 653; Arthur Leader, "An Agency's View toward Education for Practice," *Journal of Education for Social Work* 7 (Fall 1971), pp. 27–34.

10. Chris Argyris, *Intervention Theory and Method: A Behavioral Science View* (Reading, Mass.: Addison-Wesley Publishing Co., 1970).

11. Martin Bloom, *The Paradox of Helping: Introduction to the Philosophy of Scientific Practice* (New York: John Wiley & Sons, 1975), p. 81.

12. *See* Billy Tidwell, "The Black Community's Challenge to Social Work," *Journal of Education for Social Work* 7 (Fall 1971), p. 64; and Douglas Glasgow, "Black Power through Community Control," *Social Work* 17 (May 1972), p. 59.

13. Gurin and Williams, op. cit., pp. 246–247.

14. Kenneth Boulding, "A Theory of Social Protest," *ETC: A Review of General Semantics* (March 1967), p. 53.

15. Gurin and Williams, op. cit., p. 245.

Part II:

Skills in Practice

Practice through Measurement

MARTIN BLOOM

Only recently has social work had access to a feasible technology for the practitioner in the field to evaluate scientifically the progress and product of his work with a single client, regardless of theoretical orientation used.[1] The availability of this technology renews the demand for an orientation toward using evaluation as an intrinsic part of scientific practice by each worker, all the time for every case. To move a profession toward adopting a new orientation requires (1) unfreezing the myths that lock in the old perspectives, (2) moving toward a conceptualization of practice events that permits both precision information retrieval (to generate a practice based on the best available knowledge) and systematic continuing evaluation (to receive objective feedback on the client's progress), and (3) incorporating these components into the body of scientific practice.[2]

MYTHS ABOUT EVALUATION TECHNOLOGY

A continuing mystique of unmeasurability that prevents many social workers from taking full advantage of any available technology seems to exist. Kaplan captures this mystique by saying, "If you can measure it, that ain't it," meaning that the isolating of important qualities of human behavior is impossible and, hence, anyone who claims to be doing this is ipso facto wrong. To be sure, no single quantitative measurement says everything there is to say about a phenomenon—nor does a single qualitative accounting, Kaplan notes.[3] But it is fully possible to identify important elements of behavior and feelings, as well as collective events, in quantifiable form—however one's theory reconstructs them—such that changes in them would constitute significant information related to problem resolution. If this were not possible, then "helping" would be a hollow word in the helping professions. A minimum quantifiable form is the nominal level of measurement that indicates the existence or nonexistence of some event. Higher levels of measurement indicate whether a variable is more or less than another or whether certain units or ratios obtain between them. Each higher level of measurement requires more information about the events, but permits a greater range of statistical operations to be performed on them.[4]

Perlman noted another barrier in this orientation toward using measurement: "Repeatedly there has been implied the primitive fear that if we name what we know the magic will disappear from it, that if we eat of the tree of knowledge, the Eden of intuitive arts will be lost to us."[5] Adding evaluation does not subtract from the creativity of practice; although it does transfer some energy, this transfer may reap multiple rewards in the form of accurate feedback on the ongoing process of intervention. Moreover, naming what social workers know leads to further knowing what we name, that is, knowing what others have learned about the kinds of problem events we face in our clients. If we go no further than the limits of our own intuition, however gratifying it may be, we do a grave injustice to our clients.

Another threat of modern evaluation methods is that they may be highly complex and may involve statistical procedures beyond the ken of the average practitioner. Indeed, some techniques may be highly complex, but reinforcements are on the way in the form of computer programs that take almost all the effort out of the evaluation process per se.[6] Some techniques are easy to use, both in terms of the level of mathematical background needed and in the actual computation for testing the significance of intervention.[7] The simpler methods, however, purchase ease at the price of accepting statistical assumptions that yield approximate answers. Social work has yet to explore the utility of these single worker/single client evaluation models, let alone teach them systematically in schools of social work. It may be that approximate answers are quite suitable to on-the-spot practice decisions.

Another source of resistance to technological evaluation is stated in words to this effect: "I have already tested my techniques in practice and have found them satisfactory for my purposes." It is not the author's intention to minimize clinical experience, but rather to strengthen it by putting it on an empirical basis; by so doing, the test of clinical experience may be satisfactory to the worker and may also serve the purposes of public accountability. Moreover, what we can demonstrate we can also teach more effectively, thus making each generation of social workers stronger by accumulating the empirical practice wisdom of the preceding generations.

Assume, then, that qualitatively meaningful events can be isolated, that numbers can be attached to the patterns of their expression, and that the available technology can be used for identifying the level of significance which social workers' interventions have on client problems. If these assumptions are correct, the myths that have prevented social work from making evaluation an intrinsic part of its practice have been destroyed.

CONCEPTUALIZATION: BRIDGE BETWEEN PRACTICE AND EVALUATION

Professional helping involves *abstractions* as well as *concrete reality; science* as well as *art; practice,* but also *accomplishment.* In the initial service contact, the worker demonstrates his engrossment with the reality of the client's problems. But if the worker were merely engrossed, however genuinely warm and sensitive he might be, no benefit would ensue beyond what engrossment the client and his family had already shown. The worker must also be professionally removed from the problem so as to abstract and generalize on the pattern of events the client has demonstrated and reported. As the worker attaches symbolic labels to these conceptualized events, he constructs conceptual maps that suggest tentative causal systems which enable him to identify points of intervention. Thus concepts describe the client's life situation but, in important ways, go beyond it.

Concepts as Vehicles for Information Retrieval

The concepts the worker has evolved are likely to have been used by other theorists or researchers in their work, and hence the worker's concepts become points of entry for the scientific knowledge base by means of key-word (i.e., concept) retrieval devices.[8] In principle, workers can find relevant references from over 1,800 behavioral and social science journals through the *Social Science Citation Index.*[9] Furthermore, workers can obtain brief, nonevaluative summaries of selected portions of this immense literature from either general abstracts (e.g., *Abstracts for Social Workers*) or specific abstracts directed toward a specialized group of users (e.g., *Bibliography on Suicide and Suicide Prevention*). Other forms of concept-oriented retrieval, such as the key-word-in-context (KWIC) system (e.g., *The Helping Person in the Group*), present each major term of an article title permuted around the other parts of the title so that an information searcher has multiple opportunities for locating the same article. Various types of paired-concept grids, such as the *Coordinate Index Reference Guide to Community Mental Health*, represent still another way concepts are used for precision information retrieval.

The advent of information science tools in the performance of social work is new. The level of complexity of these retrieval instruments is rising, enabling users to retrieve more precisely; but it also requires more care and study in learning how to use them effectively. Law students typically spend one or two semesters learning the range of their information storage and retrieval devices. A proportionate amount of time and energy should be required of applied social scientists so they will know and use their vast literature effectively. Most reference tools only point to locations where information is stored; direct access to the specific information contained in these references still needs to be provided.

Concepts as Vehicles for Evaluation

In their abstract form, concepts cannot be measured directly; rather, an attempt is made to measure variables, a form or version of concepts that can take various values (number, rate, etc.) corresponding to real events. The process of translating from concepts to variables has been little discussed in the applied fields, even though it is vital. Tripodi describes the process as one of converting a nominal definition (in which one term is defined by means of other terms whose commonly agreed on meaning is assumed) into an operational definition (in which the measuring procedure constitutes the full extent of the definition as well as the method of observation of the phenomenon).[10] How to convert from a nominal to an operational definition is not discussed by Tripodi, and it may be questioned whether such a conversion to a *researcher's* operational definition will benefit the *practitioner's* need for a precise definition suited to the action and value contexts in which he operates.

One way to convert nominal definitions into operational ones would be to examine all the operational definitions available to see which one is the "best." Unfortunately, there may be two or two dozen competing versions of operational definitions bearing the same or a similar nominal label.[11] Which is "best?" They are all, in principle, following the *research* operational philosophy. But from a practitioner's perspective, it may be that some are more feasible than others, some more controllable, some more ethical.[12] Practitioners have learned from the research operationalist philosophy what systems theorists call equifinality, which means that an end state may be reached from different initial conditions and by using different methods.[13] But more important, they have learned that the meaning of a *practitioner operational definition* comes from the demonstrable impact the practitioner has on the client's problem.[14] There is no single, sovereign road to practice; any demonstrable method that resolves problems, at the same "cost" level and without introducing new ones, is "best." But the method must be *demonstrable;*

the worker must be able to attach numbers to events such that the pattern of numbers indicates the course of the intervention. Changes in the pattern of numbers become sensitive indicators of improvement, deterioration, or stagnation, of effectiveness and of efficiency—all of which are vital information for effecting change in the client's problems.[15]

The nature of the demonstrability of practice requires information on the following elements:

1. A statement of specific problems, the external behavior or internally reported feelings, or combinations of these, that are part of the client's difficulties.

2. A statement of specific goals—those future events that the client wants and society permits and which are realistically feasible.

3. Statements of the contextual events that may hamper, be neutral to, or facilitate goals, given the specific system of events in the problem situation.

Each element of the demonstration involves a concept abstracted from the client's situation. Each element uses a nominal definition, a symbolic label through which the worker may seek the best available information to guide his practice. Each element should also involve an operational definition as reconstructed by the practitioner so that he can have a planned and measured impact on it, regardless of whether he takes a task-centered, behavior-centered, or client-centered approach. Numbers attached to patterns of abstracted events that indicate and influence the course of intervention—this is practice through measurement.

AN ILLUSTRATION

This illustration of practice through measurement is derived in part from a case study conducted by a second-year social work student.[16] A teacher in an elementary grade school complained of the acting-out behaviors of one of her students, an 11-year-old girl; at the same time, this child's guardian was seeking help regarding the child's misbehavior at home. The student worker assumed direction of both parts of the problem. After several meetings with the people involved, she was able to reconstruct the situation as described in the following discussion.

Problem Events

The worker identified eight specific problems—five in the home, three at school—that needed to be changed if the girl was to get along satisfactorily with her guardian and teacher in the course of her development. Details are not relevant here, except to emphasize that the worker chose specific problem events, the *sum* of which was the "problem." At home, for example, the girl did not do her chores without constant nagging by the guardian; she came home late from school and sassed her guardian. At school, the girl wandered around the classroom aimlessly, had crying tantrums, and so on. Rather than use such global labels as "acting-out problems," the worker chose to deal with a cluster of specific events.

Goals

The goals were defined by the guardian and teacher (as persons responsible for this minor) as an acceptable level of performance on each problem event. For example, the girl would do her chores as she and her guardian had agreed, or she would move around the classroom only when she had some legitimate task or destination. But, implicitly, the guardian and the teacher also agreed that another goal would be to keep the neutral events neutral (if no positive change had been planned for them); at the same time, the facilitating factors would be held constant (or strengthened), and hampering factors would be reduced if possible, or at least held constant. Let us look more closely at these factors.

Contextual Events

Several currently neutral events were important but not part of the perceived problems. For example, the girl had satisfactory peer relationships and her grades in school were satisfactory. If these neutral events were to become new problems during the intervention process, they would have to be termed "iatrogenic effects." [17] If they remained unchanged, the people involved would be satisfied. If the neutral events improved, the people involved would be surprised because they had not planned on this serendipitous outcome. But some objective baseline is needed to determine which of these conditions happens.

There were some facilitating factors as well: the good intentions of both guardian and teacher and the attention they had shown the girl. Facilitating factors become points of leverage in interventions; but it would be destructive of the situation if these were to be sharply reduced. Again, some kind of evaluation is needed.

The hampering factors included the guardian's frail health and poor economic status, which limited what she was able to do with and for her ward. The size of the class limited what the teacher was able to do for any one pupil. Indeed, the worker's caseload limited her involvement as well. And the girl had preoccupations other than being involved in the social work process. Intervention should not, in principle, make any of these factors worse. For example, the guardian's health should not be affected adversely by intervention, the teacher's class should not suffer from her extra attention to one child, and the social work process should not interfere with other aspects of the girl's life any more than absolutely necessary.

Thus many complex expectations were defined and measured for their initial status and were observed during and after the intervention. If all the expectations were met, the strong logical inference that the worker's intervention had something to do with the results would be supported. Using some elements of Campbell and Fiske's convergent and discriminant analysis applied to an individual design, it can be suggested that when the expected positive changes occur and some reduction among hampering conditions also occurs, while no significant changes transpire in currently neutral events, then the inference of effectiveness of practice may be entertained seriously.[18]

Is it possible for a worker to collect data on eight separate problems as well as several contextual factors? The answer is yes; this was in fact done by the worker in this case. Some of the data already existed as part of the natural conditions: for example, grades, records concerning problematic relationships with peers, and membership in peer organizations. Interview reports of the subjective factors, based on the rapport the worker had gained with guardian and teacher, were prepared. The client was directly involved in keeping records of her behavior (e.g., a checklist of when chores were done or class assignments completed). This reduced the burden of record-keeping for the guardian and the teacher and accentuated their role as providers of positive attention (and reinforcement) for the child when she completed her work.

The guardian, teacher, and worker were directly involved in the intervention tasks of generating a contract between themselves and the child and in providing the reinforcements for appropriate behaviors.[19] Thus different people were involved in collecting or reporting different pieces of the situation. The worker maintained only summary records obtained through weekly phone calls or visits to the home or school. She monitored the progress of each of the problems and noted no changes in the neutral factors or in the negative factors. Thus the time and effort of practicing through measurement comes primarily in the organization of effort rather than the collection of raw data.

This case example with eight identified problem events in two settings may sound complex. In reality, it is probably like the average case situation seen by social work students. The apparent complexity emerges through the awareness of the realistic problems facing the child, her guardian, and her teacher—an awareness generated in part by attaching a number to each problem event. Moreover, the reporting of eight problem events suggests or announces the intention of dealing with all of them; more can be overlooked.

Numbers attached to events permit many problems to be monitored carefully and simultaneously. This allows accurate observation of what may be called the "total problem" (i.e., the sum of the identified problem vis-à-vis the goals and contextual factors). It would be difficult to maintain such a monitoring of many variables without some measurement system. In addition, concomitant variations of numbers may suggest unsuspected causal hypotheses; for example, perhaps tallies of the child's frustrations at school might be paralleled by tallies of her aggressions toward either the guardian or the teacher (sassing behavior). Continuing systematic measurement would permit the testing of specific intervention hypotheses: for example, that dealing with the frustrating circumstances would be a more fruitful approach than dealing directly with the sassing behavior.

Practice through measurement is nothing but good practice made better by having systematic feedback on its impact with client problems. The practitioner does not do less than his accustomed good practice; rather, he is enabled to do more and to do it more effectively and demonstrably. Scientific practice, therefore, involves the incorporation of information retrieval and systematic evaluation methods with the problem-solving skills that are at the core of social work. But first it requires that practitioners understand and appreciate the potential of these methods in combination with their traditional work.

NOTES

1. See Martin Bloom, *Paradox of Helping: Introduction to the Philosophy of Scientific Practice* (New York: John Wiley & Sons, 1975); John M. Gottman and Sandra R. Leiblum, *How To Do Psychotherapy and How To Evaluate It: A Manual for Beginners* (New York: Holt, Rinehart & Winston, 1974); and Michael W. Howe, "Casework Self-Evaluation: A Single-Subject Approach," *Social Service Review*, 48 (January 1974), pp. 1–23. In addition, there are a number of evaluation materials connected with specific theoretical approaches, especially the behavioral; *see*, for example, Robert M. Browning and Donald O. Stover, *Behavior Modification in Child Treatment: An Experimental and Clinical Approach* (New York: Aldine-Atherton, 1971).

2. The three-stage process of change is described by Kurt Lewin in "Frontiers in Group Dynamics: I and II," *Human Relations*, 1 (June and November 1947), pp. 2–38, 143–153.

3. Abraham Kaplan, *Conduct of Inquiry* (San Francisco: Chandler, 1964), pp. 206, 207.

4. S. S. Stevens, "A Metric for Social Consensus," *Science*, 151 (February 1966), pp. 530–541.

5. Helen H. Perlman, "The Charge to the Casework Sequence," *Social Work*, 9 (July 1964), p. 54.

6. Gottman and Leiblum, op. cit.

7. Bloom, op. cit.

8. Ibid.

9. Melvin Weinstock, "ISI's Social Science Citation Index: A New Comprehensive Multidisciplinary Information Retrieval System for Social Science Literature." Paper presented before the Annual Meeting of the American Society for Information Science, Philadelphia, 1972.

10. Tony Tripodi, *Uses and Abuses of Social Research in Social Work* (New York: Columbia University Press, 1974). *See also* G. A. Theodorson and A. G. Theodorson, *Modern Dictionary of Sociology* (New York: Thomas T. Crowell, 1969), for standard definition of "operational definitions."

11. For an indication of the variety of tests purporting to supply information on the same concept, *see* collections of tests such as the one by John P. Robinson and Phillip R. Shaver, *Measures of Social Psychological Attitudes* (Ann Arbor, Mich.: Institute for Social Research, 1969).

12. *See* Edwin J. Thomas, "Selecting Knowledge from Behavioral Science," in *Building Social Work Knowledge* (New York: National Association of Social Workers, 1964).

13. *See* James G. Miller, "Living Systems: Basic Concepts," *Behavioral Science*, 10 (July 1965), p. 233.

14. Martin Bloom, "Impact Definition: An Operational Definition for Practitioners." Unpublished manuscript, St. Louis, 1975.

15. Martin Bloom, "Effectiveness and Efficiency in Single Worker/Single Client Evaluation Methods." Paper presented before the Annual Program Meeting of the Council of Social Work Education, Chicago, 1975.

16. The author thanks Mrs. Marilyn Marby, MSW, for permission to refer to her unpublished paper on this case study.

17. *See* Richard B. Stuart, *Trick or Treatment: How and When Psychotherapy Fails* (Champaign, Ill.: Research Press, 1970).

18. Donald T. Campbell and Donald W. Fiske, "Convergent and Discriminant Validation by the Multitrait-Multimethod Matrix," *Psychological Bulletin*, 56 (March 1959), pp. 81–105.

19. *See* Roland G. Tharp and Ralph J. Wetzel, *Behavior Modification in the Natural Environment* (New York: Academic Press, 1969).

Working with Families with Scapegoated Children

WILLIAM K. MOTLONG AND
LEONARD SZYMCZAK

Practitioners in social agencies frequently deal with families in which a particular child is focused on in a negative way. Such families can be difficult to work with if the rigid maintenance of their family system has resulted in scapegoating. Based on their experience in a family agency where scapegoated children are commonly seen, the authors have developed a means of viewing scapegoating families as well as methods for altering their patterns.[1]

The first section of this article describes the framework for viewing scapegoating families, explores the functions that the scapegoat role fulfills for the family, and delineates various kinds of family patterns in which scapegoating occurs. The second section views the process of the initial involvement and early treatment of such families and deals with specific techniques that have been found valuable in altering this particularly entrenched family system.

CHARACTERISTICS OF THE FAMILY AND THE SCAPEGOATED CHILD

The Family

The authors view families as systems—interactive and interdependent organisms—wherein a change in one part of the system affects every other part. Family systems develop ongoing mechanisms (i.e., complex patterns of behaving and relating) to maintain order and balance; the family adjusts these mechanisms to the particular needs and tasks that it must face. When a family is overwhelmed by a particular issue, it will sometimes move toward a rigid, unyielding pattern that, while preventing the family from falling apart, also maintains the system in a dysfunctional way. Ordinarily, a symptom will emerge as a reflection of the dysfunction. Families that develop a scapegoat to manage internal stresses represent systems which have gone to an extreme length to maintain an equilibrium. The scapegoat is the person who takes on the role of bearing blame for family tension and conflict and becomes the recipient of strong negative feelings. (The scapegoat is not always a child; but if it is an adult, he or she is in a "child" role.)

Families with scapegoats have several characteristics in common: low self-esteem (of individual members and the family as a whole); a rigid manner in handling stress; a high degree of sensitivity to external criticism; and difficulty with direct resolution of tensions and conflicts within the family, especially between the parents. Such families extensively utilize the defense mechanisms of projection, displacement, denial, and externalization.

The Child

The scapegoated child serves a number of specific functions: (1) He can act as a *deflector* of family conflicts by shifting conflict between others onto himself. In this role he is the mediator, or buffer, between the parents and offers them a way to avoid dealing directly with each other. (2) He can serve as a *reflector* of family feeling, mirroring family anger, mourning, guilt, and so on. The scapegoat becomes the expresser of submerged feelings and is often the only one to express a particular emotion. (3) He can be the *group solidifier* by becoming the "black sheep" against whom the family rallies. This type of scapegoat helps the family achieve a pseudosense of closeness through unity of purpose, togetherness of mind, and alignment against a common target. (4) A scapegoating pattern can emerge when a child becomes the *pioneer*, or *trailblazer*, by being the first child to break the family norms or to challenge traditional rules, which results in his being scapegoated for being "different." This often becomes the case as a child enters adolescence.

The factors that influence the choice of one child to become the scapegoat include age, sex, ordinal position, or chance characteristics (e.g., having been adopted or having features like one of the parents). Although the scapegoat role is dysfunctional for the health of the child and his adjustment outside the family, the scapegoat accepts the function and thereby sacrifices his autonomy. He has a direct and active part in maintaining the scapegoating mechanism in the family. Clinicians have often viewed the scapegoat as being the most pathological person in the family. The authors have found that although this can be the case, the scapegoat can also be the least pathological member.

Family Patterns

The authors have encountered several family patterns in which a scape-goating mechanism is found. The most rigid family pattern is one in which the couple's relationship is characterized by *overt harmony*.[2] The husband and wife have a seemingly conflict-free relationship in which they appear to think, feel, and act together in relation to the scape-goated child. The open expression of conflict between the parents is rarely if ever verbalized; much of the couple's energy, communication, and conflict is directed at the scapegoated child, who serves to bring his parents together. The fear seems to be that conflict between the hus-band and wife would threaten the stability of the family system. Such expressions as "We never fight" and "If it weren't for Lenny, our family would be perfect" are commonly heard. These families are the most difficult to treat, and marital issues are rarely available for therapeutic intervention.

A slightly less rigid family pattern is one in which the couple has *occasional open conflict*, but the discord is confined to issues involving a child. The couple issues are disguised as child-focused issues in an at-tempt to resolve underlying marital conflict. Often, each parent attempts to get the scapegoated child to become his/her ally. Common expres-sions heard in such a family are "If Billy didn't mess up, we would never fight" and "We have no arguments between the two of us; we only fight about the kids." This kind of family pattern more readily allows the scapegoat target to shift to another child and can at times tolerate a focus on the marital relationship.

A third family pattern is one in which there is *deceptive disharmony* between the spouses. The marital issues are accessible, with each spouse expressing dissatisfaction with the other. Any attempts to deal with the marital conflict are blocked; however, the spouses deny that the marital conflict has any effect on the scapegoated child's behavior. The scape-goat is needed because he represents someone who has more "problems" than the parents themselves. Many times complaints about the child actually reflect complaints the parents have about each other. The paren-tal attitude seems to be "We have problems that will never change, but we're really concerned about Gloria because she has serious problems." The best treatment approach seems to be to establish a dual contract to work both on the marital relationship and on issues regarding the scapegoat.

Additional problems arise when dealing with a *single-parent family*. The family system, which as an intact family needed a scapegoating mechanism, often continues one of the patterns just discussed after the divorce, separation, or death of one of the spouses. The scapegoated child is maintained in the rigid role that had been established before the family breakup. In other families, the scapegoat mechanism does not develop until after the loss of a parent. The single parent becomes involved in reenacting unresolved areas of conflict between him/her and the former spouse. The child thus becomes the receptacle for the feelings of anger, guilt, and mourning over the loss of the spouse, and the scapegoat may even fight the absent parent's battles. Adjunctive therapy (e.g., through single parents', volunteer, or children's groups) is extremely valuable with such families.

A final family pattern, with which the authors have been in increasingly frequent contact, are *merged families,* wherein one or two single-parent families are merged into a new family network. The scapegoating mechanism in such families can become extremely complex. Any combination of the patterns discussed can occur, and the scapegoating frequently crosses blood lines, with one spouse scapegoating the other spouse's child.

INITIAL INVOLVEMENT AND TREATMENT

Families with scapegoating patterns usually do not seek help willingly or openly and, frequently, are forced into treatment. There are two typical ways in which such families become engaged with the agency with which the authors are associated.

Usually, the family is referred by an outside social institution—school, police, or court—that forces the family to seek assistance. Police referrals are often prompted by burglary, theft, running away, disorderly conduct, and drug abuse; school referrals are typically for truancy and disciplinary problems. Although the scapegoating pattern serves a vital balancing function within the family system, the behavior of the scapegoat comes into conflict with societal norms and is viewed as dysfunctional.

Sometimes the family will seek help itself. When it does, it is because the family system has spiraled out of control and the family is seeking to reestablish its delicate balance. Such families do not seek help in altering the essential scapegoating structure; rather, they wish to reestablish sufficient control over the behavior of the scapegoat.

The initial phase of therapy with the scapegoating family usually lasts from four to eight sessions and is marked by a number of therapeutically difficult factors. A high level of resistance to treatment often exists, and the family is sometimes openly antagonistic and suspicious of the therapeutic process. A marked unwillingness to examine patterns in the family, or for individual family members to look at their own part of the process, is often exhibited. There is a desire, and often a fairly powerful attempt, to force the therapist to focus on the scapegoat. Finally, whether the family will remain in treatment is a continuing question. (The average length of treatment for families who do remain is from twelve to twenty sessions.)

The essence of the authors' treatment of scapegoating families is the process of *defocusing*: decreasing the intensity and frequency of the expression of negative feeling toward the scapegoat, along with redirecting energies to other parts of the family system. Defocusing can occur at any time in treatment. Sometimes it happens fairly quickly. In a fairly high percentage of cases, some significant degree of defocusing can occur within six to twenty sessions. Sometimes the family is never able to move from the focus on the scapegoat, and the ultimate result may be removal of the child from the home (i.e., psychiatric hospitalization, commitment to a correctional facility, or institutional or foster home placement).

The authors concentrate on five points of entry into the family system. To maximize the number of options for intervention, involvement of the entire family is essential, at least during early treatment. The five points are as follows:

1. *The Family as a Whole.* The central aim of intervening with the entire family system is to define the problem as being familywide, encourage flexibility, and define the family as the problem-resolving mechanism ("If you're not part of the solution, you're part of the problem").

2. *The Parenting Subsystem.* The aim of intervention with the parents is to ally with them as the executive heads of the family, support positive and functional parenting, clarify rules and regulations, and decode double or conflicting messages.

3. *The Marriage Subsystem.* Relatively little early intervention regarding marital issues is undertaken. Attempts to deal even with obvious marital issues generally meet with heightened defensiveness and increased rigidification of the scapegoating pattern. The authors have found it more valuable at the outset to avoid any emphasis on the marriage per se; marital issues gradually becomes accessible to intervention.

4. *The Sibling Subsystem.* The central aim of this kind of intervention is to shift some of the scapegoating burden onto other siblings, decrease sibling complicity in maintaining the scapegoat mechanism, and develop supportive alliances with the scapegoat.

5. *The Scapegoat.* The main emphasis in intervening with the scapegoat is to relate to the difficult role of the "bad guy," reframe his role in a more positive way, help him become aware of his part in maintaining the pattern, and aid him in finding other ways to get his needs met.

When dealing with "overt harmony" family patterns, defocusing from the scapegoat is often the most that can be expected of treatment;

but in lengthy therapy, couple issues can be dealt with eventually. When dealing with "occasional open conflict" and "deceptive disharmony" family patterns, the treatment focus can more quickly move to marital issues, although the process may be interwoven with attempts by the family to reinstate the scapegoating mechanism. When dealing with single-parent and merged families, mourning issues must frequently be dealt with in attempting to alter the scapegoating process.

The authors have found a number of techniques that are particularly helpful in defocusing.

Derigidifying the System

This is largely aimed at the family as a whole. Because the central characteristic of scapegoating family systems is their inflexible structure, the therapist spends much of his time in the first two or three sessions in derigidifying the system. Typical ways that is done include (1) questioning the family's "diagnosis" of itself and insisting on the exploration of other ways of viewing the family system; (2) emphasizing that each person in the family has his or her unique point of view, placing value on a diversity of viewpoints, and emphasizing the need for hearing all ideas about how the family operates (while blocking attempts by one or two family members—usually a parent—to define "what we all think" about the problem); (3) talking about every problem raised by the family as being a problem of the family as a whole, conveying that what affects one member of the family affects everyone else; (4) setting an informal, relaxed, and flexible tone, in opposition to the frequently inflexible and rigid manner in which the family usually operates; and (5) utilizing experiential, nonverbal techniques (e.g., family sculpting, a spatial description of family relationships), which requires the family to actually move around the treatment room (the authors' experience is that physical flexibility promotes system flexibility).

Cushioning the Confrontation

Verbal and nonverbal confrontation and interpretation techniques are used in the early stages and, for the most part, are aimed at the family as a whole. The confrontation must be couched in such a way as not to be overly threatening because scapegoating families are particularly susceptible to fleeing from treatment. The therapist presses hard enough to begin to effect change, but not so hard as to raise anxiety high enough for the family to drop out.

Confrontations and interpretations are made easier for the family to accept when the therapist takes responsibility for his perceptions and observations about the family: for example, "Is it only me, or does anyone else experience that there is a lot of sadness in this family?" and "If I were in your family, I'd have a hard time saying what's on my mind. Is that a problem for anyone?" Confrontations can thus be directed toward the family in a nonthreatening way. If the family does not accept the interpretation or confrontation, the therapist can simply say, "Well, I guess my perception must be wrong. Tell me how it *really* is." A confrontation or interpretation can thus be accepted or rejected by family members without their feeling they are being "clobbered" by the therapist; if rejected, it can be used as a tool for further exploration into the family system.

Spreading the Symptom

This technique is particularly valuable in "overt harmony" family patterns and is aimed primarily at the sibling subsystem. The task of the intervention is to identify and encourage the family to recognize problems with *other* family members. In that way, it is possible to distribute scapegoating among several family members so that no one individual has to carry an inordinate load. It is essential for siblings to be present for this technique to work. Often, siblings will cooperate in taking some of the scapegoating burden because of the guilt they have felt about having it unfairly heaped on one person. Sometimes they will even defend the scapegoat, thereby providing him with some alliance. Although this technique does not essentially change the scapegoating process, it does serve to redirect energies more equitably and is often an interim step toward a total lessened need for scapegoating. Using this technique, the therapist can ask specifically whether other children have problems that the parents recognize; if problems are denied, the therapist can comment on how unusual that is.

Another way of spreading the symptom in the family is to take what the family defines as a difficult problem of the scapegoat and redirect it to the family as a whole; for example, the therapist can ask, "How does everyone else in the family handle their anger?" and "What do the rest of you do when you feel like being mean?" Family members will therefore have to take responsibility for their own attitudes and actions in regard to the issue.

Defocusing by Focusing

This technique is particularly effective with "overt harmony" families, and the intervention is with the scapegoat. Focusing on the scapegoat is aimed at fostering recognition of the scapegoat's attempt to maintain himself in that role. In this maneuver, the therapist implicitly agrees with the family that the child is indeed difficult and needs additional help. A support group or volunteer to aid the child can be offered, which is often done at the agency with which the authors are associated; the provision of psychological testing or a tutor would serve the same purpose. While providing additional service for the scapegoated child because "he needs all the help he can get," the therapist insists that the entire family remain involved in treatment. The technique serves to defuse the family's claims that the therapist does not recognize the seriousness of the problem. At the same time, the therapeutic intervention with the scapegoat fosters his self-esteem, provides him with models and alternative ways of interacting within his family, and lessens his need to perpetuate the scapegoat role.

Redefining and Relabeling

The aim of redefining and relabeling is to intercept family messages and restate them in a different way so that the message no longer has its original meaning or effect. Relabeling and redefining offer family members an alternative choice in the way they look at their problems and, therefore, themselves. Because most families of this sort possess a pervasive feeling of low self-esteem, redefining in a positive way helps family members to see themselves differently, which in turn directs their efforts toward discovering more productive ways of operating as a family. For example, a scapegoat's behavior—so all-consuming and attention-riveting—can be redefined as helpful to the other children because their negative behaviors go unnoticed. The position of a "perfect" child can be redefined as a lonely and isolated position in that his behavior never gives any cause for parental investment or involvement.

Also, a negative characteristic of the scapegoat can be stated in a way that virtually forces the family to view it as a positive:

PARENT: "He has too big a mouth."

THERAPIST: "I like people who are direct and say what's on their mind. Whom does he take after?"

In addition to relabeling a negative trait in positive terms, the therapist also begins to build alliances between the scapegoat and those family members who have similar traits. Thus it is difficult for the family to dismiss the relabeling without turning down a compliment.

Enhancing Esteem

This technique is aimed at all the family subsystems, but particularly the parental subsystem. Permission is given to the parents to be "selfish" and to have a life separate from their children. They are encouraged to "get away from the kids" and to have some time and space for themselves. Highlighting the parents' life serves to free up energies so that parenting functions become more giving and, at the same time, places pressure on the marital relationship so that underlying conflicts can become more available to therapeutic intervention. Parental support is particularly important for single parents because, frequently, they feel overwhelmed by parenting functions that had previously been shared.

Because of the frequent reluctance of scapegoating families to see themselves as needing help, education is used to point out that most families have difficulty in coping with the shifting demands of life. This serves to decrease the threat of treatment as well as the feelings of failure and inadequacy that often pervade scapegoating families. The therapist underscores the family's normal aspects and helps family members to view problems as part of normal family life. Presented in this way, the family can see the intensely felt immediate crisis in a longer-term perspective. This tactic not only enhances self-esteem, but also fosters hope for the successful resolution of problems.

CONCLUSION

The framework and techniques outlined represent a total process of family-focused intervention designed to cope with the pathological syndrome of scapegoating. Although scapegoating patterns present difficult therapeutic tasks, it has been the authors' experience that the family approach represents the most effective way to institute lasting change away from those patterns.

Work with scapegoating families is arduous, frustrating, and frequently discouraging. The authors feel strongly that therapists who treat fairly large numbers of such families would do well to have a peer support group (fellow professionals having experience with the same kinds of families) and/or supportive supervision to deal effectively with the feelings of frustrations, discouragement, and anger that these families evoke.

NOTES

1. The agency serves a largely blue-collar, middle-class, suburban clientele. The age range of the scapegoated children dealt with is 6–18. The authors' experience is that more boys than girls are scapegoated. But that is a clinical impression not based on formal study; also, the particular population seen by the authors has more boys than girls.

2. The "overt harmony" family pattern is essentially identical to Sylvia Schmidt's "united front" family pattern. *See* Schmidt, "Special Treatment Applications: United Front, Acting-Out Adolescent, and Only-Adopted-Child Families," in Charles H. Kramer et al., eds., *Beginning Phase of Family Treatment*, proceedings of a workshop on family therapy (Chicago: Family Institute of Chicago, 1968), pp. 39–51.

Task-Centered Treatment After Five Years

LAURA EPSTEIN

The Task-Centered Treatment Program consists of (1) a year-long course in the School of Social Service Administration at the University of Chicago, (2) a series of research projects carried out by approximately twenty-five first-year graduate students enrolled in the course, and (3) extensions of the program to eleven agencies throughout the United States and in England and Israel. The course and its research projects are directed by the developers of the task-centered treatment model.[1] The social agencies that collaborate and provide cases for the research are the agencies used for the students' fieldwork. The extensions of the program to other agencies developed because of the interest they expressed in making clinical trials of the task-centered treatment model and in carrying out research aimed at developing adaptations of the model to specific settings.[2]

The program enrolled its first group of students in 1970, after a preliminary effort in 1969. The basic content of the course is the task-centered model of treatment techniques or procedures for alleviating problems addressed to individuals, families, and groups.[3]

The task-centered model was a sequel to the research project reported in *Brief and Extended Casework*.[4] The findings of a study on that project were compatible with findings from a number of other studies available in 1969. There was reason to believe that planned short-term treatment yielded good results and could probably be used successfully when its objectives were specified and that improvement was relatively durable. Since 1969 studies conducted in the Task-Centered Treatment Program and under other auspices have strengthened these conclusions.[5]

The Task-Centered Treatment Program began with these questions: What is there about planned short-term treatment that makes it go? What techniques and what skills can be specified?

CONTEXT OF CONTEMPORARY
SOCIAL TREATMENT

The social work profession has faced the stark awareness that social treatment practices have serious limitations in their outcomes.[6] Even so, practitioners have been slow to make use of the growth of research capability. But there are signs of change. Recent writings have examined the complexities of the treatment process, and some outcome studies have concluded that social treatment does, in fact, produce beneficial results. These benefits are not necessarily found in methods customarily termed "casework" to the extent hoped for, but benefits there are. Thus the present emphasis in treatment research and development is on extracting knowledge about techniques, or practitioner acts, that work best. It is hoped that such studies of technique will develop technologies, that is, orderly and specific guidelines for systematic procedures, according to treatment phase, priorities, and problems.

A conviction is developing that social treatment practice should be instrumental: It should emphasize the current problems of clients and should be restricted to feasible goals that are specific and understandable, utilitarian, and formulated in terms explicitly acceptable to and wanted by clients. A change in viewpoint is involved in the development of this conviction. The client is being thought of as a consumer of a service for which he has contracted. Attributes of the client that are related to social class, ethnic and cultural background, expectations, assumptions about himself, and beliefs about his world are being given strong credence. These attributes lead to the idea that there should be plural methods for pursuing diverse treatment objectives. This view is in contrast to the view that considers the client as the object of interventions for which he often needs to be laboriously (and usually unsuccessfully) motivated and that has the idealistic objectives of rehabilitation, reconstruction, reform, development, and redevelopment.

A powerful morality has been driving social treatment theory and practice for decades: so-called immaturity was sinful, and the right of people to achieve the mythical state of "self-actualization" was assumed to be sacred. These ideologies have been powerful among liberal intellectuals whose values incline them toward utopias, even while their reality perception precipitates frustration and despair. To concentrate on striving for inner utopias, however desirable they seem, conditions social treatment practice to ignore pressing influences of the social environment and the profound immediacy of present stress. Growing concern about protecting the civil rights of involuntary mental patients reflects a stage in the process of revising values about treatment. Social workers may soon need to face more forthrightly what their position should be when people do not want particular interventions whose efficacy is uncertain.

A related issue is the developing belief that there has been excessive "problemization" of some types of deviant behavior, such as juvenile misconduct.[7] Also, there are advocates of "decriminalization," that is, removing from criminal sanctions proscribed acts among consenting adults—the so-called victimless crimes.[8] Consideration will probably develop to "detherapize" less harmful deviations from ideal normative conduct, not only on the grounds of financial economy but also because of poor results and unwarranted intrusion into private, personal affairs.

Alterations in the political and social climate of the country and the world are changing professionals' perceptions of what people need, want, can do, and should do in personal and social behaviors in particular circumstances. Detailed concentration on intimate relationships, while important and valuable, is not necessarily the most desired avenue for negotiating the chaos of modern life. Also, the effects of the limits to affluence and expansionist growth must be dealt with. The immediate effect on social welfare of these limits was the reintroduction of hard times, that is, shrinking resources in relation to population increase and program needs. As a result of restrictions on welfare dollars, the hard-nosed demand for accountability arose.

AIMS OF THE TASK-CENTERED
TREATMENT PROGRAM

From this sea of troubles, the Task-Centered Treatment Program has extracted certain issues to concentrate on. First and perhaps foremost, the program seeks to develop a treatment technology in the form of a model that is specific, systematic, and efficient (assuming that efficiency will both control costs and be beneficial to clients). The research conducted in the program is developing the task-centered model, which seeks to legitimate and enhance clients' interests, choice of treatment objectives, and degree and kind of investment they wish to make. The model intends to formulate its processes in a way that makes measurement and evaluative and developmental research possible and makes accounting feasible and comprehensible. It also seeks to conceptualize practice skills in a way that will reduce as much as possible the ambiguity of judgments made by practitioners at all levels of education.

Although a simpleminded set of formulas that tells a practitioner "If this, do that" will never exist, movement in that direction should be sought. It would be best if clinical judgment were to be exercised within parameters that have some relatively clear boundaries. This aim is not easy to achieve. The difficulty is, partly, that human behavior and the impact of the social environment remain mysterious. Techniques and programs based on some partial explanation tend to develop unexpected and unwanted side effects.

Another part of the difficulty is that in many social agencies sanctions for the practice of social treatment contain social control purposes: the containment and possibly the reversal of deviance, defined as "to depart from conformity with the normative standards which have come to be set up as the common culture." [9] By mixing together the aims of treatment and the aims of social control, social treatment practice incurs difficult internal dissonance, conflicts between needing to compel clients to behave in certain ways on the one hand and respecting clients' rights and autonomy on the other. The problem is, of course, not new; but a particular difficulty of present-day practice is that normative standards are in flux. Furthermore, the understanding of what constitutes deviance has changed. The modern analysis construes deviance as a social transaction, not an attribute of individuals. Deviance labels are affixed to behaviors in ways that change considerably over time, are not uniformly applicable at any time, and vary in their consequences, depending on social class, ethnic and cultural identifications, political trends, and other factors.[10]

The task-centered treatment model disclaims fundamental responsibility for using interpersonal treatment to fulfill social control requirements. At the same time, however, this model is a product of its time, which means that task-centered practice occurs under conditions of less than ideal client voluntarism. Much of its practice has been with clients who are "involuntary," that is, referred by various authorities (e.g., schools, physicians, judges) for amelioration of deviant behavior; this is an attribution about which the client may be in significant disagreement. Task-centered practice cannot disentangle social control from treatment so long as agencies are involved in this conflictful duality. Task-centered practice, therefore, attempts to put client voluntarism in an ascendant position by placing the greatest possible emphasis on the client's particular target problem or problems, exactly as perceived by him.

TASK-CENTERED TREATMENT MODEL

The task-centered treatment model has been fully described elsewhere.[11] In brief, task-centered treatment is a set of flexible procedures that has the objective of alleviating explicit target problems formulated as perceived by clients. In instances when clients are involuntary participants, there are procedures for a preliminary sequence to elicit problems and negotiate goals with referring agencies. Processes relied on to alleviate target problems are clients' commitment to selected and agreed on tasks, interventions aimed at overcoming obstacles to task achievement, and a treatment contract containing time limits. Types of interventions to produce problem reduction include the following: problem exploration, task selection and task implementation planning, task reviews, rehearsals for task action, anticipation and analysis of obstacles, encouragement and reinforcement, direction, advice, development of a rationale for work on tasks, enhancement of the client's awareness of his own and others' actions, obtaining cooperation from significant others to support task work, and procurement of needed concrete resources.

Task-centered treatment is perceived as a first-line intervention that will suffice for most situations. Developmental and maintenance therapies, those having the objectives of promoting personal growth and sustaining behaviors, should be reserved for selected clients who desire them or for whom there are explicit indications that such treatment can be effective. Criteria for developmental and maintenance therapies, however, have not as yet been developed on an empirical base and their use tends to be determined by individual practitioners' beliefs and styles.

Tasks are framed to state what the client is to do. A task may state a general direction for the client's action. These general tasks are broken down into more tangible specifications. Tasks change form and content as treatment. Some tasks drop out; others are added. Target problems change sometimes.

Assessment is concentrated in the initial phase, the first two sessions. It consists of exploration, classification, and specification of the problems and evaluation of the behaviors they consist of in the person and in his psychosocial context. Assessment is confined to the logical boundaries of the target problems. A target problem is classified according to its best fit into a typology that limits the scope of assessment. Assessment would not extend beyond problems that could be subsumed under the target problem classification. Assessments of this type are not as changeable as they are in the psychosocial model, for example. Reassessment occurs if and when the target problem has to be changed. Some recycling of the treatment design is then made.

Clinical classifications based on a psychiatric nosology have limited use in task-centered assessment. Psychiatric typologies are sometimes useful when one apparent cause of the problem is physical or neurological, when drugs or other biological interventions are being administered, or when perverse and pervasive ideational problems (e.g., delusions or hallucinations) are present. Information about etiology and history of the problems is seldom used, but information about the problem's duration and some of its changes or stability over time is sometimes helpful. Attention is given to what the problem means to the client in the present. Long duration of a problem may or may not color its meaning in the present.

A pragmatic and eclectic position is taken vis-à-vis personality theory. A practitioner can use any theory or combination of theories he believes can help him and his client understand and explain a situation. When there are obscurities or impasses to treatment, reference to personality theory is helpful in charting a direction; but reexamination of the problem is more valuable. Practitioners are combining the task-centered approach with psychoanalytically derived practices as well as with behavior modification.

Although practitioners' attitudes and styles, overt and covert behavior, feelings, beliefs, and so forth play an important part in treatment, little is known empirically about how these factors operate. The task-centered practitioner must be appropriately responsive to the client; but he concentrates on what is done, said, and communicated, not on the practitioner–client "relationship." The practitioner's main responsibility in treatment is to help the client target his problem, locate task alternatives, revise tasks as needed, and help him carry out these tasks. A useful working alliance develops from this concentration.

Obviously, some practitioner attitudes defeat a working partnership: insensitivity, defects in listening and hearing, coldness and punitiveness, self-centeredness, and the like. Some of these attitudes can be influenced through education and some cannot. In task-centered work, the strong emphasis placed on eliciting and legitimating the problems as perceived by the client is a protection to him from practitioner attitudes that result in ignoring the client's assessment of his situation or unduly influencing him, deflecting him from concentrating on those problems he wants to and can attend to.

Between 1970 and 1974, approximately one thousand cases were handled using the procedures of the task-centered treatment model; the cases were handled in twelve settings that provided fieldwork for students enrolled in the program at the School of Social Service Administration. These settings were two medical clinics, two psychiatric clinics, six public elementary schools, one home for the aged, and one group home for adolescents. Research was concentrated on a representative sample of two hundred cases. In the first three years, the research concentrated on testing the model's usefulness in various agency settings. Subsequently, a specific set of techniques, the Task Implementation Sequence (TIS), was developed; TIS is intended to strengthen the process of task achievement.[12]

At present, research is in process to study task implementation in more detail and to develop further the task-centered group work adaptation and the use of the model with the special problems of low-income families.[13] Agencies other than the School of Social Service Administration fieldwork settings that have undertaken systematic clinical trials include the following: two juvenile courts, one child guidance clinic, two private family service agencies, one public child welfare agency, and two industrial social service settings. In England, a project has been in operation in an area social services office operated by the Local Authority of Aylesbury; in Israel, a school of social work has trained staffs of several agencies to use the task-centered model.

SKILLS NEEDED FOR TASK-CENTERED WORK

Four general types of skills need to be practiced in task-centered work: (1) problem identification, (2) task selection and management, (3) formulation of the treatment contract, and (4) measurement of results. Each of these general skills have numerous facets.

Problem Identification

The target problem is the focus of attention for the treatment work. It has been common in the past to formulate problems not so much in terms of what they are but in terms of suppositions and inferences. Thus, practitioners often get statements about causality, hypotheses about why the problem exists: Miss F "struggled to find a place as an adult, both in her disturbed family and in society." Statements are made that ascribe meanings to the problem: Miss F "was seeking love, acceptance, and understanding of herself and life." Often, the problem is stated in terms of how the client ought to be: Miss F needs to develop "unique and consistent ideas, opinions, and a way of life instead of copying her friends and totally subjecting herself to their influence." These kinds of problem formulation owe their rationale to treatment theories based on fairly complex personality assessments in which problems are functions of the ascribed personality and interpersonal relationship patterns.

In task-centered work, however, attention is focused on depicting the problem: what occurs, when and how often, alone or with what others, in what place or places, with what stimulation or provocation, and with what results? The doing, thinking, and feeling (i.e., behaviors) represent too much or too little action to achieve the person's intention. This kind of specificity owes its conceptual framework to the behavior modification stream in treatment practice. A possible way to reformulate Miss F's problem in task-centered terms would be as follows: "Miss F is unhappy with her boyfriend. He wants her mainly as a companion in

drug-taking. She is without skills for employment, which she desires."
In the task-centered typology, this problem could be classified as "dissatisfaction with social relations" or "difficulty in role performance."
The general statement of the problem tells what occurs. The problem
needs specification in terms of its frequency, antecedents, and effects.
It needs assessment of its social context to be comprehensible. The possible influences for good or ill of other persons, social institutions, and
cultural and economic factors in stimulating and maintaining the problem have to be explored. From that exploration it is possible to obtain
clues about what changes could be made in the environment to change
behavior in the desired direction. The clients' own intentions and wishes
provide firm constraints on what problems are selected. The experience
of the Task-Centered Treatment Program is that clients of all ages, including children, select target problems that are moral, reasonable, and
relevant—if allowed to follow their own bent. Occasionally, a client
has to be presented with alternatives if what he wants is not feasible.

Task Selection and Management

Tasks are what a client is to do to alleviate his problems. Tasks are
broken down into small segments, replaced as often as needed when
they are done, and exchanged for others when they are not done; tasks
are added as new facets of the work emerge. Examples of task segments
from an elementary school setting, where the most common problem is
academic underachievement (difficulty in role performance) are to get
an appointment with the teacher; find out what he or she thinks is wrong;
attend a tutoring session; and so on. Task segment examples in dealing
with a woman's problem of depression are to get medication, hold a
family conference with the teenage children, assert what household
duties the children are to do, encourage the client to join a women's
group, and so on. These tasks are operational and normally occur as a
changing group of task segments, or subtasks. These smaller bits are
analyzed and planned for, and clients are assisted in acquiring the skills
to make them go. Experience in the program is that psychological well-
being accompanies work on and follows achievement of tasks. While
being responsive to a client's unhappiness, sadness, and tension, the
practitioner concentrates on such feelings per se only when they are
obdurate obstacles. Techniques for dealing directly with feelings are
verbal recognition of their characteristics, frequency, and the conditions
under which they occur and do not occur; an explanation of their probable cause; reassurance about their universality; and guidance on ways to
endure them and reduce the length of time they debilitate the client.

In addition to learning how to break down tasks into small pieces, practitioners need to accustom themselves to recasting the objective or goal of the tasks, primarily under two conditions: (1) when the tasks are intended to change someone else and fail to do so and (2) when the problem alters during treatment. In task-centered work, it is not necessary to convince a person that he must change if he believes the responsibility is that of another. Thus a parent who wants his child to change will be helped to accomplish this. It has been observed that these others often will and can change. It is when they do not that the client can re-analyze his target problems and tasks to face what he must do for himself to get relief.

Practitioners need to learn to be aggressive in recommending tasks to clients who are ambivalent or confused. Clients welcome strong advice when it is congruent with their interests. They usually alter the advice, but it starts them off.

Obstacles to task achievement are of many sorts. But, in general, it may be said that these obstacles are located in the fears and lack of problem-solving skills of the clients, in an intractable situation, and in practitioner discouragement.

Many client fears are directly produced by their not knowing how to take certain actions normally expected to produce a desired result. These fears run the gamut from dread to slight apprehension. Fear may be addressed from the viewpoint of etiology, nature of the feeling, consequences of the feeling, and reactions of the person and others to the feeling and its expression in words, demeanor, and acts. In task-centered work, the intention is to help clients overcome fears by teaching them skills to accomplish tasks and by arranging for significant others to aid, support, and reinforce these efforts.

Many problems in living are intractable. Often, there is a dearth of available knowledge suitable for use in helping a client. The complexity of some problems defies intervention repertoires. Many times resources do not exist or are inaccessible. Under such circumstances, the sense of the task-centered model is to reformulate the target problems to identify a particular facet that is malleable and to recycle the treatment sequence.

Practitioner discouragement is an obstacle when it is transmitted to a client and produces a withdrawal of effort. Discouragement seems to be associated with inexperience, expectations of global change, and beliefs that problems have such tenacious underlayers that a reconstruction of personality and life-style is required.

Formulation of the Treatment Contract

The characteristics of treatment-contracting in task-centered practice are more explicit than the general, emerging, revising, tentative characteristics common in open-ended treatment. The contract has to be specific about stating the end product, the time to be taken, the frequency of contact, and the persons to be participants. Treatment-contracting appears to diminish a client's uncertainties about the present intentions and future expectations of the practitioner. A businesslike arrangement means that the client preserves his autonomy and that the possibilities for transference difficulties are diminished. The need for relationship engagement and management is transformed into a *temporary* working alliance or partnership.

Duration is an arbitrary matter. What is optimum is not known. Experience indicates that from five to ten contracts over two to three months are feasible. Extensions are possible if they occur with full client participation and are planned. Duration statements seem to be productive in reducing unplanned discontinuance (dropout).

The skills practitioners need to acquire in treatment-contracting have to do with attitude more than anything else—an attitude of willingness to "let go." Treatment-contracting is a way to put into effect principles having to do with limited goals and client self-determination. This process requires unlearning the practice habits of stating treatment objectives in global, vague terms that are often incongruent with the client's objectives. New practitioners on the whole have little difficulty with acquiring the needed skills. Young practitioners, however, are often zealous about demanding, of themselves and clients, adherence to extraordinary goals and time to work at them. Idealism and inexperience partly explain this zeal.

But there is confusion, particularly in the public agency sector, about goals imposed by agencies' views of their functions. When agencies present themselves in public positions as intending wholesale reform of the life-styles of poor and buffeted families, and when eager young practitioners invest great effort to wrest better lives for clients from the social system, difficulties in letting go and frustrations because of poor outcomes result. Also therapy-oriented practitioners seem sad when clients are satisfied after brief treatment; practitioners presumably would like clients to go on to more complex changes. Clients can stay in open-ended treatment, profitably or not, only when they stay voluntarily, with knowledge about what they are staying for and with conviction that their investment is worthwhile.

The practice of treatment-contracting runs into most difficulty when clients are required to maintain contact with an agency (as in foster care) or are under authoritative duress resulting from a court order and when agencies have assumed an obligation to maintain surveillance over them. Such situations have nothing to do with skill and are not treatment practice problems. They are problems of agency and social policy. A trend today is for social welfare agencies to extricate themselves from the surveillance obligation. As yet, however, there is no solution to the conflict between a social control mandate and a treatment contract. Practitioners and agencies are caught within this unsolvable dilemma. In the absence of comprehensive, readily accessible resources, the backup use of social workers to hover over deviant people, different people, troublesome people, is questionable. New administrative practices have to be designed to provide practitioners with adequate sanctions for goal-oriented services. Furthermore, extensive rethinking of social control functions will eventually be necessary if these are to be separated from treatment.

Measurement of Results

The task-centered approach lends itself to measurements of various types, which promotes credibility in a time of widespread questioning about the worthwhileness and expense of many social treatment programs. The fact is that people who apply for and receive social welfare benefits continue to want and need direct services. People need to locate services they consider suitable and get the best use from such concrete services as homemakers, foster homes, day care, and vocational training. There does not appear to be any diminution in people's demand for counseling to help with private psychological pain and living problems connected to stress in interpersonal relations. Although counseling is not in danger of being obliterated, heavy pressure that it be accountable and productive does exist.

The demand for accountability cannot be attributed only to restrictive, conservative social policies. Some politicians have attempted to justify the reduction of services on the grounds of defects in social welfare technology. Evaluative research has sometimes been viewed by practitioners as an attack by researchers, as the private antagonism of researchers against the values and practices of social treatment—especially casework. Accountability raises the central questions of efficiency and effectiveness in reducing social problems.[14] Programs have to address real problems that can be remedied. If society makes resources available, techniques that can do the work in the manner promised are needed. The purpose of social welfare is to minimize problems, and the work ought to be done as economically as possible. Experiments, mistakes, and waste are ubiquitous and endurable; they inevitably occur in a live organization and program. But the maintenance of practices that are harmful or of low utility, no matter what proper-sounding rationale is given, are not endurable. The political processes of government identify, allocate, and legitimate the means and resources intended to achieve social welfare purposes. Resources are finite, and choices among options must be made. Such choices are always politically influenced.

Social welfare policy in the United States seems to be based on such goals as reducing dependence on public assistance, child welfare, and mental health services and reducing delinquency, drug use, and other critical problems. While denigrating social work for its inability to produce a widespread reduction of social problems, government officials, media commentators, and some segments of the general public hold the profession responsible for achieving simplistic solutions to exceedingly complex problems. There is, in such views, insufficient attention to inadequate administration of social welfare agencies, to the large gap between what social workers are expected to do and the minimal resources provided, and to the realistic limits of existing technology.

Nevertheless, the present demand for accountability is justified on political, humanitarian, and professional grounds. Professional objectives, in the past, have been stated in "input" terms: number of interviews, number of persons served, number of children placed. Today, to be honest and responsible, the evaluation of services has to be in terms of "outputs," or results.

To evaluate a program, there has to be clarity from the beginning about its objectives, its target population and problems, the interventions to be used, and the criteria for the effectiveness and efficiency of the work. Practitioners, administrators, and researchers need to have explicit information about those factors and an understanding of the changes made during the course of a program. Measurements can be built into ongoing work processes and can be simple and manageable. Practitioners and administrators can use some measurement techniques without elaborate or esoteric training. Some practitioners seem to think that researchers are involved in dazzling and impenetrable issues, and practitioners have been known to intimidate researchers with esoterica. Differences in perspective between researchers and practitioners often do not seem easily resolved. But their debates are valuable because they enlighten problems and issues in practice. Conflict between them ought to lessen if practitioners acquire more education about research aims and methods.

Relatively objective, simple means can be constructed for evaluative research on an ongoing basis. In task-centered work, for example, follow-up interviews with clients are customarily conducted to tap client responses to treatment. Pretreatment and posttreatment information can be secured from observation and from significant others who are friendly to the client and who may be or may have been participants in the treatment. Referral sources, who often make important judgments about the outcomes of treatment, can provide useful information when interviewed through the use of a structured questionnaire. Practitioners, clients, and observers can make organized judgments about target problems, task achievement, and problem reduction. All these can be recorded on simple forms that yield readily analyzable data. Measurements taken in the course of treatment are immensely valuable aids for recycling a treatment design that is not working.

Larger-scale evaluative studies are sometimes called for. But in the absence of ongoing evaluative information, large-scale studies can develop into catastrophes that are difficult to respond to and absorb. Small-scale, ongoing, practitioner-focused studies could possibly heal the wounds of evaluative research disasters and guide daily practice into a flexible responsiveness to empiricism.

The types of skills needed for practitioner studies would include, for example, explicit recording of the behaviors and social conditions that demonstrate a target problem; recording of goals, that is, the results expected by clients and practitioner; regular charting of behavioral and social condition changes, concentrating on major areas of the target problems; recording, according to a prescribed listing, what interventive techniques were used and what results were obtained within a specified time; making regular follow-up inquiries, according to a structured questionnaire format, after a case is closed; and using audio and audiovisual recordings to study processes in some depth on a selective basis.

Analysis of the information secured by such means could, over a period of time, provide concrete information about what problems were addressed in treatment and with what intentions; what interventions were made; what clients' responses were; and what changes did or did not take place. Information of that sort does not constitute proof of effectiveness of treatment or identification of basic problems in a program. Such information does, however, begin a process of thinking concretely, of collecting a body of information about what is and what is not happening. Practitioners who get into the habit of studying their practice with attention to specifics are in a better position to produce credible information about a social treatment program, and they can use research consultation and collaborate with researchers profitably.

CONCLUSION

The task-centered model is a social treatment technology that can make goal-oriented, efficient practice possible and accountable. It may be cost-effective after the costs of staff training and any needed revisions in recording and supervision have been overcome. There is good reason to believe that it is effective under the important condition that its goals are instrumental, that is, designed to achieve problem reduction in explicitly designated problems.

NOTES

1. *See* William J. Reid and Laura Epstein, *Task-Centered Casework* (New York: Columbia University Press, 1972); and William J. Reid, "A Test of a Task-Centered Approach," *Social Work*, 20 (January 1975), pp. 3–9.

2. William J. Reid and Laura Epstein, eds., *Task-Centered Practice* (New York: Columbia University Press, 1976).

3. Charles Garvin, "Task-Centered Group Work," *Social Service Review*, 48 (December 1974), pp. 494–507.

4. William J. Reid and Ann W. Shyne, *Brief and Extended Casework* (New York: Columbia University Press, 1969).

5. *See*, for example, Harvey H. Barten and Sybil S. Barten, eds., *Children and Their Parents in Brief Therapy* (New York: Behavioral Publications, 1973); Harvey H. Barten, ed., *Brief Therapies* (New York: Behavioral Publications, 1971); Dorothy Fahs Beck and Mary Ann Jones, "A New Look at Clientele and Services of Family Agencies," *Social Casework*, 55 (December 1974), pp. 589–599; Magrit Cohen and Patricia Ewalt, "An Intensive Program for Severely Disturbed Children," *Social Casework*, 56 (June 1975), pp. 334–336; Judith Long, "Planned Short-Term Treatment in a Family Agency," *Social Casework*, 55 (June 1974), pp. 369–374; Karl Kay Levin, *Brief Psychotherapy* (St. Louis: Warren H. Green, 1970); James Mann, *Time-Limited Psychotherapy* (Cambridge, Mass.: Harvard University Press, 1973); Genevieve B. Oxley, "Short-Term Therapy with Student Couples," *Social Casework*, 54 (April 1973), pp. 216–223; Patrick V. Riley, "Practice Changes Based on Research Findings," *Social Casework*, 56 (April 1975), pp. 242–250; Blanca N. Rosenberg, "Planned Short-Term Treatment in Developmental Crises," *Social Casework*, 56 (April 1975), pp. 195–204; Peter E. Sifneos, *Short-Term Psychotherapy and Emotional Crisis* (Cambridge, Mass.: Harvard University Press, 1972); Leonard Small, *The Briefer Psychotherapies* (New York: Brunner/Mazel, 1971); and Brenda Wattie, "Evaluating Short-Term Casework in a Family Agency," *Social Casework*, 54 (December 1973), pp. 609–616.

6. *See*, for example, Allen E. Bergin, "The Evaluation of Therapeutic Outcomes," in Allen E. Bergin and Sol L. Garfield, eds., *Handbook of Psychotherapy and Behavior Change* (New York: John Wiley & Sons, 1971), pp. 217–270; William C. Berleman, James R. Seaberg, and Thomas W. Steinburn, "The Delinquency

Prevention Experiment of the Seattle Atlantic Street Center," *Social Service Review*, 46 (September 1972), pp. 323–346; Joel Fischer, "Is Casework Effective? A Review," *Social Work*, 18 (January 1973), pp. 5–21; Edward J. Mullen, James R. Dumpson, and associates, *Evaluation of Social Intervention* (San Francisco: Jossey-Bass, 1972); Edward J. Mullen, Robert M. Chazin, and David M. Feldstein, "Services for the Newly Dependent: An Assessment," *Social Service Review*, 46 (September 1972), pp. 309–322; and Kenneth P. Wilkinson and Peggy J. Ross, "Evaluation of the Mississippi AFDC Experiment," *Social Service Review*, 46 (September 1972), pp. 363–377.

7. Margaret K. Rosenheim, "Notes on Helping: Normalizing Juvenile Nuisances," *Social Service Review*, 50 (June 1976), pp. 177–193.

8. Edwin M. Schur, *Crimes Without Victims* (Englewood Cliffs, N.J.: Prentice-Hall, 1967).

9. Talcott Parsons, *The Social System* (New York: Free Press, 1951), p. 206. *See also* Joel F. Handler, *The Coercive Social Worker* (New York: Academic Press, 1973); and Raymond Plant, *Social and Moral Theory in Casework* (London: Routledge & Kegan Paul, 1970).

10. Schur, op. cit.

11. Reid and Epstein, *Task-Centered Casework*.

12. Reid, op. cit.

13. Research is supported in part by Grant No. 18–P–57774/5–01 from the Social and Rehabilitation Service of the U.S. Department of Health, Education, and Welfare.

14. This discussion is based on Edward Newman and Jerry Turem, "The Crisis of Accountability," *Social Work*, 19 (January 1974), pp. 5–16.

Assertive Training and Social Work Practice

EILEEN D. GAMBRILL

Assertive training is designed to increase the influence a person exerts over his or her interpersonal environment by increasing the appropriate expression of both positive and negative feelings. It is assumed that people have a right to express their feelings in a manner which subjugates neither others nor oneself and that personal well-being includes the expression of feelings.[1] Training is thus for those who are overly aggressive as well as for those who are overly reticent in their encounters. The former achieve their rights at someone else's expense whereas the latter fail to assert their rights. The role of assertive behavior was first emphasized by Salter and then by Wolpe.[2]

Assertive training has been used with beneficial results with a range of both outpatient and inpatient psychiatric populations, including some patients diagnosed as psychotic whose behavior had previously been controlled with medication.[3] It has also been used with nonpsychiatric populations.[4] A lack of assertion has been implicated in a broad range of presenting problems of interest to social workers; these include marital discord, inappropriate sexual behavior, antisocial aggressive behavior, and depression.[5] This is not surprising when the consequences of a lack of assertion and the array of situations in which it may take place are examined. A lack of assertion places the individual at a disadvantage in relation to others. Opportunities are lost and punishing events tolerated. For example, an employee may not obtain a coveted job promotion; a woman may do things she does not really want to do because of an inability to say no. Such consequences affect the individual's internal dialogue in that he may engage in a range of negative self-statements and ruminations. A high frequency of such thoughts may cause overreactions in other situations and consequent criticism from others because of these inappropriate reactions. Stressful physiological responses may also result. In addition, behavior that reduces unpleasant thoughts and feelings, such as excessive drinking, social isolation, or attention to physical symptoms, may be exhibited.

In the following sections, assertive behavior is defined and assessment and training procedures are described. The final section considers the relevance of assertive training to social work practice.

TOWARD A DEFINITION OF ASSERTIVE BEHAVIOR

Assertion is the open expression of preferences by words or actions in a manner that causes others to take them into account. Although the most common assertive responses involved in clinical work relate to the expression of negative feelings, the term *assertive behavior* is used to refer to all socially acceptable expressions of personal rights and feelings. Assertion is differentiated from both *aggression* and *submission*. Aggression has been defined as the "hostile expression of preferences by words or deeds in a manner which coerces others to give in to these preferences; any act which suppresses or takes away the rights of another person." Submission has been defined as "the act of allowing one's rights to be ignored, as any act which yields humbly to the preferences of another person." [6]

Say that you have been waiting in line to get into a movie theater and, as you get near the ticket office, the person in front of you lets in six people. An aggressive reaction might be, "Hey, get back there. What the hell is going on?" This reaction conveys antagonism; strong opposition to others' behavior is indicated. An assertive reaction entails the statement of a request or demand for a behavior change showing minimal negative emotion, such as, "Listen, we've been waiting for a long while. Why don't you move to the end of the line?" Personal attacks are avoided in assertive behavior. A submissive reaction may be the expression of annoyance in a manner that is not readily noticeable, such as coughing or sighing; a complete absence of overt reaction, that is, simply allowing the people to move in the line; or a departure from the situation. [7] Only one systematic attempt, using all three response possibilities, has been made to gather normative data describing how selected populations define various behaviors in given situations. [8] There is a need for additional information of this type.

What is considered a right depends on the particular context. Thus assertion requires appropriate behaviors as well as an appropriate identification of the situations in which to display them. Appropriateness also relates to individual value judgments as to how things should be. In this sense, not only a social, but also an individual, judgment is involved in the definition of assertive behavior. For example, a woman may feel it fair to attempt to contribute more during staff meetings; she may feel she has a perfect right to do this. Her resulting new behavior may, however, be considered aggressive by her peers. As long as value judgments are involved in the definition of assertive behavior, individuals may vary in what they consider an assertive reaction.

The consequences of assertion may differ for various interactants in a situation. The consequences should be positive to the individual in that pleasant opportunities are gained or unpleasant ones removed. The consequences of assertion may not, however, always be positive to those with whom the person interacts. For example, a welfare worker may not be at all pleased when his clients start to express what they feel are their rights in relation to welfare payments. Usually, however, the effects of increased assertive behavior are positive for all involved parties in that mutual respect is encouraged and feeling of resentment removed.

The range of behaviors encompassed by the term "assertive behavior," together with the situations in which they occur, have yet to be identified and categorized adequately. Examples of assertive behaviors include refusing requests; requesting behavior changes; complimenting others; disagreeing with others; responding to criticism; initiating and terminating conversations; stating opinions; arranging future meetings; introducing topics of conversation; and changing the topic. People rated high in overall assertiveness speak louder, respond more rapidly, give longer replies, evidence more profound affect, show less compliance, and request more changes in other people's behavior than those rated low in assertiveness.[9] Nonverbal as well as verbal behaviors are important components of assertive behavior.[10]

IDENTIFYING ASSERTIVE PROBLEMS

Assertive difficulties are typically situational, that is, a person experiences difficulty only in certain situations. A variety of dimensions may affect assertive behavior, including (1) the degree of intimacy involved in the situation; (2) whether the feeling is positive or negative; (3) the various characteristics of relevant people, including status, age, and sex; (4) the perceived status of self in the situation; and (5) the number of people present.[11] The situational nature of assertive behavior is illustrated in a recent study in which sixty male hospitalized psychiatric patients were requested to participate in thirty-two role-played situations that required assertive responding.[12] Half the scenes required the expression of positive feelings such as praise, appreciation, or liking, and the other half required the expression of negative feelings such as anger, displeasure, or disappointment toward the role-played partner. Partners were of the same sex in half the role-played situations and of the opposite sex in the other half. Half the scenes required interaction with a role-played familiar other, such as a wife or employer, and the other half required interaction with an unfamiliar other, such as a cashier or waitress. Behavior varied as a function of the situational context. Responses to negative scenes were characterized by longer replies, more eye contact, greater affect, increased speech volume, and increased latency of response. The patients tended to talk longer to men than to women and were significantly more assertive with women than with men. Situational differences related to sex were also found in a study that required women to respond to twelve taped situations concerning initiation of contacts with unfamiliar others.[13] Half of the scenes involved a male and the other half involved a woman. There were twice as many failures to respond in situations involving a male.

Often, a client who has an assertive problem does not mention it during initial contact with a social worker. With the growing popularity of assertive training and the availability of assertive training manuals to the public, however, client recognition of a problem may occur more frequently in the future.[14] Indications of an assertive problem and its relationship to the presenting problem may be gained from information gathered during interviews. The client may display an undue deference to the counselor, offer examples of interactions that indicate a lack of assertion, or interact with a significant other in an unassertive manner in the office situation. Or, indications of a lack of assertion may be uncovered when the client is questioned about what happens just before and after incidences of his presenting problem. He may, for example, report that it is only after his supervisor unjustly criticizes him or his wife arranges social events he does not like that he starts to drink excessively.

Paper-and-pencil inventories, such as the Assertion Inventory, may be used to gain an overview of assertive behavior.[15] Situations may be presented *in vivo* or via film, audiotape, or videotape and the client's responses observed and recorded for assessment purposes.[16] The client may be requested to keep a log of relevant situations that actually occur, noting what he said and did and what he would like to have said or done. Such methods offer information concerning the range of situations in which a lack of assertion occurs.

Role-playing is a valuable tool for assessing a client's behavior. The client is requested to role-play his behavior so the verbal and nonverbal components of relevant social behaviors can be observed. The social worker often assumes reciprocal roles. Needed information may also be gained by observing the client in actual situations. The information collected is carefully reviewed; possible relationships between a lack of effective social behavior and the presenting problem, and the situations in which this occurs, are noted. A careful search during assessment often reveals many appropriate social behaviors that simply have to be prompted in other situations. For example, a client may have available appropriate ways of saying no to a spouse; these ways of saying no may be of utility in work situations, but he may not be using them.

COGNITIVE AND BEHAVIORAL ASPECTS OF ASSERTIVE TRAINING

A critical aspect of assertive training is to develop a conceptualization of assertive behavior as important. Specific situations are selected in which nonassertive behavior has occurred, and these are carefully examined; negative consequences, such as doing things one did not wish to do, aggravating others unnecessarily, losing opportunities, and experiencing such unpleasant feelings as anxiety and resentment are pointed out. The client comes to recognize the losses entailed through ineffective behavior and the possible relationship of this to his presenting problem. Possible detrimental effects on others are also highlighted.

Often, the unassertive client initially feels that to be assertive is to be aggressive; that he will hurt other people's feelings; that they will not like him; that he has no right to impose his preferences on others. Misconceptions may interfere with a willingness to become more assertive, and discussion may be necessary to alter these misconceptions. Various beliefs may have to be challenged, such as the belief that one should never hurt people's feelings and that therefore one should never criticize others or justly complain or that one must always please others. Attention is devoted to discriminating among submissive, assertive, and aggressive behavior and encouraging the belief that one has a right to express his feelings. It is also important to help the client to identify instances when he should not assert himself. For example, if it is obvious that a person is upset, or if the annoyance is a minor one, it may be best to remain quiet or select another time to express one's preferences.

Assertion training usually consists of a variety of components, including model presentation, instructions, behavior rehearsal in a role-playing situation, feedback on specific target behaviors, and homework assignments. Selection of procedural mix depends on the nature of each client's cognitive and behavioral deficits, surfeits, and assets in relation to relevant situations. If appropriate behaviors exist but are not performed because of anxiety, the focus is on training in anxiety-management skills. A lack of assertive behavior is often related to negative self-statements and instructions, in which case there would also be a focus on developing positive self-instructions.[17] The importance of self-statements is highlighted by studies that have found cognitive restructuring methods to be just as effective as rehearsal and model presentation in altering social be-haviors.[18] If skills are absent, procedures geared to develop them, such as model presentation and behavior rehearsal, are selected. Discrimina-tion training is required when skills are available but not performed at appropriate times.

Live models may be presented, or films, videotapes, or audiotapes may be used.[19] Nonverbal behaviors, which are so important in social inter-action, can be demonstrated, as can verbal behaviors—and the client's attention can be drawn to those that are especially vital. For example, the client may be requested to notice the model's eye contact, his hand motions, and the orientation of his posture toward others. Sometimes written scripts are used to establish appropriate verbal skills. The client is requested to imitate the modeled behavior. If he is too uncomfortable to do this at first, he can start by reading a prepared script. Instructions given before the client rehearses a behavior "prompt" him to engage in certain behaviors rather than others. Perhaps he did not look at a role-played partner, so is coached to look at others while speaking. Care is taken to identify specific behaviors. Positive feedback is offered follow-ing each rehearsal; that is, positive aspects of the client's performance are carefully noted and praised. Focus is on what the client did in a better way, noting even small improvements.[20]

The cycle of model presentation, rehearsal, and feedback is repeated until the client has attained requisite skill and comfort levels. Hierarchies attenuated in terms of the degree of anxiety or anger that imagined, ac-tual, or role-played situations induce are used to gradually establish as-sertive skills. For example, one hierarchy used with a 22-year-old male who engaged in destructive acts concerned making requests of the nursing staff.[21] The hierarchy contained eight scenes that varied staff response (yes or no) and the latency of the reply (five seconds to no response at all). Rehearsal began with scenes that induced a small degree of anger or anxiety; as these were mastered, higher-level scenes were introduced. Only after needed skill and comfort levels are attained are assignments that the client will carry out in actual situations mutually agreed on. Only those that offer a high probability of success at a low cost in terms of discomfort are chosen.

An assumption in assertive training is that it is best to assert oneself in as positive a way as possible. This implies the use of the "minimal ef-fective response": one that requires a minimum of effort and negative emotion and a high probability of positive consequences.[22] To avoid the possibility of negative outcomes, there is a need for adequate understand-ing of various relationships in which assertive behavior is proposed.[23] The client should be prepared to handle possible stress reactions in situa-tions in which negative reaction may occur, as in the example in which a woman decided to be more active during staff meetings. The client can be prepared for such situations through the development of cognitive and behavioral coping skills.[24] If negative consequences are likely to follow new behavior, the short- and long-term benefits and costs of engaging in more effective behavior are discussed, and the client must make a decision as to his preferred alternative.[25] As can be seen, the client is an active participant during training. Self-reinforcement training has been found important in developing assertive skills.[26] Also, groups can provide a useful context for assertive training; this setting provides a variety of models and multiple sources of support for trying out new behaviors.[27]

RELEVANCE OF ASSERTIVE TRAINING TO SOCIAL WORK PRACTICE

Assertive training offers social workers a technology and a cognitive framework for encouraging and aiding clients to influence their environment. Thus the aim of such training is in accord with social work values. It can be of value to a range of clients, both children and adults.[28] Assertive training has been used to teach teenagers to deal with peer pressures to drink when on parole.[29] Women and men have been trained to initiate more social contacts.[30] Assertive training emphasizes taking more initiative in meeting people and offers skills for initiating and maintaining conversations, arranging future meetings, and increasing the frequency of opinion statements. Assertive training has been used successfully to decrease abusive behavior toward others.[31] For example, psychiatric inpatients who have a history of antisocial behavior were trained to decrease irrelevant and hostile comments and inappropriate requests (e.g., "Move, or I'll throw you off the bus") and to increase looking time and appropriate requests (e.g., "Please move. I have to sit down").[32]

Assertive training can be a useful adjunct in advocacy. For example, the tenant who has a legitimate complaint can be trained how and when to express it in a way that will evoke a high probability that his request will be granted. Assertive training relates to family as well as work problems. A husband who is dominated by his wife can learn to make requests for changes in her behavior in such a way that they are likely to be followed by compliance and an increase in mutual pleasure in the marriage; the employee who has been consistently refused a job promotion can learn new ways and optimal times to request a promotion; and the social worker who wishes to make changes in his agency that will benefit clients can learn skills for interacting with supervisors and administrators in a way which will maximize his probability of success and minimize the cost to himself. Assertive training offers a valuable addition to social work practice.

NOTES

1. Joseph Wolpe and Arnold A. Lazarus, *Behavior Therapy Techniques* (New York: Pergamon Press, 1966). For a recent review of the literature concerning the development of assertive behavior, *see* Michel Hersen, Richard M. Eisler, and Peter M. Miller, "Development of Assertive Responses: Clinical Measurement and Research Considerations," *Behaviour Research and Therapy*, 11 (November 1973), pp. 505–521.

2. Andrew Salter, *Conditioned Reflex Therapy* (New York: Farrar, Straus, 1949); and Joseph Wolpe, *Psychotherapy by Reciprocal Inhibition* (Stanford, Calif.: Stanford University Press, 1958).

3. *See* Michel Hersen and Alan S. Bellack, "Social Skills Training for Chronic Psychiatric Patients: Rationale, Research Findings, and Future Directions." To be published in a forthcoming issue of *Comprehensive Psychiatry*.

4. *See*, for example, Craig T. Twentyman and Richard M. McFall, "Behavioral Training of Social Skills in Shy Males," *Journal of Consulting and Clinical Psychology*, 43 (June 1975), pp. 384–395; Richard M. McFall and Diane B. Lillesand, "Behavior Rehearsal with Modeling and Coaching in Assertion Training," *Journal of Abnormal Psychology*, 77 (June 1971), pp. 313–323.

5. *See*, for example, Herbert Fensterheim, "Assertive Problems and Marital Problems," in Richard D. Rubin et al., eds., *Advances in Behavior Therapy* (New York: Academic Press, 1972); Richard M. Eisler et al., "Assertive Training in Marital Interaction," *Archives of General Psychiatry*, 11 (May 1974), pp. 643–652; Arnold A. Lazarus, *Behavior Therapy and Beyond* (New York: McGraw-Hill Book Co., 1971); Neil B. Edwards, "Case Conference: Assertive Training in a Case of Homosexual Pedophilia," *Journal of Behavior Therapy and Experimental Psychiatry*, 3 (March 1972), pp. 55–63; Charles J. Wallace et al., "Destructive Behavior Treated by Contingency Contracts and Assertive Training: A Case Study," *Journal of Behavior Therapy and Experimental Psychiatry*, 4 (September 1973), pp. 273–274; and Lazarus, op. cit.

6. These definitions of submission, assertion, and aggression are based on those developed by Marian MacDonald in "A Behavioral Assessment Methodology as Applied to the Measurement of Assertion." Unpublished doctoral dissertation, University of Illinois, 1974.

7. Ibid.

8. Ibid.

9. Richard M. Eisler, Peter Miller, and Michel Hersen, "Components of Assertive Behavior," *Journal of Clinical Psychology*, 29 (July 1973), pp. 295–299.

10. Ibid, *See also* Michael Serber, "Teaching the Non-verbal Components of Assertive Training," *Journal of Behavior Therapy and Experimental Psychiatry*, 3 (September 1972), pp. 179–183.

11. Marian MacDonald, "Teaching Assertion: A Paradigm for Therapeutic Intervention," *Psychotherapy: Theory, Research and Practice*, 12 (Spring 1975), pp. 60–67.

12. Richard M. Eisler et al., "Situational Determinants of Assertive Behavior," *Journal of Consulting and Clinical Psychology*, 43 (June 1975), pp. 330–340.

13. Eileen D. Gambrill, "A Behavioral Program for Increasing Social Interaction." Paper presented at the Seventh Annual Convention of the Association of Behavior Therapy, Miami, Florida, December 1973.

14. *See*, for example, Stanlee Phelps and Nancy Austin, *The Assertive Woman* (San Luis Obispo, Calif.: Impact, 1975); Manuel J. Smith, *When I Say No, I Feel Guilty* (New York: Dial Press, 1975); Herbert Fensterheim and Jean Baer, *Don't Say Yes When You Want To Say No* (New York: David McKay Co., 1975); and Robert E. Alberti and Michael L. Emmons, *Your Perfect Right: A Guide to Assertive Behavior* (2d ed.; San Luis Obispo, Calif.: Impact, 1974); and Eileen D. Gambrill and Cheryl A. Richey, *"It's Up to You": Developing Assertive Social Skills* (Millbrae, Calif.: Les Femmes, 1976).

15. Eileen D. Gambrill and Cheryl A. Richey, "An Assertion Inventory for Use in Assessment and Research," *Behavior Therapy*, 6 (July 1975), pp. 550–561; An Interpersonal Situation Inventory consisting of fifty-five problematic interpersonal situations was developed by Jean B. Goldsmith and Richard M. McFall and is described in "Development and Evaluation of an Interpersonal Skill-Training Program for Psychiatric Patients, *Journal of Abnormal Psychology*, 84 (February 1975), pp. 51–58.

16. Eisler, Miller, and Hersen have developed a fourteen-item Behavioral Assertiveness Test that is administered *in vivo* by a female research assistant (*see* Eisler, Hersen, and Miller, op. cit.). A film for the assessment of the assertive behavior of women was developed by Patricia Jakubowski-Spector, J. Pearlman, and K. Coburn. It is titled *Assertive Training for Women: A Stimulus Film* (Washington, D.C.: American Personnel and Guidance Association). Audiotapes have been used by a number of investigators. *See*, for example, Lynn P. Rehm, and Albert R. Marston, "Reduction of Social Anxiety through Modification of Self-Reinforcement: An Instigation Therapy Technique," *Journal of Consulting and Clinical Psychology*, 32 (October 1968), pp. 565–574.

17. *See*, for example, Donald Meichenbaum, "Self-Instructional Methods," in Frederick H. Kanfer and Arnold P. Goldstein, eds., *Helping People Change* (New York: Pergamon Press, 1975), pp. 357–392.

18. *See*, for example, C. Glass, "Response Acquisition and Cognitive Self-Statement Modification Approaches to Dating Behavior Training." Unpublished doctoral dissertation, Indiana University, 1974.

19. *See* Richard M. McFall and Diane B. Lillesand, "Behavior Rehearsal with Modeling and Coaching in Assertive Training," *Journal of Abnormal Psychology*, 77 (June 1971), pp. 313–323; Michel Hersen, Richard M. Eisler, and Peter M.

Miller, "Effects of Practice, Instructions, and Modeling on Components of Assertive Behavior," *Behaviour Research and Therapy*, 11 (November 1973), pp. 443–451.

20. For a helpful trainer's guide, *see* Robert P. Liberman et al., *Personal Effectiveness: Guiding People to Assert Themselves and Improve Their Social Skills* (Champaign, Ill.: Research Press, 1975).

21. Wallace et al., op. cit.

22. David C. Rimm and John C. Masters, *Behavior Therapy: Techniques and Empirical Findings* (New York: Academic Press, 1974), p. 98.

23. Wolpe, op. cit.

24. Meichenbaum, op. cit.

25. MacDonald, op. cit.

26. *See* Cheryl A. Richey, "Increased Female Assertiveness through Self-Reinforcement." Unpublished doctoral dissertation, University of California, Berkeley, 1974; and Rehm and Marston, op. cit.

27. *See* Sheldon D. Rose, "In Pursuit of Social Competence," *Social Work*, 20 (January 1975), pp. 33–39.

28. *See*, for example, Roger L. Patterson, "Time-out and Assertive Training for Dependent Children," *Behavior Therapy*, 3 (July 1972), pp. 466–468.

29. I. G. Sarason and V. J. Ganzer, "Social Influence Techniques in Clinical and Community Psychology," in C. D. Spielberger, ed., *Current Topics in Clinical and Community Psychology*, Vol. 1 (New York: Academic Press, 1969); Harold H. Bloomfield, "Assertive Training in an Outpatient Group of Schizophrenics: A Preliminary Report," *Behavior Therapy*, 4 (March 1973), pp. 277–281.

30. *See* Footnotes 4 and 13.

31. *See*, for example, Lee W. Frederikson et al., "Social Skills Training to Modify Abusive Verbal Outbursts in Adults," *Journal of Applied Behavior Analysis*, 9 (Summer 1976), pp. 117–125; Wallace et al., op. cit.; David W. Foy, Richard M. Eisler, and Susan Pinkston, "Modeled Assertion in a Case of Explosive Rages," *Journal of Behavior Therapy and Experimental Psychiatry*, 6 (August 1975), pp. 135–138.

32. Frederikson et al., op. cit.

Systematizing Advocacy for Anonymous Clients

ADRIENNE AHLGREN HAEUSER

Professional social work participation in the formulation of economic policies, labor force policies, and service structures to promote the general welfare is of tremendous importance. The state of the economy and current manpower shortages are made all too clear in the daily newspapers as well as in the professional literature. For example, Demone and Schulberg introduce their comprehensive article on human service trends with a warning summation: "After many decades of geometric growth and expansion, the human services are stabilizing, even contracting in the face of adverse economic conditions." [1] As professionals, social workers are equally and perhaps even more painfully aware that their service structures are often fragmented, bureaucratic, dehumanizing, and residual. Furthermore, although preventive intervention has recently been suggested as a social work goal, it has also been called "a goal in search of a method." [2] In short, service structures have not been amenable to contact by all who seek or need assistance, nor have they been amenable to an institutionalized preventive emphasis. The profession must face this deficit at a time of contracting funding and manpower shortages. [3]

This paper describes advocacy, program development, self-help groups, and hotlines as responses to these conditions. It then describes a specific program developed for anonymous clients, in this case parents in need of help.

ADVOCACY AND PROGRAM DEVELOPMENT

Social workers' failure to achieve effective and systematized outreach, which is the key to preventive intervention, probably reflects the magnitude of the alienation and isolation characteristic of today's technological, urbanized and suburbanized society. It further suggests that despite social workers' best professional intentions and skills, society still stigmatizes problems for which assistance represents "public admission" and the threat of stigmatization.

Two professional skills that social work can bring to bear on this situation are (1) advocacy, both case and cause, for those hostile to or otherwise disconnected from needed services and (2) the development of outreach programs that not only adapt to contemporary conditions but also expedite the use of alternative programs when professional services are unacceptable.

The skills of advocacy and program development are not new to social work. In fact "the social worker as advocate; the champion of social victims" is probably the keystone of the profession.[4] Moreover, whenever championship for the victim is institutionalized, can program development be far behind? The recently rekindled interest in advocacy as a professional obligation, however, stems directly from the complexity of contemporary urban society and admits that, as a profession, social work has indeed failed in its outreach to substantial numbers of individuals and groups. This failure is embedded in the tardy emergence of an institutional approach to social welfare, which assumes that social interventions are necessary to enable *all* people to cope with a changing society.

Instead, social welfare has tenaciously maintained a residual approach, which assumes that most "normal" people do not require social interventions and that their problems are temporary, accidental, or result from their own failings. Richan and others have detailed the characteristics of contemporary advocacy as a professional skill, but the fundamental construct is "partisanship in a conflict."[5] When social isolation and professional fragmentation, bureaucracy, dehumanization of clients, or residual orientation deter or prevent those needing help from seeking assistance, skilled social work advocacy may dictate partisanship with the client, with the potential client who hurts but cannot identify a problem, or with the delivery of services by nonprofessionals. The development of outreach programs following from these partisanship positions maximizes accessibility through programs dissociated from the established service system. Thus while social work does not condone stigmatization of clients, program development through alternative systems recognizes that stigmatization by the public does in fact occur.

SELF-HELP GROUPS AND HOTLINES

Professional partisanship with nonprofessionals has been taking two major programmatic forms, namely, a renewed interest in self-help groups and the more recently developed volunteer-staffed "hotlines" under professional guidance. Both concepts emphasize anonymity for the person seeking assistance and the availability of immediate, no-red-tape help. Both have evolved largely because of some hostility to professionals and social agencies, while professionals have viewed hotlines and self-help groups with some suspicion and have generally discounted their value until recently.

A review of recent social work literature, however, indicates a new respect for at least self-help groups as an alternative support to the professional system.[6] As one author puts it, "The professional position then has progressed beyond recognition and advocacy of the self-help technique to explicit proposals for direct professional involvement in stimulating, organizing, and maintaining the activities of self-help groups."[7] Self-help groups usually focus on a single, often socially unacceptable, problem, such as drinking, gambling, overeating, mental illness, or even child abuse. The groups use the "twelve-step" principle of Alcoholics Anonymous as a model. This principle organizes self-help according to a progression of actions or resolutions that begins with admission of the problem and concludes with a commitment to carrying the group's message to others, no step of which is undertaken without successful mastery of the preceding steps. It is described as a "way of life" that requires daily effort and focuses on one day at a time.

For social workers, the challenge is to define the professional role as facilitator and catalyst rather than provider of direct treatment. This does not imply that direct professional treatment by an individual clinician is incompatible with self-help—although this is not a settled issue—but it does highlight the group theory and organizational skills required by the professional advocate for a self-help group. It further suggests that self-determinism continues to be a basic professional principle which social workers frequently abuse through overly giving, active, and authoritative roles.

Hotlines, a telephone crisis intervention technique, are a newer development. Suicide prevention center hotlines emerged in the early 1960s; but hotlines for other problems did not evolve significantly until the early 1970s, when their effectiveness as a response to campus turmoil and the drug-related problems of youths was generalized to other areas and promoted the development of helplines. While hotlines are characterized by twenty-four-hour-a-day availability for crisis intervention, helplines generally promote their availability for problems of any proportion and are often targeted to early intervention. Helpline hours vary considerably, but usually they provide more than eight hours but less than twenty-four-hour coverage; when the hours are quite limited, they may be known as "warm lines." In the past five years, both hotlines and helplines have mushroomed across the nation.[8] A few are monitored rigidly as extensions of agency programs. Most appear to be loosely structured, not so precisely supervised, and generally without stable funding and administration. Most offer assistance for a specific problem—drugs, rape, alcoholism—and a smaller number, usually the helplines, focus on their availability for everyday coping problems.

Two important distinctions between the hotline-helpline approach to service accessibility and the information and referral (IR) approach must be emphasized. IR ordinarily is part of the established service system and focuses on referral within that system. More important, it usually requires that the caller know what the problem is. Hotlines and helplines refer both within and outside the established system and have time to help callers who simply feel "troubled" identify the problem for which assistance may be needed. Although hotlines and helplines have not been covered extensively in the professional literature, Lester and Brockopp's *Crisis Intervention and Counseling by Telephone* is a noteworthy contribution.[9]

The literature does report on that critical aspect of most hotline programs which permits their availability beyond normal office hours: the use of trained volunteers. As early as 1961, a pilot study undertaken by the National Institute of Mental Health responded to the Joint Commission on Mental Illness and Health's warning of an acute manpower shortage with clear evidence that nonprofessionals could be trained to perform effectively in facilitating the solution to people's problems.[10] More recent literature substantiates this position and goes further, suggesting that "graduate training might even retard or contribute to the deterioration of the trainee's ability to offer these [effective treatment] conditions."[11] Systematic assessments of the clinical effectiveness of nonprofessional and professional telephone workers reported by Knickerbocker and McGee indicate that volunteers are as high or higher on all scales of clinical effectiveness; they are notably higher with respect to warmth, which previous studies have identified as the most significant predictor of positive outcome for verbal clients.[12]

Thus it has been recognized that self-help groups can be a feasible substitute for unwanted professional service or an alternative support to the professional system; it has also been recognized that trained volunteer-staffed hotlines can effectively break the isolation barrier between many persons and various formal as well as informal community resources. In view of such recognition, professional social workers, who are so frequently frustrated by the hard-to-reach, unserved, or unresponsive population, may well ask where indeed are our skills hiding? Can we walk that delicate tightrope as a professional partisan for the nonprofessional? If we truly respect as well as understand the respective "turfs," we can.

Using these advocacy skills, could we not proceed to develop programs that interrelate the nonprofessional activities of hotlines and self-help groups to maximize the benefits of each and, in effect, create an alternative system that is acceptable to those who reject professional help?

OUTPOST–PARENTS HELPLINE

In answer to the questions just posed, the School of Social Welfare at the University of Wisconsin-Milwaukee developed Outpost–Parents Helpline and, from that clientele, an embryonic Parents Anonymous group for actual or potential child abusers.[13] The State of Wisconsin Department of Health and Social Services and the School of Social Welfare believed that the growing national interest in the issue of child abuse and neglect— now exemplified in the Child Abuse Prevention and Treatment Act of 1974—clearly invited practice and program innovation focusing on outreach to parents and families. A grant from the state permitted the school to undertake a research project in 1973 to study the factors associated with parental satisfactions and dissatisfactions and to set up a demonstration of a hotline or helpline for parents.[14]

Believing that the inevitably authoritarian role of protective service agencies stigmatized parents and discouraged fearful parents from seeking early assistance, and believing that prevention was at least as important as treatment, the school proposed to demonstrate a helpline for the early prevention of parent–child problems including, but not limited to, child abuse. The objective was primary as well as secondary prevention. The school assigned a field education unit of five students and the author, as faculty supervisor, to develop the program. Unit members discovered twenty-six lines, including both hotlines and helplines, of various kinds and availability in the Milwaukee area. Only one, Outpost, then serving a general clientele, was amenable to focusing on parents. At that point the one-year-old Outpost was struggling to stay alive as a totally volunteer program having no professional affiliations. Outpost welcomed the opportunity to become associated with the School of Social Welfare, and Outpost–Parents Helpline became operational in early January 1974.

By offering anonymity and availability, the goal is to break the isolation barrier for parents and others hostile to, threatened by, or otherwise unable to use the established service system in the Greater Milwaukee area. Services include brief telephone counseling; information about parent education programs, social services, and other formal and informal community resources; referral; and just plain empathic listening to angry parents who need to ventilate and emotionally hungry parents who need comforting. In effect, the helpline can at least temporarily defuse the anger or frustration of parents on the verge of losing control. Helpline staff also offer callers alternative parenting behaviors and help parents identify and reinforce positive behaviors and eliminate negative ones. Several families known to the Milwaukee County Department of Public Welfare's Protective Services Agency call the helpline regularly when their frustrations begin to mount and they need support and guidance regarding child-rearing practices. As a secondary goal, the helpline is promoted as a backup for baby-sitters.

Outpost–Parents Helpline receives about one hundred calls a week on two lines with a single number. In space donated by a church, the helpline is open for calls from 9:00 A.M. to 11:00 P.M. every day. The goal is to become a true hotline by remaining open twenty-four hours every day. Regularly, however, the largest number of calls are received in the morning, and the number declines throughout the day.[15] This may indicate that the helpline is in fact achieving its early intervention rather than crisis objective.

The helpline is advertised through cards and brochures; public service announcements on radio and television; ads in buses and posters throughout the community; numerous speaking engagements of volunteer staff members and the executive director; and mailings to target groups, ranging from pediatricians to apartment managers. The ads invite calls from "confused, angry, or frustrated parents" and suggest that "sometimes parents need help too." This low-key approach was chosen in view of the helpline's early intervention objectives. The term "child abuse" was rejected as stigmatizing and, instead, reference is made to "cooling, relieving, and preventing parental stress."

Staffing and Home Visits

In developing Outpost–Parents Helpline, the School of Social Welfare recognized and respected the value and necessity of volunteers as staff. The immediate challenge was to train the small group of Outpost volunteers with whom the project began and then commence with further recruitment, screening, training of prospective volunteers, supervision, and in-service training. The helpline is now staffed by about forty volunteers, from three to six graduate students, two paraprofessional aides who are paid to cover Sundays and Friday nights, and a half-time paid executive director. Two MSWs from the community volunteer time regularly as consultants, review the daily log in which all calls are recorded, and attend the monthly staff meetings.

Outpost–Parents Helpline relies primarily on screening and training to maintain the quality of the program. Whereas the school's role is advocacy of a cause or development of a program based on partisanship with all abusive or potentially abusive parents and respect for their feelings about identification, the volunteer's role is case advocacy based on partisanship with the individual parent caller and the individual parent's needs. As case advocate, the volunteer requires active listening skills and social brokerage skills so he can select and use appropriate resources. The twelve-hour training program for prospective volunteers covers awareness and use of self; active listening and reflective response; background and management of particularly difficult kinds of calls and callers, including those related to child abuse; and use of community resources. A volunteer handbook that includes additional training materials complements the actual training sessions.

Toward the end of the first year, there was increasing awareness of staff frustrations in dealing with many resistant callers hostile to professionals and established agencies. Staff were surprised by the number of these resistant callers—two or three times a week—who verbalized or suggested concern about child abuse and who seemed to live socially isolated lives without connections to friends, family, or community.

Convinced of the need to extend staff outreach to deal with these problems, Outposts–Parents Helpline began offering home visits by graduate students to these callers. These visits do not provide ongoing casework but, rather, help parents overcome hostility or resistance in utilizing community resources; a circular given to each family on the first visit notes that the students will be able to make a maximum of four visits. Many parents accept the home visit offer, apparently because (1) the visitors are students and not yet professionals, (2) only an address and not a last name is necessary for the contact, and (3) the helpline's staff have made a comfortable impression. The initial visit is made by a male and a female student; the follow-up is handled and subsequent visits made by whichever student is most appropriate for the situation. Volunteers or paraprofessionals could be trained to fulfill this student function.

Parents Anonymous

The students quickly discovered that for some of these parents, case advocacy entailed locating resources, ranging from homemakers to education and recreation programs, whose use dissipated the parental stress and concern about child abuse. An approximately equal number of parents, however, appeared too alienated and fearful of their parenting behavior to be substantially affected by tangible resources. They had dependency needs and no one they trusted or felt they could depend on. At the very least, helpline staff could put these parents in touch with each other, and the faculty supervisor agreed to pilot Milwaukee's first Parents Anonymous group. Jolly K., the national founder of Parents Anonymous, said in a recent interview that "the feeling most parents talk about in P.A. is fear—fear of what they're doing, fear of what will happen if they don't get help and fear of what will happen if they do." [16]

As the Milwaukee Parents Anonymous group began to meet, one of the alternatives offered through the home visits was the option of joining. The student–parent relationship was utilized to support the fearful parent's entry into the group, even to the extent that students provided baby-sitting during meetings and transportation. Once present at a Parents Anonymous meeting, most parents recognize the safety of the group and reach out for each other. They become available to each other for friendships as well as for support in time of crisis. They may or may not continue to call the helpline at times of stress.

CONCLUSIONS AND ISSUES TO BE EXPLORED

The Milwaukee experience in systematizing advocacy for anonymous parents with respect to child abuse, moving from a helpline for early intervention to identification of parents wanting further but unthreatening help in a group such as Parents Anonymous, corroborates other professionals' conclusions, for example: "Most abusive parents suffer from the fear that they have no one to turn to when they are in need. Whether the isolation is emotional or realistic, there is a defective communication system and a weak support system within the client's environment." [17]

At the same time the burgeoning development of hotlines and self-help groups raises major issues for further exploration:

1. In relating to nonprofessional alternative service systems, how can social workers systematically evaluate them without diminishing the unique uninstitutionalized appeal that makes them acceptable to hard-to-reach groups?

2. Would participation by stigmatized persons, such as child abusers, in the design of professional programs and service delivery better serve these persons than professional advocacy for alternative systems?

3. Would the hard-to-reach be better served by concentrating social work skills on analysis formulation of policies to guarantee income, employment, health, and housing for all persons and to promote an explicit family policy in the United States?

Until these questions are answered, the Milwaukee experience in systematizing advocacy for anonymous clients suggests that the functions of a helpline can effectively be enlarged to encompass preventive, unthreatening intervention as well as crisis counseling and to provide a

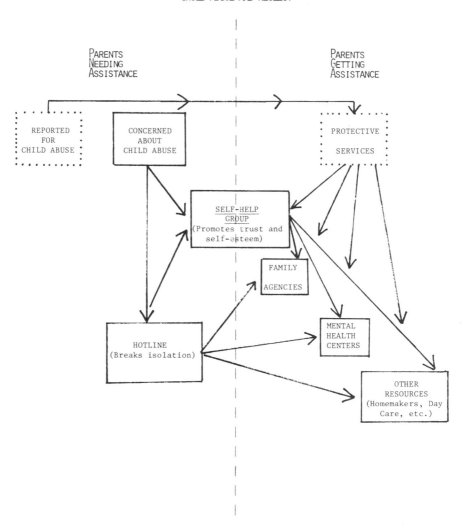

SYSTEMATIZED OUTREACH FOR PREVENTION OF
CHILD ABUSE AND NEGLECT

cross-response system matching resources and needs and a system to promote self-help when professionals are unavailable or unacceptable. By doing so, the helpline will also become a system that is a force for social change. The professional skills required for this response to social isolation, professional fragmentation, bureaucracy, and client dehumanization are advocacy and innovative outreach program development.

NOTES

1. Harold W. Demone, Jr., and Herbert C. Schulberg, "Human Service Trends in the Mid-1970's," *Social Casework*, 56 (May 1975), p. 268.

2. Carol H. Meyer, "Introduction/Preventive Intervention: A Goal in Search of a Method" (Washington, D.C.: National Association of Social Workers, 1974).

3. On May 14, 1975, in National Coalition for Mental Health Manpower testimony before the Labor, Health, Education, and Welfare Subcommittee of the House Appropriations Committee, it was said that "the contention that there is now a surplus of mental health professionals is pure myth. . . . A national crisis in manpower continues to exist." This was reported in *NASW News*, 20 (June 1975), p. 11.

4. *See* NASW Ad Hoc Committee on Advocacy, "The Social Worker as Advocate: Champion of Social Victims," *Social Work*, 14 (April 1969), pp. 16–22.

5. Willard C. Richan and Marvin Rosenberg, *The Advo-Kit, a Self-Administered Training Program for the Social Worker Advocate* (privately printed, 1971); and Arnold Panitch, "Advocacy in Practice," *Social Work*, 19 (May 1974), p. 326.

6. *See*, for example, Herbert Barish, "Self-Help Groups," in *Encyclopedia of Social Work* (New York: National Association of Social Workers, 1971), Vol. 2, p. 1164; Demone and Schulberg, op. cit., p. 278; James M. Jertson, "Self-Help Groups," *Social Work*, 20 (March 1975), pp. 144–145; and Thomas Scheff, "Reevaluation Counseling: Social Implications," *Journal of Humanistic Psychology*, 12 (Spring 1972), pp. 69–74.

7. Jertson, "Self-Help Groups," p. 145.

8. The 1973 *National Directory of Hotlines and Youth Crisis Centers*, distributed by The Exchange, 311 Cedar Avenue, Minneapolis, Minn. 55404, includes approximately fourteen hundred listings in all fifty states. The transient or unstructured nature of many lines often operating in isolation from each other precludes exact tabulation.

9. David Lester and Gene Brockopp, eds., *Crisis Intervention and Counseling by Telephone* (Springfield, Ill.: Charles C Thomas Publisher, 1973). *See also* Ursula Delworth, Edward H. Rudow, and Janet Taub, *Crisis Center/Hotline: A Guidebook to Beginning and Operating* (Springfield, Ill.: Charles C Thomas Publisher, 1972); and Carolyn M. Forsman, *Crisis Information Centers: A Resource Guide* (Minneapolis, Minn.: The Exchange, April 1973).

10. Margaret Rioch et al., "NIMH Pilot Study in Training Mental Health Counselors," *American Journal of Orthopsychiatry*, 33 (April 1963), pp. 678–689.

11. Robert R. Carkhuff, "Training and Counseling in Therapeutic Practices," in Joel Fischer, ed., *Interpersonal Helping: Emerging Approaches for Social Work Practice* (Springfield, Ill.: Charles C Thomas Publisher, 1973), p. 371.

12. D. Knickerbocker and R. McGee, "Clinical Effectiveness of Nonprofessional and Professional Telephone Workers in a Crisis Intervention Center," in Lester and Brockopp, op. cit., pp. 305–307.

13. Andre L. Olton includes Outpost–Parents Helpline as one of eleven programs surveyed in "An Evaluation Survey of Crisis Intervention Centers and Hotlines in Milwaukee." Unpublished master's degree thesis, University of Wisconsin-Milwaukee School of Education, 1975.

14. Following the suggestion of Prof. Max Kurz at the University of Wisconsin-Milwaukee School of Social Welfare, Prof. Catherine Chilman, Ph.D., developed and directed the study and outlined the proposal for the hotline demonstration.

15. In 1974 nine hundred calls in the morning, eight hundred calls in early afternoon, seven hundred calls in late afternoon, and six hundred calls at night were received.

16. Jolly K., in an interview with Judith Reed, "Working With Abusive Parents," *Children Today*, 4 (May–June 1975), p. 6.

17. Sally A. Holmes et al., "Working with the Parent in Child-Abuse Cases," *Social Casework*, 56 (January 1975), p. 11.

Data-Based Advocacy

PAUL K. H. KIM AND

KENNARD W. WELLONS

The impetus for this paper came from the authors' study of advocacy in the field of aging.[1] Time and again during the course of the study the need for information-based advocacy was emphasized, especially by politicians in strategic decision-making positions. They made statements such as, "Kind-hearted concern without information has little influence on the legislative process," and "The exertion of power strategies not reinforced with factual information is not likely to have much impact." These statements by political officeholders, the targets of advocacy efforts, imply the purpose and perspective of this paper: to delineate and to advocate for research-grounded strategies of political advocacy. It is not the authors' purpose to develop a model of advocacy delineating strategies and techniques, but to provide the essential grounding on which a technology might be built and without which political advocacy is devitalized.

ADVOCACY DEFINED

Advocacy, as conceptualized here, connotes a research-based professional activity having the purpose of exerting influence, in the arena of public policy and legislation, for eliciting change—or causing the veto of proposed change—for the benefit of a particular class or group interest.[2] This focus on advocacy in the public, or governmental, arena was selected because public policy and legislative change generally have potentially wider impact and greater legitimacy and permanence than policy change within private organizations; more important, an effective way for research to influence public policy has not yet been found.

Social workers have traditionally been hindered in their advocacy efforts for three reasons: (1) traditional particularistic service or case-oriented goals, (2) agency-bound role constraints (i.e., agencies have not traditionally assigned advocacy responsibilities to social work staff), and (3) the well-known reluctance of social workers to engage in any activity even loosely defined as research. The first two of these hindering factors are indeed in the process of change. Social workers in increasing numbers are insisting on performing advocacy roles, are being trained as advocates by schools of social work, and are performing legitimate roles in agencies to advocate on behalf of client groups as a primary job function. In fact, the major recent movement within the profession is in the direction of broadening the base of intervention from individuals and families to wider social systems. These advances are diluted, however, by the failure of social work (the profession, the professional organization, and the schools of social work) to inculcate a sense of systematic inquiry among professional practitioners and to allay the myth that research is a highly esoteric, oversophisticated, unmasterable phenomenon to be practiced only by research specialists and to be avoided at all costs by the intimidated majority of practitioners.

The situation is an untenable one. For too long social workers have relied on their convictions, effecting public policy changes and program development by "appeals to the heart" rather than data-supported appeals to the intellect. Certainly, social workers have supported and have been involved in political action; however, the issue is how they were involved and the types of strategies they used. During the mid-1960s the profession made what Thursz has called a radical departure from the traditional professional posture.[3] It did so by making a rather easily attained transition to the widely accepted notion that political action on the part of professionals was "the only effective tool for social reform."[4] The strategies of confrontation and conflict and the techniques attached to each were rapidly developed, labeled, and implemented. But all too often actions were not supported by systematically obtained valid data. Social workers learned painfully that when their social reform efforts did not include the critical element of a valid information-based approach, and when they lacked the empirical foundations for the numerous social programs for which they advocated, they had contributed significantly to the lack of success of programs; to the growing disenchantment of the public with social programs; and to the increasing demand for accountability and clearly defined and attainable program objectives.

WHY DATA?

The term "data," as used here, refers to factual material and information upon which policy decisions regarding social service programs are based, and with which communication between the public and the social work profession is facilitated with minimal misunderstanding.

Data for Decision-Making

Like it or not, a new federalism is developing in this country in that political decision-making on most local, state, and federal issues, including the issues related to social welfare, are being made increasingly at the federal level. Numerous bills related to social workers' professional concerns are introduced each year, and numerous major acts and titles are legislated. It is estimated that approximately fourteen to fifteen thousand bills are introduced in both Houses each year, approximately 10 percent of which involve areas of concern to social work.[5] The historic move of the National Association of Social Workers from New York to Washington, D.C., appeared to be influenced by professional accountability to, and desire for communication with, the national administrative and legislative processes.

"Total federal and state expenditures on human services exceed $160 billion annually. They have more than tripled since 1960, with the largest dollar increase being in social security and public education costs," says Rep. Martha W. Griffiths of Michigan. She continues, "HEW currently administers more than 300 separate social welfare programs. About $9 billion is spent each year to finance these narrowly defined service programs." [6] There is also evidence of a welfare future shock: "In order to extend services to all of those eligible, HEW programs could cost well over $200 billion more than is currently being spent on them; nearly 15 million more trained people would be needed." [7] It appears, then, that a vicious competition over limited resources is imperative and unavoidable.

Not unlike social workers' decision-making processes at numerous hierarchical echelons, national administrative and legislative decisions are made based on available factual information, that is, data. The instigation of new service programs and the continuation of existing programs are simply contingent on factual demonstrations that solidify the justification for the programs. Since 1970 social service programs have been monitored closely as a result of the federal demand for the evaluation of programs.[8] A systematic means of evaluation has also been established at the state level. California's Lanterman-Petris-Short Act for evaluating the effectiveness of the mental health program, Massachusetts's law requiring utilization reviews, and Missouri's procedures for the evaluation of community mental health centers are major examples.[9] Sen. Walter F. Mondale's proposal for large-scale program evaluation rather than "piecemeal, *ad hoc* arrangements" was passed by the Senate in 1972.[10] The American Institute for Research and the National Institute of Mental Health, based on their survey of members of the National Council of Community Mental Health Centers, concluded that the primary concern of the centers was program evaluation.[11] These concerns about program evaluation will contribute to the utilization of data, in the decision-making processes, that indicate program outcomes precisely and eventually justify the value of program and redirective rationales.

The lack of data relative to program instigation and continuation creates great concern among political decision-makers. This was the very concern of the Senate Appropriations Committee in 1972 relative to the lack of control of federal income security programs.[12] Even today many legislative committees and subcommittees related to such social programs as aging and health are searching for data on which to base appropriate and feasible decisions. History has demonstrated that when social work practitioners and organizations cannot provide appropriate data to political decision-makers, while others with competing interests can, social work practice as advocacy becomes unwittingly inefficient, ineffective, and consequently significant to no one. When social workers did not have counterbalance data available, they lost the Head Start program despite inconclusive evaluation findings; when they were unable to demonstrate the effect of social service in nursing homes, the value of social service was questioned and, through legislation, became a nonreimbursable service under Medicare law. On the other hand, when they had data, however painfully collected, they experienced success, as witnessed by such effective social work advocates as Dorothea Dix for mental hospital reformation and Charity Organization Society advocates for poverty and settlement programs.

The trend of the social work profession in the utilization of data is discouraging. Social work data per se have been disappearing in the name of (1) misunderstood interdisciplinary practice and (2) the tendency of social workers to become data consumers rather than data producers. Nevertheless, social work advocates are expected to work with data to complement their compassion for those for whom they advocate.

Data for Communication

Social accountability is an often repeated theme at countless national and local professional meetings. The term "social accountability" seems to be the professional slogan for the 1970s and potentially for the 1980s. One of many implications of social accountability is professional responsibility for communication (written, verbal, and otherwise) with (1) people (taxpayers, program supporters, voters, etc.), (2) government or private funding resources, (3) related systems surrounding social service systems, and (4) related scientific disciplines.

A crucial communication issue is that all people understand differently; that is, the same words convey different meanings to different people. Ironically, the more educated people are, the more difficult communication will be. As people receive education from kindergarten through bachelor's, master's, or doctorate (even post-doctorate) degrees, they gradually become limited to designated turf and language systems and eventually become "educationally disabled specialists." People's communication methods and skills are continually differentiated as their unique process of life experience unfolds, and thus the requirement for a common language is paramount if one is to communicate effectively in the contemporary professional arena.

One way people can communicate with the fewest problems in understanding is to communicate with data. Data add a quantified definition to reality and not only represent abstract definition but also operationalize a precise definition. For example, a numerical expression of height ("He is six feet tall") is much more precise than simply saying, "He is tall." Such a statement as "There are many poor people" is truly ambiguous because it lacks such critical parameters of poverty as frequency (i.e., the number of people who are poor) and the intensity and duration of people's poverty.

According to the advocacy study conducted by the authors, the most important indicator of the successful advocate is the quality of his data-based communication with political decision-makers.[13] A rather simplistic episode described by one of the legislators interviewed for the study illustrates the point. An agency representative appeared before a grant appropriation committee and said, "We need more vans to transport our senior citizens." This was followed by an avalanche of questions by the committee members: "How many vans do you have now? How many do you need? Why? How many senior citizens are there who need your service?" If an agency representative does not prepare the appropriate answers to the questions (which unfortunately was the case), the chances of success are diminished greatly.

Social workers cannot just speak loquaciously or write in terms of convincing, esoteric, unmeasurable constructs. They have to communicate precisely and explicitly with their numerous audiences what they mean when they say or write such terms as "more," "effective," "improved," "happier," "extremely successful," and so on. When they say "more," they should indicate how many; when they say "effective program," they should discuss effect; when they say "improved," they should demonstrate a difference. In brief, in the advocating process, data-based statements are imperative for communicating what they intend to communicate and, eventually, for achieving that for which they are advocating.

CRITICAL COMMENT

Numerous myths surround the research enterprise: For example, research activities are carried out regardless of the methodological handicaps and meaninglessly esoteric findings; the research process is executed subjectively and therefore has limited utility, if any; research, as a process of computer analysis, is a game of "garbage in, garbage out"; research is numerical and thus not human; and data are manipulated to find what the researcher is looking for. Such myths primarily arose from and are maintained by two groups of people: (1) disillusioned research "experts" and (2) the "ambivalent empiricists." Disillusioned research experts complain vigorously of the shortcomings of research, but continue to conduct research. Ambivalent empiricists are basically unsure about research findings and do not have research capability, but strongly feel the need of research.

Realistically, most knowledge imparted throughout all levels of education is research based, and the advances of modern civilization and technology are by and large consequences of rigorous research activity. These research uses and advances offer strong testimony as to the methodological integrity and capabilities of research. Therefore the disillusioned research experts should be cautious with their criticisms of the mythical methodological handicaps and other shortcomings of research and should instead devote their energies to the development and refinement of existing research processes. The ambivalent empiricists should seriously go about learning research and its methodologies and become capable of discerning whether they do good or bad research—whether they are involved in the "garbage in, garbage out" game. To know what is garbage, it is also necessary to know what is not garbage. Data collected from bad research are less useful than data collected from no research. In other words, questionable data are worse than no data. To eliminate questionable data, well-designed research is needed, and to conduct well-designed research, more effective learning of research processes and methodologies needs to be promoted.

SUMMARY AND RECOMMENDATIONS

Political advocacy as a social work methodology has been apparent since the mid-1960s, and professional involvement in various political decision-making processes is imperative if functional, humane social legislation is to evolve. If social workers are to advocate successfully in the political arena for social reform, they must make considerable progress in the use of organized data to develop, account for, and test the theoretical and practical effects of social work programs. Data are the bases of political decision-making, and data are the most precise and explicit tools for professional communication with the people who are the potential benefactors of social work programs.

For data-based (or research-based) advocacy to develop effectively, it is imperative that the research component of social work education be strengthened; that interventive strategies become viewed as inseparable from the evaluative research function; and, thus, that community agencies begin to engage in evaluation research of practice as a matter of course, not as a special, isolated activity conducted only in collaboration with or by a research specialist. A burgeoning computer technology, coupled with the increasing capability of the social work profession to identify and gather relevant information on clients, problems, goals, techniques of intervention, expectable outcomes, and costs, makes possible the development of a national information system. Such a system offers the potential for the accumulation and storage of infinite amounts of rapidly retrievable data, manipulations permitting elaborate investigations of relationships among variables, and the results of prior research, programs, and interventive strategies.

These are the types of information demanded by those politicians who are the potential sponsors of legislation aimed at social reform. Such information is also demanded by the sponsors of human service programs, by those social workers most interested and involved in the advancement and maintenance of the profession, and eventually, it is hoped, by every person engaged in the practice of social work.

NOTES

1. *Advocacy in the Field of Aging* (San Francisco: U.S. Human Resources Corporation, 1975). This was a five-state advocacy study in the field of aging. The authors conducted the Kentucky component and wrote the sections that relate specifically to Kentucky.

2. "Advocacy as a Process," in *Field Manual* (San Francisco: U.S. Human Resources Corporation, 1975).

3. *See*, for example, Daniel Thursz, "Social Action as a Professional Responsibility," *Social Work*, 11 (July 1966), pp. 12–21.

4. James D. Orten, "Political Action: End or Means?" *Social Work*, 17 (November 1972), pp. 4, 105–106.

5. These estimations were made by a staff person of the National Association of Social Workers office in Washington, D.C. The figure was identified as a conservative estimate.

6. Martha W. Griffiths, "Replies to Position Paper," *Evaluation* (special issue, Spring 1974), p. 12.

7. Laurance E. Lynn, Jr., and Susan Salasin, "Human Services: Should We, Can We Make Them Available to Everyone?" *Evaluation* (special issue, Spring 1974), p. 4.

8. Garth N. Buchanan and Joseph S. Wholey, "Federal Level Evaluation," *Evaluation*, 1 (Fall 1972), p. 21.

9. Howard R. Davis, "A Solution for Crisis," *Evaluation*, 1 (Fall 1972), p. 3.

10. Walter F. Mondale, "Social Accounting, Evaluation, and the Future of the Human Services," *Evaluation*, 1 (Fall 1972), pp. 29–34.

11. Davis, op. cit.

12. Elmer B. Staats, "The Challenge of Evaluating Federal Social Programs," *Evaluation*, 1 (1973), p. 53.

13. *Advocacy in the Field of Aging*, op. cit.

Combating Racism in a State Hospital

ARAMINTA SMITH AND JANE BIERDEMAN

The late Whitney M. Young, Jr., called racism America's No. 1 mental health problem.[1] That racism distorts reality, feeds paranoia, degrades human beings, and turns human institutions into dehumanized mockeries of American values has been well documented. Institutionalized racism insidiously invades social agencies and institutions, especially those in which large numbers of persons who are members of ethnic minorities are committed for care, treatment, rehabilitation, and protection of themselves or society.

During the whole history of our profession, social workers have had an inescapable mandate to combat racism actively and vigorously and to replace its dehumanization with creative programs of human development.[2] How to operationalize this mandate is the real challenge. How do we make our values come alive? What knowledge base do we need? What practice skills should we use?

This paper analyzes the strategies utilized in one institutional setting, where social work leadership seriously examined its value commitments and then set about to combat racism in everyday practice. This experience has significance for any setting in which minority-group members are present, such as welfare systems, juvenile courts, and correctional institutions, as well as medical and psychiatric hospitals.

THE SETTING AND THE PROBLEM OF INSTITUTIONAL SUBORDINATION

The Forensic Unit of Fulton State Hospital houses the only maximum-security unit for mentally ill male offenders in the state of Missouri. (Forensic units are designed primarily for the care and treatment of mentally ill offenders and others who exhibit extremely dangerous behavior. Such units may be part of a large public psychiatric hospital, such as at

Fulton, part of a correctional system, or administratively autonomous. Historically, they have served males only because the care and treatment of mentally ill female offenders has been largely ignored and neglected. Usually there are minimum-, medium-, and maximum-security areas within such units.[3]) Fulton is located in the center of the state equidistant from St. Louis and Kansas City. Of the 300 men housed in the unit, over one-third are blacks from urban centers; almost all the 175 staff members are white males with rural backgrounds. The urban black male finds himself in a truly alien culture in such a setting. He is discriminated against because (1) his skin is not white; (2) males, especially black males, are regarded as aggressive and physically dangerous; (3) he has come into conflict with the law and is labeled by society as a criminal who must be punished; and (4) he has been committed to a mental institution and is stereotyped, like other mental patients, as impulse-ridden, "crazy," or retarded.

In the late 1960s and early 1970s, positive action to combat racism, reduce the black patients' culture shock, and change institutional practices became mandatory to preserve human rights and create an atmosphere conducive to treatment. The Social Service Department's administrative and key supervisory staff recognized the problem and began a detailed assessment of theory and strategies. Working together, they decided to focus on the goal of changing the behaviors rather than the basic attitudes of staff and to direct change strategies toward influencing the hospital culture to the point where an awareness of the human rights of all persons and quality treatment for black patients could become normative.

Theories of social change were studied and methods weighed. Combinations of leadership and power theory, institution-building theory, organizational theory, social policy work, and educational method utilization were studied, discussed, and tested. No one theory or methodology was consciously selected above all others. Instead, these theories and methods were utilized eclectically, and attempts were continuously made to link together to create logical strategies and actions. Internal as well as external variables were scrutinized and utilized when deemed appropriate.

ASSESSMENT OF INTERNAL INSTITUTIONAL VARIABLES

The first step was to identify, study, and assess the major institutional variables that explain systemic behavior. The second step, closely intertwined with the first, was to determine how these variables could be utilized creatively to promote and sustain positive institutional change.

The major institutional variables, as identified in the literature on institution building, are (1) leadership, (2) internal structure, (3) doctrine, (4) program, and (5) resources.[4]

Leadership

Leadership is considered the single most critical element in institution building because deliberately induced change processes require intensive, skillful, and highly committed management of both internal and environmental relationships. Leadership can be centered in one person; however, there is usually a leadership group comprised of those who hold formally designated positions and those who informally exercise important, continuing influence. Among the variables usually identified as leadership characteristics are political viability, professional status, technical and organizational competence, and continuity.[5] In the assessment period, leadership had to be viewed in two dimensions. First, it meant finding out where leadership and power were centered and who had the authority necessary to sanction the internal changes necessary to begin and continue efforts to combat institutional racism. Second, it meant assessing the leadership role and power of the Social Service Department and to what extent its power could be risked in pursuit of this task.

In the classical medical model, the doctor and nurse are in the formal ascribed positions of leadership and power. In a professional environment, however, power can be achieved through knowledge and competence.[6] Fortunately, there were elements in the social work subsystem that enabled it to compete with ascribed power centers fairly and effectively and to use its achieved power for leadership credibility. The Social Service Department was generally recognized for competently performing tasks essential to the system. These factors made it highly propitious for the department to carry out "the idea whose time had come" and to use its achieved power constructively in the risk-taking necessary in the role of patient advocate and systems change agent. The achieved leadership position also made it possible to enlist and obtain the cooperation of identified allies in the medical and nursing administration, as well as in other professional departments. Strong, permanent, as well as ad hoc, linkages had already been developed and could be mobilized for the goal of combating institutional racism in the total culture of the hospital and in the specific subculture of its Forensic Unit.

Internal Structure

Closely intertwined with the leadership component is the internal structure in which the leaders act. This institutional variable includes (1) the distribution of functions and authority, (2) the processes of communication and decision-making, (3) the identification of participants within the institution, (4) the consistency of structure with doctrine and program, and (5) the structure's adaptability to shifts in program emphasis and cultural changes.[7] In the assessment period, social service leadership had to analyze all key elements in the internal structure and identify, define, and attempt to anticipate how each could be used in advancing the goal of combating institutional racism.

In any state hospital setting, the internal structure is highly authoritarian and formalized, and it is even more so in a forensic unit. The superintendent of the total institution must take direct responsibility for the forensic unit because of the gravity of its task and the political and social implications of its mission. At Fulton, the superintendent's unqualified sanction and commitment to the goal of combating racism was, therefore, essential. Formal communication patterns included daily administrative meetings of key staff; clinical case review of patients in the Forensic Unit, over which the superintendent presided; other interdisciplinary meetings to plan collaborative treatment efforts; and interdepartmental staff training functions.

Essential also to assessing the internal structure was the recognition of the informal communication system, or "the grapevine." Generally, informal systems are used to express opinions that are different from or critical of formal policy. Because it was the official position of the institution—through the formal authority of the superintendent—to be committed to the goal of combating racism, the grapevine would be the communication channel most apt to be used by staff opposed to this policy. It was also the means through which their strategies of opposition would most likely be developed.[8] Fortunately, there was much casual and informal communication taking place at all levels in the Forensic Unit. It was therefore easy for staff favorable to change to penetrate this communication network, correct misinformation and rumors, and use the informal system to create and develop communication positive to the goal of combating institutional racism.

Doctrine

Doctrine is defined as the action-oriented "expression of the institution's major objectives, purposes, and methods of operation."[9] It takes the objectives and converts them into a concrete set of policies that give definite direction to the institution's activities. More simply, it is "applied ideology."[10]

Intellectually, the values of the mental hospital system place the treatment of the patient and restoration of mental health as conscious primary goals. In the medical model, however, the needs of staff in the system, especially those with ascribed power, often take precedence over doctrine; this happens all too often in social institutions. But the doctrine of patient primacy can be utilized consciously by those with leadership power and motivation to operationalize change on behalf of patient treatment.

The doctrine of treating mental illness and restoring the patient to independent functioning could easily be translated by social work leadership into combating racism because racism is a form of mental illness and racial supremacy is often equated with paranoia. Indeed, in the total assessment, the doctrine of Fulton State Hospital unquestionably supported the social work leadership and its change-agent role of combating institutional racism.

Program

Program fulfills the goal of the organization as set forth in legal mandates and official doctrine. Program is the translation of doctrine into concrete patterns of action; it also includes the allocation of resources within the institution itself and in the external environment. Subvariables relative to the program include consistency, stability, and contribution to societal needs.[11]

Simply stated, the program of the mental hospital is treatment translated into the practical modalities that will produce the desired results. This means not only treatment of the patient, but treatment of the system for the sake of the patient. To treat the system means dealing with staff at all levels of administrative and treatment capacities. Therefore, in the planning and carrying out of the specific program to combat racism, the social work leadership had to design a program model that would reach both staff and patients and accomplish this within approximately the same time frame. The overall program would have to have consistency with the doctrine and contribute to the needs of the total system in demonstrable patient improvement and staff betterment through knowledge-building and morale enhancement. Furthermore, the overall program should be designed to benefit the teaching and/or research function of the system to bring about further bonuses.

The social work leadership first decided to begin on those aspects of a black studies program related to staff. They realized that intensive staff development designed to overcome the intellectual and emotional deficits of the white majority had to be carried on prior to any program of patient treatment. The formal sanction of the superintendent and major department heads was obtained; informal testing of the idea for a human relations program had preceded the formal approval.

The social work leadership started the staff development program at what was thought to be the most receptive and least stressful part of the system, namely, the Social Service Department itself.[12] Sessions on white racism, institutional racism, the black response to white racism, black history, and the black family were planned. Detailed factual content was developed and presented in a series of meetings on each of these major topics. Case illustrations led to discussion and exploration of the attitudes and feelings of the participants. Methodology included the use of lectures and audiovisual materials, large group discussions, and more intensive small group sessions. Black professional social work staff and other social workers who had special education in Afro-American history and race relations served as leaders.

The initial sessions presented in July and August 1971 were well received and evoked curiosity on the part of staff and administrators of other departments and program units. The social work leadership decided quickly to extend the staff development program to administrative staff and key clinical staff. By October 1971, social workers were approached by the Nursing Education Department to design and present a series of staff development programs, first to registered nurse supervisors, then to nonprofessional nursing service supervisors. The latter group worked directly with the psychiatric aides who have responsibility for individual wards and all assigned hospital attendant staff. These, of course, are the key personnel who have the most continuous and direct relationship with patients.

In late 1971 plans for an intensified training program for social work staff assigned specifically to the Forensic Unit were developed. This program was begun in the early summer of 1972, and it developed from once weekly to daily discussions on an intensive feeling level. Toward the end of the summer, it culminated in a marathon weekend program in a retreat setting. This group was picked for the most intensive and confrontive training because of its frontline position in assessment and action and because the social workers, of all the groups in the maximum-security unit, were judged to be the least resistant and most amenable to change.[13]

The staff development program for Forensic Unit personnel was also used as part of the learning experience for social work students from the University of Missouri School of Social Work and for students from two undergraduate colleges. The Research Department in the hospital, as well as the students, utilized various aspects of the staff development program for scientific investigation.

The social work leadership next studied how best to treat the black forensic patient and how individual staff members and volunteers, as well as other program resources—such as films, discussions, lectures, records, and so on—could be utilized to achieve the best results. In white-dominated mental hospitals, correctional settings, and welfare systems, the black patient frequently behaves in learned stereotyped roles of feigned stupidity, withdrawal, patronizing attitudes, and superficial conformity—never letting real problems, true behavior, and genuine feelings, come through in front of white staff. In a therapeutic treatment system run by skilled black therapists, however, these facades do not work and can be penetrated easily.[14] Genuine personal problems can be separated from societal injustices, and both can be dealt with realistically.

An enriched black studies program that combined an education and treatment model was chosen as the primary way to help black patients overcome the detrimental effects of the prejudices experienced by black male forensic patients. It was thought that the positive presentation of the facts of black history, with past and present achievements of black persons, by responsible, effective black staff members would be appropriate. These staff members could serve as role models; effectively dissipate poor self-images; debunk the degrading cultural stereotypes; encourage control in self-gratifying, impulse-ridden individuals; and give hope and challenge to those seeking self-esteem.

The patient-centered program began with informal discussions between black patients and black staff. These progressed to the joint development of program goals and content. Again, audiovisual aids were utilized extensively, as were records of black musicians. Since January 1972 the birth of Martin Luther King, Jr., has been the occasion for special programs that include films, music, dramatics, and an open-house reception to which black patients invite all patients and staff.

Resources

Resources are the physical, financial, personnel, informational, and other inputs required for the functioning of the institution.[15] These are the physical and human resources available for the performance of a total program. How could their availability be directed toward the innovative programs for staff and patients to combat institutional racism and promote positive human interaction?

Before any resource change could be expected, it was judged absolutely necessary that black leadership serve as the major resource in planning and executing the program. Fortunately, through previous recruitment efforts, the Social Service Department had two experienced black staff members with master's degrees in social work who could be the key planners and advisers in initiating and carrying out the overall program. During their student training, these staff members had collaborated with a black leader on the faculty of the University of Missouri School of Social Work in developing curriculum content on Afro-American history and its implications for social work practice. Several white staff members had also had the opportunity to take this course and were eager to participate, especially in programs concentrated on staff development for white administrative staff, the various echelons of the nursing service, as well as social workers.

In a bureaucracy, one of the easiest ways to defeat an innovative program, particularly one that may evoke strong cultural resistance to change, is to deny it either financial or staff resources. To circumvent such a possibility, the social service director, in early 1972, explored outside funding resources and decided to write a grant proposal requesting Mental Health Authority funds (federal funds available for small seed-money grants to start innovative mental health programs). The grant request was approved for approximately $6,000 to (1) hire a qualified black social work supervisor and an assistant to develop and carry out the patient treatment and staff training aspects of the program on a full-time basis during the summer of 1972 and then (2) to finance the treatment program on a part-time consultative basis for the remainder of the fiscal year, or through June 1973. This period of continuous funding provided the program a substantial time frame in which to prove its usefulness to the system and to become accepted and an expected part of the everyday treatment program. While the initial grant-funded program was in process, the social service director negotiated concurrently with the hospital administration for incorporation of this program into the regular hospital budget. She was successful and, since fiscal year 1973–74, this program has been regularly funded as any other accepted and proved hospital program.

Another essential resource was the black faculty member from the University of Missouri School of Social Work who became the technical consultant to the program practically from its inception. She served first as a volunteer, then as part-time employee; she was funded initially through grant resources and, later and up to the present, through the regular hospital budget. Since 1970 she has been the university-employed field instructor responsible for graduate and undergraduate student programs at the hospital. In this capacity, she had gained special knowledge of the hospital system and had already earned acceptance and respect from hospital staff and administration. She has been an invaluable resource in helping regular hospital staff develop program directions, allocate time for change efforts, and develop the skills to effect change.[16] Her role is that of technical assistant or change strategist who brings outside help, not as an unwelcome intruder, but as a vehicle through which a purposive, cooperative transfer of knowledge takes place. Her presence has enabled hospital staff to become more creatively involved in their own change efforts.[17]

LINKAGES AND TRANSACTIONS AS EXTERNAL VARIABLES

Linkages and transactions are defined as "The interdependencies which exist between an institution and other relevant parts of the society. No institutionalized organization exists in isolation; it must establish and maintain a network of complementaries to survive and function. The institution must communicate with a limited number of organizations and engage in transactions for the purpose of gaining support, overcoming resistances, exchanging resources, restructuring the environment, and transferring norms and values."[18] Some of the Social Service Department's most significant linkages were its long-standing relationships with the University of Missouri School of Social Work and with the National Association of Social Workers (NASW). These two organizations provided substantial goal definition and direction to the leadership of the Social Service Department. The university provided technical assistance, leadership, and recruitment resources. NASW, through action by its Delegate Assembly of 1969, established the dual priorities of eliminating poverty and racism. Through this action, the professional association motivated and challenged its members to develop and sustain specific programs and practice techniques to attain these ends. Three members of the Social Service Department's administrative staff had participated in the NASW Leadership Training Program for Social Workers in Mental Health, which was carried out from 1966 through 1974.[19]

Relationships with the persons to whom the Mental Health Authority had been delegated in Missouri, and those who thereby controlled these federal funds, provided the opportunity for the social work leadership to learn about, apply for, and obtain the initial grant. There were also linkages with legal aid groups and others interested in the patient's rights movement. The overall Black Studies Program, both for staff training and patient treatment, actually predated any organized activities of these groups in Missouri. But, when their presence did become visible and they confronted the hospital administration, the existence of the overall Black Studies Program tempered charges of patient neglect and abuse and made the program all the more valuable to the system.

THE TIME DIMENSION

If used constructively, time can foster the productive use of internal and external resources. The dimensions of timing are synchronization, sequence, and rate.[20] As mentioned earlier, the overall Black Studies Program was an "idea whose time had come." The 1960s and early 1970s had seen development and acceleration of the civil rights movement, the prisoners' rights movement, and the patients' rights movement. By synchronizing the overall Black Studies Program with these major social movements in the outside culture, the social work leadership created a vehicle for translating the elements from them into constructive internal programming. In both its staff and patient aspects, the total Black Studies Program helped the hospital system anticipate, predate, and to some extent diffuse the negative and extreme elements of these social movements as they affected the hospital system.

Also, the pressures from these outside forces enabled the social work leadership to accelerate the development of the total Black Studies Program, expand its base insofar as staff limitations would permit, and assure its regular funding. There were times when the pressures for acceleration and expansion of the total program were so great that the social work leadership was tempted to expand the program beyond the limited staff resources and before the staff training and treatment aspects were solidly based. The director steadfastly resisted these pressures, however.

Undoubtedly, one of the most dangerous temptations to those who have produced a successful program is to overexpand prematurely with inexperienced or unsuitable staff and insufficient resources. Consequently, an important concept of institution building has to do with knowing when not to build, when to simply maintain the status quo, when to regroup, and even when to retreat. This is, perhaps, one of the hardest parts of the process to assess because it runs counter to the American propensity to do everything "bigger and better."

MEASURING THE SUCCESS OF INSTITUTION BUILDING

Institutionalization is the process by which an invention or practice is accepted and is given significance, utility, or value by members of the group in which it takes place so that their behavior toward it can be determined and relevant social structures and processes can develop.[21] Many authors have addressed the question of when the institution-building process has been completed. Esman identifies certain tests of institutionalization, including (1) the ability to survive; (2) being viewed by an organization (or an environment) as having intrinsic value which, in turn, can be tested by the autonomy the institutionalized culture has gained; (3) the influence the institutionalized process exercises; and, (4) the spread effect of its activity, that is, whether specific relationships and action patterns embodied in the organization have become normative for other social units with which the institutionalized process interacts.[22]

If measured by Esman's criteria, the program of combating institutional racism through social work leadership and practice has become institutionalized, as attested by the following facts:

1. *Survival:* The program has been in continuous operation since the summer of 1971; it has continued to expand slowly as staff resources have permitted.

2. *Intrinsic Value and Its Own Autonomy:* The program is well entrenched in the regular budget process of the overall hospital and at times of budgetary crisis has been given priority over other programs by both clinical and business elements in the hospital power structure.

3. *Influence:* There are many specific concrete changes that have taken place as a result of the overall Black Studies Program in both its staff development and patient treatment aspects.

a. Staff identified with the program are constantly used as consultants on human relations questions or problems by all levels of administrative and program personnel.

b. Content on black history and culture, and their meaning in the treatment of black patients is now a permanent part of the nursing education curriculum as presented to all levels of nursing service personnel.

c. Content of black history and culture and their meaning for treatment have been incorporated permanently into the overall hospital orientation program for all disciplines and levels of staff.

d. The administration has backed merit increases for staff members on the basis of their participation and creative contribution to the total Black Studies Program as it affects both other staff and patients.

e. Specific changes in overall patient treatment have taken place:

(1) Black patients are now employed in industrial therapy assignments requiring managerial, clerical, and sales capacity rather than being employed only in laundry, food service, and janitorial jobs.[23]

(2) Black patients are now allowed to associate together more freely for recreational and social activities without the undue suspicion of white staff members.

(3) Black patients state that derogatory name-calling and overt racist slurs have diminished markedly.

(4) Special products manufactured for black clientele, such as those manufactured for grooming and hair dressing, are now regularly stocked and sold in hospital canteens. Previously, these items were not available or were available only in limited supply.

(5) Black patients who wish to now attend Moslem religious services.

(6) Charges of overmedication by black patients are now exceedingly rare.

(7) Black patients are now assigned to rooms and ward locations more suited to their psychiatric condition in the maximum-security Forensic Unit and are able to participate more freely in ward government and other activities. Study prior to the beginning of the overall Black Studies Program showed that black patients tended to be clustered in less desired locations on wards and in the maximum-security unit, and their participation in various programming was more limited than that of white patients with comparable psychiatric conditions.

4. *Spread Effect:*

a. The presence of the Black Studies Program has helped in the recruitment of more black staff, especially social workers. When the program started in 1971, there were only two MSW social workers. At this time there are seven full-time and one part-time black professional social workers in a staff of sixty-five serving inpatients and outpatients.

b. The content and methodology of the overall Black Studies Program, both in its staff development and clinical aspects, has been presented at statewide meetings of social workers employed by the Missouri Department of Mental Health. Through this, the program has influenced programming in other hospitals and mental health clinics for the retarded and the mentally ill.

c. The director of social service and a black supervisor, together with a technical consultant, presented two programs at the regional meeting of the American Public Welfare Association held in St. Louis in 1972.

d. A black social work supervisor serves as consultant to the Human Relations Program of the Missouri Department of Mental Health in setting up statewide training programs on human relations.

e. A black social work supervisor is chairman of the hospital's Human Relations Committee, which has jurisdiction over staff and patient complaints of discrimination.

f. Some content and process were presented informally to some participants in the NASW Leadership Training Program for Social Workers in Mental Health in its 1972, 1973, and 1974 sessions.

g. This paper was presented at the 1975 NASW Professional Symposium and was published in this book.

Despite these gains, all the human relations problems among staff and patients are not solved. Institutionalized racism still exists in the outer community as well as in the hospital system, and the negative social forces that would perpetuate this form of dehumanization are ever present. That the program for combating racism is now institutionalized, however, makes it harder for those forces to undermine and infect the mental health of both staff and patients. The practice skills of social workers as leaders, change agents, and institution builders have contributed significantly to the combating of institutional racism in this system. It is hoped that they can be duplicated in similar settings.

NOTES

1. This remark was made at the closing general session of the National Conference on Social Welfare held in San Francisco, Calif., in May 1968.

2. The Code of Ethics of the National Association of Social Workers states: "I will not discriminate because of race, color, religion, age, sex, or national ancestry, and in my job capacity will work to prevent and eliminate such discrimination in rendering service, in work assignments, and in employment practices."

3. *See* Jane Bierdeman, ed., *State of Missouri Standards for Psychiatric Hospitals and Clinics* (Jefferson City, Mo.: Missouri Department of Mental Health, November 1975), p. 108, which states: "Maximum security facilities have the responsibility and function to evaluate, contain, and treat those individuals who have demonstrated a probability of doing great bodily harm to themselves or others, whether they are civilly or criminally committed."

4. Milton J. Esman, *"The Institution Building Concepts—An Interim Appraisal."* (Pittsburgh, Pa.: University of Pittsburgh, Graduate School of Public and International Affairs, 1967), pp. 3–4. (Mimeographed).

5. Ibid.

6. John Wax, "Developing Social Work Power in a Medical Organization," *Social Work*, 13 (October 1968), p. 66.

7. Hans C. Blaise, "The Process and Strategy of Institution Building in National Development: A Case Study in Cambodia," pp. 207–208. Unpublished Ph.D. thesis, University of Pittsburgh, 1964.

8. Wax, op. cit., pp. 67–68.

9. Esman, op. cit.

10. J. Silva de Corvahlo, "EBAP: An Experiment in Institution Building," pp. 32–33. Unpublished Ph.D. thesis, University of Southern California, Los Angeles, January 1968.

11. Esman, op. cit.

12. *See* Kenneth D. Benne and Max Birnbaum, "Principles of Changing," in Warren G. Bennis, Kenneth D. Benne, and Robert Chin, eds., *The Planning of Change* (2nd ed., New York: Holt, Rinehart & Winston, 1968), p. 333.

13. Ibid.

14. James H. Carter and Barbara M. Jordan, "Inpatient Therapy for Black Paranoid Men," *Hospital and Community Psychiatry*, 23 (June 1972), p. 182.

15. *See* Blaise, op. cit., p. 206.

16. *See* James Dykens et al., *Strategies of Mental Hospital Change* (Boston: Commonwealth of Massachusetts, Department of Mental Health, 1964), p. 186.

17. Ibid., p. 187.

18. Esman, op. cit., p. 5.

19. George W. Magner, "Evolution of the Leadership Training Program," in George W. Magner and Thomas L. Briggs, eds., *Leadership Training in Mental Health* (New York: National Association of Social Workers, 1970), pp. 9–21.

20. Norman T. Uphoff and Warren F. Ilchman, "The Time Dimensions in Institution Building," in Joseph W. Eaton, ed., *Institution Building and Development: From Concepts to Application* (Beverly Hills, Calif.: Sage Publications, 1972), pp. 109–136.

21. Melvin G. Blase, *Institution Building: A Source Book* (Washington, D.C.: Agency for International Development, U.S. Department of State, 1973), p. 278.

22. Esman, op. cit., pp. 5–6.

23. The hospital conducts a continuous Industrial Therapy Program as part of the individualized treatment plan of some patients. Patients are paid wages for their services in accordance with the Fair Labor Standards Act, Part 529.

Working with Minority Populations: The Dual Perspective

DOLORES G. NORTON

In a society composed of different racial, ethnic, and socioeconomic groups, such as the United States, the goal of social work practice must be to meet the needs of its total client system. A large proportion of social workers work with at least one of the oppressed minority groups in America: Asian-Americans, American Indians, blacks, Mexican-Americans, or Puerto Ricans. This paper proposes that the use of dual perspective can help in broadening the view of the social worker to better understand the life situations of various groups in a pluralistic society and to produce more effective intervention with them.

DEFINITION OF THE DUAL PERSPECTIVE

The "dual perspective" is a misnomer. In reality, a "multiperspective" is meant, but at the minimum two perspectives must be recognized as being present and must be taken into consideration. The concept of the dual perspective grew out of the idea that every individual is embedded in two systems: The larger system is that of the dominant society; in this larger system is the second system—the more immediate society, the immediate physical and social environment. All human beings have the same duality of life systems, but those whose racial, ethnic, and socioeconomic status most nearly meets that of the larger society have a congruence between the major environmental system and their immediate environmental system. This congruence does not usually exist for minority individuals, and that makes the dual perspective important in understanding and working with them. The dual perspective involves understanding both these systems and the interaction between them; it forces the social worker to take both systems into account simultaneously. The history, culture, life-style, acculturation processes, and values of the immediate environmental system are weighed against those of the dominant environmental system for congruence, conflict, and interaction between the two systems. The social worker must also be aware of his own beliefs and values. The dual perspective provides the backdrop, or frame of reference, within which assessing, understanding, and determining a course of action take place.

The concept of the dual perspective will not sound dissimilar to what most social workers have been taught. To have empathy, to begin where the client is, and to view the client's situation nonjudgmentally and with self-awareness of one's biases is a familiar litany in most social work education. The dual perspective implies all of this and adds something more by setting forth, in juxtaposition to implicit dominant societal norms, another specific set of criteria by which to assess the situation. It permits the social worker to examine the problems of minority clients, groups, and communities from both the minority and the majority frames of reference, as well as his own.

THEORY BEHIND THE DUAL PERSPECTIVE

As already stated, the concept of the dual perspective grew out of the idea that the individual is embedded in two systems. This idea of duality is supported theoretically. Chestang writes of the duality of the black experience.[1] He calls the larger and dominant system the "sustaining system." It houses the instrumental needs of man—goods and services, political power, economic resources—and through these factors confers status and power. Chestang refers to the more immediate society, the immediate physical and social environment, as the "nurturing environment." A person's basic sense of identity grows out of the more immediate society, which includes the family and the surrounding emotional and physical community. One can easily see how the dual perspective can be applied to Chestang's two worlds.

Mead's concept of the "generalized other" can also be used to understand the dual perspective.[2] He defines the generalized other as taking on the attitude of the wider society in regard to oneself. In this way one learns to become an object to himself, to have an identity, to know oneself through role-taking and the reflection from others. In acting out the roles of others, the child discovers that they belong to his own nature and he begins to know himself. From the many roles taken on, a generalized other gradually arises. It is this attitude of the generalized other, or organized community attitude, that gives unity of self to the individual as he incorporates society's response and reacts accordingly.

Mead speaks of only one generalized other. The minority person who assumes the attitude of the generalized other of the wider society, however, has a strong possibility of seeing himself as devalued. The more he incorporates a negative image into his identity, the more he is devalued in his own image. But minority persons do attain a good sense of self. It is the author's assumption that there is an alternative generalized other (a dual generalized other, if you wish) that balances or compensates for the potential destruction of self-worth which may come from the wider society.

The alternative generalized other is the attitude of the minority social order—the family and immediate community environment, the nurturing environment. The minority child can receive the love and care from his family that can lead to a positive sense of self. Because the minority person is usually somewhat isolated from the white community physically and socially, the attitude of the minority generalized other can develop, restore, or help him maintain his self-esteem. He can use it as a buffer against the effects of the attitude of the dominant generalized other as he experiences the wider community. This cannot be accomplished totally, though, because he and the minority community, being interdependent within the total system, are aware of the attitude of the dominant generalized other. If the mechanisms of socialization in the nurturing environment, or minority generalized other, are positive, they can enable people to balance the destructive image coming in from the larger community.

If both the minority and majority generalized other reflect the same image of the individual, he incorporates them as a total generalized other without conflict and interacts accordingly. Some individuals may receive positive reflections and attitudes from both the minority and majority generalized other, leading to a good sense of self-worth and harmony in functioning. When the two systems are congruent or similar, the dual perspective still exists; but it is not crucial to evaluation because the perspectives are alike. The social worker has little trouble evaluating and understanding the situation.

For many minority persons, conflict exists between the two systems because the frames of reference of the minority group, though embedded in and affected by the major society, can be quite different in certain variables. To assess the situation in its totality and to base intervention on the interaction between them, it is necessary to understand and have awareness of both systems. Thus the use of the dual perspective becomes crucial. The dual perspective, then, is not something to be applied solely to minority people and groups. It enhances an understanding of all people, but is particularly vital to the assessment and understanding of those people whose minority generalized other might differ or be in conflict with the majority generalized other. These are more likely to be minority people. The dual perspective forces the social worker to be aware of the possible difference and seek knowledge of the minority generalized other.

USE OF THE DUAL PERSPECTIVE IN PRACTICE

Development of the dual perspective requires a mind-set, a sensitivity for what Piaget refers to as "reversible thought." [3] This is the ability to go out in thought to the situation being observed; to make certain observations, then return these observations to one's own mental operations, and then process these observations by the knowledge there; to modify and add information with which to make an evaluation; and to execute reasoned, effective action. In the conscious flowing out of the mental facilities to observe and the coming back to oneself to consciously evaluate, the social worker begins to develop the mind-set of the dual perspective. Thus the first requirement of the dual perspective is a mind-set of constantly reversing thought. The social worker observes the situation, looking for points of difference, conflict, or congruence with the larger society. This assumes knowledge of several systems and an awareness of one's own attitudes.

The second requirement is the specific knowledge to guide the activities of the mind-set. The social worker must have specific knowledge about the group with which he is involved. He cannot assess correctly without specific cultural knowledge of the nurturing environment or the alternative generalized other. For example, although a social worker may know normal adolescent needs and behavior, he cannot evaluate the behavior of a specific minority adolescent until he knows the prescriptions for adolescent behavior within that group. The worker evaluates the adolescent's observed behavior against the theoretical knowledge about adolescents, then evaluates the observed behavior against the specific ethnic or cultural knowledge of the adolescent's cultural group. Some synthesis is made, and this synthesis is evaluated against the values of the social worker to determine possible individual bias; valid knowledge is necessary to avoid stereotyping. The acceptance of certain behavioral characteristics because of stereotyped knowledge about a certain group is *not* the dual perspective. Synthesis of the reversible mind-set, plus verifiable and valid specific knowledge are the major requirements of the dual perspective.

An example of the use of the mind-set without valid knowledge occurred when a student social worker was working in a black neighbor-hood agency with a 19-year-old black woman. She had four children by four different fathers, and each of the relationships with the fathers had been destructive to her in some way. The young woman came to the agency for help with a housing problem. After the problem was solved, however, she continued to stop in at the agency two or three times a week to talk about her activities and discuss her newest boyfriend with "someone who doesn't know him and can see the whole mess from all sides." The student, applying the first half of the dual perspective, the mind-set, made an attempt to be aware of her own background. She was white, middle-class, and middle-aged; when she compared her-self with the client, she wisely decided that they may not have the same values. She then tried to add knowledge and remembered reading somewhere that black adolescents are less inhibited sexually than white adolescents. Accepting these facts as valid, she decided that discussion of the client's life-style was inappropriate because it fitted in with the client's particular background, and she terminated the case. The student had short-circuited the dual perspective and was stereotyping, despite her good intentions. The use of the dual perspective in this case required not only the mind-set of reversible thought, but also valid knowledge about the client and the minority group to which she belonged.

How would using the full process of the dual perspective have changed the assessment and intervention in this case to more clearly fit the client's wishes and needs? If the budding social worker had con-tinued the process of the dual perspective and had sought verification of her knowledge of the sexual life-style of black adolescents, she would have found that (1) there is a dearth of valid information on the black adolescent; (2) what exists is often conflicting and speculative; and (3) there is a group of theorists, among them Chestang, Comer, and Poussaint, who are beginning to apply knowledge of human develop-ment to black identity within the context of the black environment and its relation to the wider society.[4] She would have reversed thought and known that her information could be questioned. She would have sought information on general adolescent needs in the major society and would have reversed thought to compare these needs with her client's life experiences. Finding many of them unfulfilled, she would have ex-amined how her client attempted to meet her needs within the limits of the resources of her immediate environment and she would have evaluated whether the results were satisfactory to the client. She would have compared this knowledge to knowledge of the immediate environ-ment gained from her research of the literature and her continued dis-cussions with the client. She would have come to some understanding of the needs and resources of the particular client and how these compare with the life-style of the immediate environment. Study of the community life-style should lead her into the community.

A final assessment should have involved some knowledge of the degree of personal, immediate environmental and larger environmental barriers involved. This should have led to some conclusion as to where the major source of stress lies and should have indicated at what level, or levels, the social worker should intervene. Does she continue to see the client regarding problems as the client presents them? Does she refer the client to Planned Parenthood? Or does she campaign for a neighborhood birth control clinic? If the last course is one of the indicated intervention choices, the social worker, if she has truly carried out the process of the dual perspective, will know that she will probably be accused by some members of the black community of promoting genocide. But if she has involved the community in her ever widening net of reversible thought and information-gathering, she can be more sure of her decision in following such a course of action.

Pursuing such a process is a large order, but social workers have long known that the ability to understand anyone's life in its broadest perspective and to take effective, appropriate action is a difficult task. To serve its total clientele, social work must embark on this arduous challenge. Admittedly, a shortage of valid information on minorities exists. Perhaps, after assessing practice situations from the dual perspective, social workers may decide that one of their major priorities is to encourage, support, and push for the continuing development of knowledge about minorities.

IMPORTANCE OF THE DUAL PERSPECTIVE IN PRACTICE

The frame of reference of the dual perspective informs practice by helping the social worker to evaluate disparate systems and to evaluate more accurately where the major stressors lie. Social policy and planning from the dual perspective force the social worker to really answer the question of whether he should move to work with the immediate environment, the dominant environment, or both systems or whether he should intervene at all.

The dual perspective is also needed to understand the institutionalized disadvantages of minorities. Structural barriers in the dominant system have been erected against individuals and groups because of their membership in certain minorities. Often, these structural barriers are not readily apparent from the perspective of either the minority generalized other or the nurturing environment. This situation should lead to action on the part of the social worker to work toward changing those socioeconomic and political barriers that foster inequality of opportunity.

The dual perspective is as important in other areas of social work as in direct service. Cafferty, writing on bilingual education and Puerto Ricans, states that bilingualism among Puerto Ricans living outside Puerto Rico reflects not only cultural pluralism, but also their periodic returns to their home island.[5] Often, the children attend school while in Puerto Rico, then return to their schools on the mainland. As a result, they have an assimilation problem different from that of other immigrant groups. The dual perspective would push social workers involved in educational policy with the Puerto Rican community to be aware of this specific history and need. And, if they are to develop effective education programs for this community, social workers would compare the Puerto Ricans' situation to the dominant U.S. societal thrust of monolingualism and realize that special programs must be created.

Grossman, in her study on ethnicity and health delivery systems, observes that the "utilization of medical care is linked to differential experiences of life" and describes specifically how different ethnic groups respond to illness and its treatment.[6] She suggests that cultural pluralism needs to become an added dimension in dealing with illness and health and the organization of health delivery systems. Using the dual perspective, health delivery systems could not be planned without this added dimension.

The dual perspective can also aid the social worker in clarifying his personal and professional value system from a minority perspective. The social worker is forced into awareness and evaluation of how his values differ from or coincide with those of his clients. Minority, as well majority, social workers must operate from the dual perspective. Their perspective may not be that of their nonminority clients or that of their minority clients. Many minority social workers tend to reject passive, uninvolved minority clients and groups. The dual perspective forces them to consider the client's nurturing system, with its history and values, and gives cues as to why the client may never reach the social worker's level of involvement in minority issues. Brown states aptly that accurate assessment must mean awareness of the variability of life circumstances, life-styles, and aspirations within minority groups.[7] Accurate assessment also means the recognition of the interrelationships among depriving conditions, social stress, and behavior.

A word of caution is needed. A racial or minority label does not presume monolithic thought, values, or behavior for all members of a minority group. Although certain characteristics do seem to be deeply rooted because of shared experiences, individuals do react as individuals. The particular individual must be observed within this particular milieu. Knowledge of the specific individual or group, the specific culture, the major society, and one's own beliefs and their meanings is part of the constantly reversing mind-set informed by valid knowledge that makes up the dual perspective.

NOTES

1. Leon Chestang, "Environmental Influences on Social Functioning: The Black Experience," in Pastora San Juan Cafferty and Leon Chestang, eds., *The Diverse Society: Implications for Social Policy* (Washington, D.C.: National Association of Social Workers, 1976).

2. George H. Mead, *Mind, Self and Society* (Chicago: University of Chicago Press, 1934).

3. Jean Piaget, *Logic and Psychology* (New York: Basic Books, 1957), pp. 10–12.

4. *See* Leon Chestang, *Character Development in a Hostile Environment,* occasional paper (Chicago: University of Chicago Press, 1972); J. P. Comer, "The Black Family: An Adaptive Perspective" (mimeographed paper presented at Yale University, Spring 1971); J. P. Comer, *Beyond Black and White* (New York: Quadrangle Books, 1972); and A. F. Poussaint and J. P. Comer, *Black Child Care* (New York: Simon & Schuster, 1975).

5. Pastora San Juan Cafferty, "Bilingualism in America," in Cafferty and Chestang, op. cit.

6. Leona Grossman, "Ethnicity and Health Delivery Systems," in Cafferty and Chestang, op. cit.

7. June Brown, "Can Social Work Education Prepare Practitioners To Contribute to a Cogent Challenge to American Racism?" in *Black Perspectives on Social Work Education* (New York: Council on Social Work Education, 1974), pp. 1–12.

Skills for Administrative and Policy Roles

ROSEMARY C. SARRI

Administrative, policymaking, and planning roles in social work are directed toward problem-solving at the community, state, regional, national, and international levels. Even though a recurrent theme throughout the professional literature is the need for training and employing social workers as administrators, planners, and policymakers, the level of success achieved has been disappointing. Except in a few states and in selected types of agencies (for example, mental health clinics and family service and child welfare agencies), administrators and policymakers have been trained in other professional disciplines, or direct service practitioners have been promoted into these roles without formal preparation for them. Only in the past two decades have the federal and state governments given greater priority in their resource allocations for the initial and continuing education of administrators. Schools of social work and the National Association of Social Workers (NASW) have recently given greater attention to the need for macrolevel competence by large numbers of social workers.

The need for further immediate action is imperative, however; otherwise, businessmen and professionals from fields other than social work will control policymaking and administration in social welfare. If the social work profession is to regain and then retain control over the design and delivery of social services by human service organizations, a far higher priority must be assigned to the development of planning, policymaking, and administrative skills. Unless the profession can demonstrate conclusively that it can assist effectively in the resolution of critical social problems, in the design and delivery of services, and in the evaluation of program outcomes, social workers will be relegated to handmaiden and subordinate roles. It is woefully insufficient to be merely social critics or lay advocates for social values and programs.[1] Social workers must actively pursue the organizational means for implementing those programs.

In this paper, a common body of knowledge and competencies for persons who are variously termed "managers," "administrators," "policy-makers," and/or "planners" will be referred to. Although sometimes the skills linked only to one of these roles will be delineated, the focus will be on those skills that, according to some level of consensus, are required by all who intervene at the macrolevel. This does not imply that direct service microlevel practitioners do not require some of this same knowledge and competence; but for them it is secondary rather than primary.

CHARACTERISTICS OF HUMAN SERVICE ORGANIZATIONS

Social welfare organizations constitute a major sector of American life today. In terms of the numbers of people served, the sums of money expended, and the numbers of employees, welfare organizations are comparable in size and complexity to large industries. Social welfare expenditures are the largest item in many state budgets, surpassing education, which had been the largest. A noted business management expert, Peter Drucker, has said that because demands for skill, knowledge, and performance in public service organizations have tripled in the past quarter century, these organizations can be considered the "real growth sector of a modern society." [2] He observes:

> Every citizen in the developed, industrialized, urbanized societies depends for his very survival on the performance of the public service institutions. These institutions also embody the values of developed societies. For it is in the form of education and health care (social welfare), knowledge and mobility—rather than primarily in the form of "food, clothing, and shelter"—that our society obtains the fruits of its increased economic capacities and productivity.[3]

Until now, most of the knowledge and technology for administration and policy have been borrowed from business and/or public administration. Drucker argues that such borrowing may be quite inappropriate because of important qualitative differences in the essential characteristics of human service organizations. Among the differences he identifies are the intangibility of goals and objectives; the criteria for determining efficiency; the basis for budgetary allocations; indeterminacy in the measurement of outputs and outcomes; and the criteria for successful performance.[4]

The author's research and experience, plus that of many other students of human service organizations, are in accord with Drucker's observations that there are distinctive features which must be taken into consideration in the administration of these agencies: [5]

1. The substantive goals of the organization are to process and change people. Moreover, persons who are served are both the major input and output of the organization. Problems arise because goals for these persons are ambiguous, indeterminate and precarious in the larger society. A multiplicity of goals is frequently confronted, and this too is problematic because priorities must be established among potentially contradictory objectives—such as control, rehabilitation, protection, custody— and the provision of opportunity for employment, education, and so forth.

2. Despite the increase in the variety of new technologies to serve clientele in human service organizations, they still rely most heavily on human relations technologies and professional personnel who have high levels of autonomy and few requirements for accountability in the practice of these technologies. More often than not, the ends and means are not clearly operationalized by an organization, which results in serious performance evaluation problems. Also, the tendency is to engage in much innovation in the utilization of new technology fads, but little fundamental change occurs in organizational behavior.

3. Human service bureaucracies can also be distinguished on the basis of the high proportion of nonroutine events they confront. Clients are reactive social beings whose behavior is often unpredictable, thus producing one source of nonroutine events. Events in the larger society are even more critical sources of instability and disruption, as is obvious not only in the United States but throughout the world. Thus the organization must be directed in such a manner as to permit flexibility in adaptation to changed internal and external events.

The distinctive features of human service organizations must be recognized and addressed in any attempt to delineate the skills essential for social work practice at the administrative and policy levels. If efficiency and effectiveness are to be optimized to meet societal demands, the competent performance of organizational functions is necessary. But these functions must be performed in accord with societal and professional ethics and values and within the knowledge base of social work practice developed from the social and behavioral sciences and from codified practice experiences (that is, systematically organized practice knowledge based on the accumulated experience of many practitioners). Therefore it seems obvious that the social work profession must assume leadership in manpower development in social welfare administration through preprofessional and professional education and, perhaps even more important, through the continuing education of social workers for management and policy roles.

In many regions of the country, these training responsibilities are being contracted to business and public administration, with little participation by social workers in the design and implementation of the programs. Furthermore, many agencies are employing larger numbers of persons professionally trained in business or public administration with little apparent awareness of the possible negative consequences that may arise. No one is satisfied with the level of performance in administration achieved by social work thus far. But, given the characteristics of human service organizations, the strict application of business principles is not likely to be any more successful.[6]

A FRAMEWORK FOR MACROLEVEL ROLES

Any conceptual framework for the delineation of planning, policy, and administrative skills must link methods and field of practice at the macrolevel. This linkage is essential because there are qualitative differences in the several fields of practice that constrain the way in which management and administration must operate. The differences among community mental health, criminal justice, public assistance, or services to the aged are of such magnitude that they must be addressed directly in the delineation of practice skills.

Parsons's framework for the analysis of functional problems of the social system has been useful in linking skills and methods with fields of practice. Parsons suggests that there are four functional processes of the social system: adaptation, integration, goal attainment, and pattern maintenance. *Adaptation* involves relating the system to the environment and developing generalized means for pursuing various goals. *Goal attainment* involves relating the system to the environment through organization for the effective pursuit of particular system goals. Bureaucracy and the polity are the primary means through which this is accomplished ("polity" refers to the federal, state, and local governments collectively). *Integration* refers to internal and consummatory functions that arise in situations of conflict, breakdown of mutual expectations, or lack of complementary role performance. Restorative and social control activities of social work involve integrative functions. *Pattern maintenance* refers to the problem of developing generalized resources for dealing with internal disturbances to insure the maintenance of commitment to general patterns of the normative social order.[7]

Figure 1 represents an attempt to use Parson's classificatory scheme to link social work methods at the macrolevel with social-problem areas.

Fig. 1. A Framework for Conceptualizing Macrolevel Social Work Roles

Social System Function	Problem Area	Illustrative Macrolevel Role [a]		
		Policy	Planning	Administration
Adaptation	Income maintenance Housing Public health Aging services Retardation Urban planning	Legislative assistant	State department of social service planning assistant	County welfare director
Integration	Addiction Racism Mental illness Physical illness Vocational rehabilitation Corrections	Program analyst in mental health	Criminal justice planning specialist	Program director in a county detoxification center
Pattern maintenance	Family Education Cultural deprivation Community relations	Senate committee staff assistant	Youth service board secretary	YWCA director

[a] Goal-attainment functions under the Parsons framework would include policy, planning, and administration in all the substantive areas of practice.

It can be seen that goal-attainment functions primarily involve the polity and the bureaucracy—in this case, the methods of policy, planning, and administration. The knowledge bases for the accompanying roles come primarily from political science, macrosociology, economics, law, and codified social work knowledge. Relating these methods to Parsons's goal-attainment functions highlights the political aspects of the roles.

The classification of social-problem areas under adaptation, integration, and pattern maintenance requires arbitrary decisions, and it is recognized that any given social-problem area involves more than one of these functions. But here the interest is in first-order consequences; therefore the classification has at least heuristic value. Adaptation, as already suggested, involves relating the system to the environment, with primary emphasis on the economic system. Thus the following can be classified under this rubric: income maintenance, housing, public health, services to the aged, mental retardation, and urban planning. Integration involves social control and restorative functions, thereby including addiction, racism, mental illness, physical illness, vocational rehabilitation, and corrections. Pattern maintenance involves the social values and maintenance of commitment to the normative order. Involved here are the family, education, cultural deprivation, and community relations.

The next step in completing this framework requires the delineation of the major skills and competencies required for each of the macrolevel roles (e.g., legislative assistant) shown in Figure 1. The skills are essentially analytic rather than the product of empirical study of role behavior, but they can be supported with some data from research on the behavior of social work administrators and planners. It is readily apparent that the skills are not mutually exclusive with respect to each of the three methods. They were developed to present the essential characteristics of each of the roles and methods rather than to define their specific domains.

Social Policy

Policy is that method of practice concerned with the analysis, development, and formulation of statutes, administrative roles, and informal regulations which are systematically applied in social programs in human service and related governmental organizations. It includes the following knowledge and skill areas:

1. Study and interpretation of policy documents and preparation of reports, analyses, and expositions.

2. Application of scientific theory and knowledge to the processes of clarifying and selecting policy alternatives, including the formulation of concrete proposals.

3. Facilitation of continuous redefinition of policy elements by em-

pirical assessment of intended and unintended consequences of policy actions.

4. Application of systems analysis in both quantitative and qualitative forms to improve the prediction of policy outcomes; simulation techniques to evaluate alternative outcomes are often utilized.

5. Development of mechanisms for generating policy-relevant information for decision-making and evaluation.

6. Explication of benefit-cost criteria to apply in policy formulation; skills in assessment of both costs and benefits and in operational research are particularly valuable.

7. The drafting of statutes and other quasi-legal documents to incorporate social policy content.

8. Assessment of the physical and social impact of alternative policies on a long-term and short-term basis for recipients as well as service providers.

9. Consultation and assistance to legislators and other committees in conducting hearings, reviewing and analyzing proposed statutes, and synthesizing proposals; lobbying, personal persuasion, and other techniques may also be required.[8]

Social Planning

Planning is that method of practice concerned with the processes involved in the implementation of social policies and programs into operational means for achieving social goals. It involves knowledge and skill in the following:

1. Operationalization of agency mandates and priorities for reaching stated multiple goals.

2. Specification of the means necessary to reach operationalized ends, including organizational structures, technologies, staffing, and so forth.

3. Specification of resources required to attain ends through the means chosen, including how and when such resources are to be generated and acquired.

4. Assessment of client group needs, constraints, and resources relative to operationalized goals and means so as to derive relative "goodness of fit" for the alternative means proposed.

5. Planning process skills such as Delphi forecasting, social indicators, PPBS, MBO, PERT, and other similar planning tools.[9]

6. Design of specific plans for program or policy implementation, along with systems for managing the implementation.

7. Secondary skills, which usually include survey research, advocacy,

social forecasting, statistical analysis, report writing, grantsmanship, and statutory analysis.

Administration

Administration is the method of social work practice concerned with the management and direction of organizational behavior so that goal outcomes are achieved as efficiently as possible within the framework of social work values and socially accepted conditions of fairness, humaneness, and justice. It involves skills in the following:

1. Translation of societal mandates into operational policies and programs through environmental surveys and intelligence systems.

2. Program planning and development, including determining program objectives, alternative program formats, and decisional choice criteria.

3. Design of organizational structures and process through which goals can be achieved. Skills in technology selection and engineering, along with skills in scheduling, coordinating, and decision-making are required.

4. Obtaining resources in the form of clients, staff, and societal legitimation for goal attainment and organizational survival.

5. Fiscal management, including resource solicitation and procurement, use of alternative budgetary systems, forecasting, cost analysis, expenditure control, and grants management.

6. Personnel management and employee relations, including recruitment, selection, assignment, training, and supervision of paraprofessional and professional staff; formulation of personnel policies and relating to various employee associations through bargaining, negotiation, and so on.

7. Evaluation of organizational performance to assess short- and long-term outcomes and to facilitate systematic and continuous problem-solving and accountability.

8. Organizational development through leadership in innovation and change, infusion and maintenance of ethical behavior, motivation of staff, handling of organizational conflict and public relations, and mechanisms for coping with ambiguity and hostility.

A set of skills related specifically to program evaluation might also be delineated, but these skills are common to all the macrolevel roles. They are, however, operationally manifested in distinct ways. Moreover, there are direct service practitioner roles that also involve program evaluation, so it seems unwise to identify program evaluation as a specific role limited to administration and policy.

TRAINING FOR ADMINISTRATIVE ROLES

One source of information about knowledge and competency requirements for social work administration is a recent survey, by the Council
on Social Work Education, of the fifty-three schools that have a curriculum in this area.[10] This survey obtained information pertaining to
the objectives of the curriculum; curriculum content areas; procedures
and instruments for admissions; and evaluation of the faculty, student
body and graduates, and the field for practicum training. Many facets of
this study are not germane to this discussion, but the responses about content areas are of interest. First of all, there is a fairly widely accepted
core of content areas that is deemed essential for administrative practice.
Fourteen areas were selected from a list of twenty-four alternatives as receiving the greatest amount of emphasis in the schools' curricula.
Ranked from 1 to 14, these include the following:

1. Political and social factors affecting service delivery.
2. Organizational theory and analysis.
3. Policy development roles in social work practice.
4. Supervision theory and practice.
5. Use of supervision for professional development and service delivery.
6. Evaluation.
7. Short- and long-range planning and program development.
8. Professional accountability and caseload management.
9. Decision-making.
10. Statistical and narrative reporting—rationale and methods.
11. Consultation theory and practice.
12. Administrative technology.
13. Personnel administration.
14. Budgeting process and fiscal control.

Because the data were obtained in early 1975, these responses are
as up-to-date as any information available about the preparation of persons for administrative roles. They indicate that there are many carry-
overs from areas that have long been emphasized in social work practice
(for example, supervision and consultation). On the other hand, a skill
of critical importance today, fiscal management, was ranked last. It is
doubtful that a much different ranking would be obtained if information
were available about in-service training by agencies or professional associations. Responses in the survey that pertained to continuing education indicated considerable demand for content in administration; but
supervision technology was clearly a first choice, followed by management technology, program evaluation, fiscal management, and consultation, in that order.

When these findings are compared with those obtained from other analyses of the performance requirements in administration and policy, it is apparent that much remains undone in professional and continuing education of social workers for administrative positions. Moreover, because preprofessional and professional education has been almost exclusively in direct service methods, the need for continuing education is most urgent for persons in administrative, policy, and planning roles.

This paper discusses some of the broad areas for which training is necessary. The next step is to delineate these into knowledge components and into primary and secondary skill areas. Following that, a variety of alternative means can be developed for obtaining the necessary competencies. Obviously, a professional association such as NASW can contribute substantially to the implementation of these alternative means throughout the country. According to recent NASW data, 43 percent of NASW members occupy administrative or planning roles. Thus it seems obvious that continuing education must be an important alternative.

BUREAUCRATIZATION, PROFESSIONALIZATION, AND THE CLIENT

To assert that there is an urgent and high priority for the development of administrative and policy competencies by social workers is not enough. This question must be asked: To what ends shall these skills be applied? Societal mandates to social agencies are being redefined rapidly through laws, judicial decisions, administrative orders, funding patterns, and technical knowledge. New forms of agency structure and service delivery can be observed almost daily. If social workers were trained to have the necessary formal knowledge and skill, would it make a difference in the service delivered to clients? Despite the case which has been developed for greater competency in social welfare administration, one must remain skeptical that it will be sufficient to facilitate achievement of the desired goals and objectives.

In a recent, provocative paper, Street asserts that bureaucratization and professionalization have interacted in social welfare organizations to perpetuate poverty, inequality, and injustice.[11] This is a disturbing charge, but his analysis of public schools and public welfare shows that there has been a tremendous growth in the bureaucratization of inequality through the extension and elaboration of governmental services which redefine, but do not change, the procedures under which inequality is maintained. He goes further to describe and document the professionalization of reform efforts whereby social workers and other human service professionals have defined social problems as the special province of the professions. They assess poor persons and their behavior to provide additional social definitions that catch the poor in a web of multiple reifications. But they provide no means for "diversion," or movement out of the status of being poor, handicapped, or labeled deviant. Wilensky comes to a similar conclusion in his recent reanalysis of the welfare state.[12]

Social work professionals have received broad discretion to define and implement their own interpretations of reform and also to assert exclusive rights for program implementation of reform proposals. Needless to say, society has seldom provided the necessary resources for these programs—perhaps because so many of the persons to be served are disesteemed or disadvantaged with respect to the characteristics valued by the majority. Nevertheless, the technologies of the profession have been insufficient to modify the perceptions and values of the majority. For example, perceptions of problems of poverty, illness, and criminality as rooted in the individual have been largely accepted by the profession and, correspondingly, technologies have focused on change targets for individuals. An understanding of this perception is critical to an understanding of other efforts at social reform.

At the present time, social workers are expressing a great interest in the enhancement of the profession. If social workers are to participate actively in a genuine solution rather than a pseudosolution of social problems, they will need to develop capabilities and skills that will permit more frontal attacks on social problems instead of indirect reform efforts. The professionalization of the public services in much of Western Europe has primarily addressed the enhancement of policy-oriented public services. In contrast, much of the recent unionization and professionalization of human services in the United States has been associated with a civil service mentality and protectionist behavior.

As professionals coalesce into strong social communities rather than continue as social movements, there may well be a tendency to place a greater priority on self-interest and esoteric technologies than on effective resolution of the social phenomena that they were mandated by society to resolve or deal with. This problem is not unique to social workers as professionals. But as social workers reflect on the development of essential social work skill, we must keep in mind "skill for what?" and "skill for whom?" It is hoped that if NASW convenes a symposium in the year 2000 to consider the progress made in a quarter century, we will be able to point explicitly to the ways social work skill has been applied and has, in fact, helped to achieve reductions in poverty, illness, inequality, and injustice.

NOTES

1. *See* Robert Morris, "Overcoming Cultural and Professional Myopia in Education for Human Service," *Journal of Education for Social Work*, 6 (Spring 1970), pp. 41–52; and Harold Richman, "Social Welfare Policy as a Specialization in the Graduate Social Work Curriculum," *Journal of Education for Social Work*, 6 (Spring 1970), pp. 53–60.

2. Peter Drucker, "On Managing the Public Service Institution," *The Public Interest*, No. 33 (Fall 1973), pp. 43–60.

3. Ibid., p. 44.

4. Ibid., pp. 48–52.

5. *See* Yeheskel Hasenfeld and Richard English, *Human Service Organizations* (Ann Arbor: University of Michigan Press, 1973); Robert D. Vinter, "The Analysis of Treatment Organizations," *Social Work*, 8 (July 1965), pp. 3–15; and Stanton Wheeler, "The Structure of Formally Organized Socialization Agencies," in Orville Brim and Stanton Wheeler, *Socialization After Childhood* (New York: John Wiley & Sons, 1965), pp. 51–116.

6. Ward Edwards, Marcia Guttentag, and Kurt Snapper, "A Decision-Theoretic Approach to Evaluation Research," in Elmer Struening and Marcia Guttentag, eds., *Handbook of Evaluation Research* (Beverly Hills, Calif.: Sage Publications, 1975), pp. 139–182; and Joseph Helfgot, "Professional Reform Organizations and the Symbolic Representation of the Poor," *American Sociological Review*, 39 (August 1974), pp. 475–491.

7. Talcott Parsons, *The System of Modern Societies* (Englewood Cliffs, N.J.: Prentice-Hall, 1971).

8. The author has benefited enormously from input from many faculty colleagues at the University of Michigan in the identification of these skill areas, especially Yeheskel Hasenfeld, Milan Dluhy, John Tropman, and Robert Vinter, as well as from the members of the Advisory Committee on Administration and Management of the Council on Social Work Education.

'9. Delphi forecasting is a tool adapted from the field of technological forecasting in which expert opinion is solicited in efforts to predict the future or to take all relevant considerations into account in the process of policymaking. PERT is Program Evaluation and Review Technique; PPBS is Program Planning and Budgeting System; and MBO is Management by Objectives.

10. Kenneth Kazmerski and David Macarov, *Administration in the Social Work Curriculum: Report of a Survey* (New York: Council on Social Work Education, 1976).

11. David Street, "Bureaucratization, Professionalization and the Poor," in Kirsten Gronberg, David Street, and Gerald Suttles, *Poverty and Social Change*. To be published by Prentice-Hall in 1976.

12. Harold L. Wilensky, *The Welfare State and Equality: Structural and Ideological Roots of Public Expenditures* (Berkeley: University of California Press, 1975).

Lobbying as Advocacy

BUDD BELL AND WILLIAM G. BELL

The concept of *social action* has achieved credence and acceptability in the literature on social work practice.[1] Stimulated in large measure by the recognition of the differential power held by groups in society and the consequences of allocations of public funds for groups at the lower end of the economic scale, the notion of an advocacy posture by human-service-oriented professionals gained strength in the mid-1960s.[2] To synthesize a concept advanced by Davidoff, *advocacy* means the exercise of one's professional function on behalf of a specified individual or group rather than a broadly defined societal or public interest.[3] Thus advocacy may be viewed as a useful strategy in the social worker's arsenal of social action. By contrast, *lobbying*, the exercise of political influence through group action, has been treated sparsely in the literature.[4] Cohen was among the first to see lobbying, a legitimate activity by social workers to alter social policy or to intervene in the legislative process, as a strategy underutilized by the profession.[5]

The intent of this paper is threefold: (1) to explore possible reasons why social workers have tended to avoid lobbying as a professional activity, (2) to identify skills deemed salient in successful lobbying in the human services, derived from the practical experiences over a five-year period of one state unit (the Florida Chapter lobby) of the National Association of Social Workers (NASW), and (3) to argue for an expansion of lobbying at state levels of the association.

LOBBYING AND PROFESSIONAL SOCIAL WORKERS

Lobbying is an acceptable and potent activity within the American political process.[6] It is a technique highly utilized by a variety of interest groups—drawn primarily from business, agriculture, commerce, and the professions—to exercise influence on decisions made by Congress and state legislatures. Why is it that social workers, who are not "issue neutral," seem to shrink from exercising their right to lobby in the interest of achieving changes in inequitable, inadequate, or punitive social policies? There are four possible reasons.

Rothman provides a first clue with this empirical generalization: "In the minds of the public in the recent past there is apparently a separation between the concepts of 'government' and 'politics.' The public generally has looked approvingly upon that which it perceives as 'government' and suspiciously upon that which it perceives as 'politics.' " [7] Like other citizens, social workers tend to view politicians as remote and inaccessible or simply beyond the reach of individual electors. As Rothman cautions, however, "A contemporary practitioner who fails to understand the implications for community practice of the political realm, and neglects to prepare himself with the requisite skills to make an impact there, is tying his own hands and may be shortchanging his clients or constituents." [8]

A second reason may lie in the social worker's view of his contribution to policy development. Social workers usually see their function as operationalizing social policies designed by others; they rarely see their function as helping to shape the direction of social policy. Social workers, who more than any other professionals see the consequences of punitive or neglectful policies daily, inadvertently give strength and support to the status quo by staying out of the arena of political influence.

Third, the critical issue of risk-taking is suggested by the act of lobbying. The risks are both professional and personal. It is within the ethos of the profession that social workers, in the conduct of their practice, are required by "their professional responsibility to give first priority to the rights and needs of their clients." [9] It follows, however, that "unless social workers can be protected against retaliation by their agencies and other special interest groups in the community, few of them will venture into the advocacy role, ethical prescripts notwithstanding." [10] Perhaps one of the strengths of the lobbyist whose experiences are described later in this paper was that she served as a volunteer having no current ties to a social agency; she was thus unencumbered in practicing her legislative skills.

Research in the area of advocacy suggests that support exists for forms of social action among rank-and-file social workers when the focus is on issues removed from one's work assignments. For example, Rothman indicates that "professionals are more likely to be mobilized for activist roles in areas more removed from their central domain" and that "the greater the client-role orientation, the greater the approval of radical roles." [11] In view of the potential risks associated with the lobbying-advocacy role, the decision to perform in this area rests on the individual's willingness to undertake such risks in support of his or her professional commitment.

Fourth, the inadequate resources possessed by social work organizations and their representatives act as a deterrent to lobbying. To function effectively as a lobbyist in the current political milieu requires both political skills and money. Social workers and social work organizations are not endowed liberally with either of these resources.

To illustrate the comparison in legislative resources of an NASW state chapter with analogous resources of more powerful state lobbying groups: In 1975 the Florida NASW lobby, headed by a volunteer director who was aided by a part-time paid assistant and several unpaid university students, operated on a budget of $5,600. None of these limited funds were allocated to campaign contributions for politicians seeking state office. Contrast this with the disclosures in the *Miami Herald* on the amounts of money spent on the 1975 election campaigns of ten state legislators by ten major lobbying groups in Florida: [12]

Beer Distributors Good Government Committee	$24,225
Florida Business Forum	24,025
Florida Wholesale Spirits Committee of Continuing Existence	22,625
Florida Medical Political Action Committee	22,520
Real Estate Political Action Committee	20,900
Florida Action Committee for Rural Electrification	14,250
Dental Political Action Committee	12,200
Bankers Political Action Committee	12,178
W. C. Herrell: Agriculture	8,870
Florida Lawyers Action Group	8,605
Total	$170,398

To summarize, the underutilization of lobbying as a professional activity by social work organizations may be attributed in part to four factors: (1) some practitioners' view of politics as an inappropriate activity for professionals, (2) a self-imposed separation from the tasks of policy development, (3) attitudes toward risk-taking, and (4) an awareness of inadequate skills and insufficient funds to carry out successful lobbying efforts.

LEGISLATIVE SKILLS IN LOBBYING

Three goals in particular provided the focus for the NASW legislative unit (i.e., lobby) in Florida. The first was to exercise a positive impact on the content and passage of human services legislation. The second was to work systematically for a more equitable set of state social policies. The third was to monitor the implementation of human services legislation by the state's human resources agency through continuing scrutiny of its operational procedures on relevant social legislation.

In a search for both allies and adversaries, the state lobbyist should undertake a careful analysis of the value set and prior legislative behavior of influential individuals and groups with whom he expects to interact. These include elected legislators; year-round staff aides of key legislators and those in the governor's office; aides serving the speaker of the house and the senate president, or their equivalent in one's state; lobbyists for major interest groups, particularly those likely to be opponents on specific social legislation; and key administrative staff in the state bureaucracy, especially those in the human services, state planning, and budgeting departments.

Among the range of skills that evolved over time in the course of legislative activities by one NASW unit over a five-year period, nine specific skills have been selected for discussion and illustration because of their potential for replication by social work lobbyists elsewhere: (1) selecting legislative priorities, (2) modeling, (3) motivating chapter members, (4) building networks, (5) building coalitions, (6) using the media, (7) collecting professional expertise, (8) maintaining a legislative presence, and (9) generating new legislation.[13]

Selecting Legislative Priorities

Because staff resources of the NASW legislative unit in Florida were limited from the outset, state legislative action by necessity had to adhere to the reality of legislative priorities. To identify a realistic set of legislative bills to which the chapter membership would throw its support by working aggressively for its passage may generate some initial conflict within the chapter. The conflict is likely to be of two kinds: (1) conflict generated by reason of the priorities selected and their consequences for some members of the chapter and (2) conflict generated by a style of action by the legislative unit acting within the normal pressures of a legislative milieu.

Conflict as a Consequence of the Priorities Selected

A potential source of conflict within the chapter membership may lie in the priorities identified; these priorities may call for a change in the policies or procedures of the state human services agency, where many NASW members may be employed. It was determined early in the Florida experience that an advocacy stance had to be consistent if it was to attain credibility with either legislators or clients of the human services agency. In the normal course of legislative action, the state-employed NASW members were sometimes put on the spot, as in the struggle for patients' rights in mental health and mental retardation programs, in the battle for improved child care programs, and in the insistence on workable alternatives to institutionalization for the aging. In these instances, the questions raised by the lobbying arm of the Florida Chapter distressed NASW members in administrative positions in the state bureaucracy. The legislative objectives were pursued with reasoned persistence; when possible, a confrontation with colleagues was minimized, but fundamental challenge was not avoided when it was necessary. Line workers in the state human services agency were often grateful for the NASW intervention.

Conflict Generated by a Style of Action

To establish legislative priorities means to have the chapter take a position. To support a position taken may require immediate reaction to legislative developments that call on the NASW chapter to speak out forcefully at the proper moment. There may be no time for committees to meet and hammer out a response. Urgent assignments of this nature must be entrusted to competent and articulate members of the organization. This style of responding to legislative demands tends to run counter to more traditional patterns of decision-making and may affront those social workers who prefer the consensual model of organizational action.

Modeling

Modeling refers to replication within subunits of the state chapter of a limited version of legislative-oriented activities pursued by the state lobby. It is a productive strategy having reciprocal value for the state legislative unit and its substate counterparts. Each unit of the Florida Chapter had an opportunity to determine social policy priorities for action in the legislature. The members of each unit were stimulated to undertake interaction with their elected legislative representatives back home prior to leaving for the capitol and to establish an ongoing relationship with legislators that paid off in later contact.

Thursz makes the point that "knowledge of the way in which legislators react to public pressure is crucial. . . . The development of an ongoing relationship with legislators is a far more productive activity than the occasional visit at times of crisis." [14] His point is confirmed by Rothman's observation that "the more a legislator experiences interaction with interest groups the more likely he is to respond positively to interest-group situations." [15]

The state NASW lobbyist used role-playing with chapter members when appropriate to help break down the innate fear of legislators held by some social workers. In addition, she provided technical assistance by moving around the state; she attended regional hearings with local members in the course of testimony and accompanied local members of the state network who journeyed to the capitol, often with consumers, to give testimony or meet with their local state representatives. ("Network" refers to a response network, that is, a group of preselected individuals who were prepared to set in motion a series of contacts with other NASW members as the occasion arose or on an emergency basis.) In these ways novices engaging with the political process had, in the more experienced state lobbyist, a model for observation and a guide for their own behavior in the political arena.

Motivating Chapter Members

While the idea of developing a legislative posture by the NASW chapter in Florida was in the formative stage, a deliberate effort was made to motivate a potential group of political activists within the association. This effort was initiated by means of a legislative institute that was sustained in major part by a modest continuing education grant from national NASW. The institute was held for the first time in 1972 as a method to infuse and reinfuse NASW members in Florida with the importance and value of legislative action.[16] The institute took place in an atmosphere of crisis because health and welfare agencies, their staffs, their practices, and their clients were then under consistent attack. The aim of the meeting was to bring a rational perspective to social issues, which were being dealt with irrationally by some legislators and some members of the press. The institute was held in the state capitol *while the legislature was in session*, which enabled social workers to visit their area delegations or local representative to make known their views on pending legislation.

Motivating social workers to responsively counteract the libel on welfare clients then current in the state was deemed a prerequisite to developing a practical advocacy position on behalf of minorities and the poor. The legislative institute was designed as a vehicle for raising the prospect of a new direction in political activity by social workers. Its effect on the group who attended was profound. This effect was attributable in major part to the realization that social workers at the institute were no longer talking to themselves but were interacting appropriately with legislators, economists, lawyers, state officials, and consumers, who accepted collectively the legitimacy of working with social workers for common ends.

Building Networks

Because legislators frequently cite "constituents' attitudes and sentiments" on controversial issues—from no-fault insurance to expanded day care services—support for human services legislative programs must demonstrate or reflect a constituency base. One of the most crucial strategies for achieving institutional change on behalf of clients, then, was to put into position an effective response network in every community throughout the state where groups of social workers could be identified and mobilized. In urbanized areas, where subchapters existed, task forces on legislative issues were assembled; telephone feedback systems (to get reaction at the local level to a particular bill on pending action) were instituted; telephone pyramid systems (whereby one individual may call several others, each of whom calls another set of people, and so on) were developed; letter-writing and telegram alerts were instituted; legislative workshops were held with county delegations; and biweekly legislative newsletters were mailed to the entire state membership. As the response network developed, emergency network bulletins were issued; these included position statements to and from the state lobby from chapter specialists in various practice settings.

Building Coalitions

Of all the skills used in political intervention, coalition-building has the most exciting potential for both politically astute and politically inexperienced professional social workers. This technique is sometimes conceptualized by Swedish planners as "rings upon the water," referring to the ripple effect of gathering together diverse groups to collaborate on a common cause. Three variations of coalitions are (1) friendly groups joined together to seek the passage of a particular bill and subsequently dissolved, (2) a temporary alliance of one group with a lobbying group or groups not normally friendly to one's overall purposes, and (3) the temporary melding of groups that tend to be competitive within a given field for the purpose of joint study and action on a commonly accepted legislative goal.

Recognizing that some groups share a common concern with social workers on issues of human betterment, the state lobby developed temporary working arrangements with several groups. Besides helping to attain the successful passage of particular bills, such linkages were productive in that each successful legislative act generated by a coalition had a discernible and vivid impact on chapter membership. Social workers new to the legislative process discovered pragmatically that the political system can yield and be responsive under conditions of marshaled power. An experience with a successful coalition combats feelings of powerlessness; subsequent risk-taking by political beginners becomes less threatening, and they begin to view the political system as more accessible. Four illustrations can be cited to describe the successful coalitions initiated by the state legislative office.

Passage of a Licensure Bill on Day Care for Children

To attain the long-delayed passage of a minimum health and safety bill for day care centers, it was possible to bring together in a massive coalition representatives from almost every early childhood academic program in the state; child psychiatrists from the medical schools; black, white, and Chicano mothers; private day care operators who wanted good standards; Title IV-A providers of services; parents' and teachers' associations; and the League of Women Voters. All these groups stood together against the proponents of separate (private) schools who challenged the licensing of child care as the beginning of "social engineering" and the "toe in the door to teaching the theory of evolution." Some 175 proponents came to the state capitol from a radius of five hundred miles for the final committee hearing on the bill. This was an impressive exhibition of mass action on child care, which had its undeniable effect on legislators, and the bill was passed.

Migrant Anti-Hiring Hall Bill

A statewide social movement evolved after the Florida Christian Migrant Ministry turned to the NASW state lobby for help in defeating a bill that would have eliminated the hiring hall for migrants. The effect of the bill would have been to return migrant farm workers to a peonage that once existed in Florida and other states. The final coalition included every group that was even remotely concerned with social justice and the elimination of racism and poverty. The lobbyists were the farm workers themselves. The overall plan was orchestrated by a steering group drawn from sixteen rural areas where migrants work. Migrant workers walked the legislative halls at the state capitol with university students, ministers walked with lay leaders. As sympathetic legislators were identified, they became an overt part of the coalition and the bill was defeated.

Ad Hoc Mental Health Coalition

The significance of this coalition is that it constituted a temporary assemblage of mental health agencies and boards and professional groups that had previously tended to be competitive. For years the Florida Chapter of NASW had documented the lack of mental health programs for children and the aging, but without appreciable effect. Six state organizations were persuaded to pool limited but critical sums of money for the short-term employment of two recently graduated social workers to work under the aegis of the state lobby on behalf of the coalition. The six state groups that formed the coalition included the Florida Psychiatric Association, the Florida Psychological Association, the Florida Council of Mental Health Clinic Directors, the Florida Association of Community Mental Health Boards, the voluntary Mental Health Association of Florida, and the NASW chapter. The task of the two social workers was to marshal statewide support for a state appropriation of $5 million, $2.5 million each for children and the aging.

The major tool for gathering and sustaining pressure on the legislature was a leased WATS line. Working under the direction of the state lobbyist, the social workers were in constant contact with powerful lay board members as well as mental health professionals and others in the service delivery systems. The social workers kept those individuals involved in the response network apprised of developments and urged them to meet with local representatives on weekends when they returned home or to visit them in the state capitol. In effect, the social workers forged a loop between the mental health system and the legislature.

The lobbying effort of the coalition culminated in a state meeting in the capitol, with a geriatric psychiatrist from a neighboring state as the main speaker. The sympathetic chairman of the House Appropriations Committee was persuaded to attend. The result? A major victory: a legislative allocation of $2.5 million (half the objective) for mental health services for children and the aging!

Passage of the Food Stamp Bill

An important variation of the coalition is the temporary alliance that brings together groups normally in legislative opposition but in harmony on a specific bill. This was demonstrated in 1972, when the national food stamp program was offered to states by the U.S. Department of Agriculture. Many of the Florida state legislators who were strongly opposed to the existing surplus food program suddenly became enamored of the food stamp program. They were not enamored for the reason advanced by the NASW state lobby, namely, that it was less dehumanizing than the surplus commodity program. The conversion came about because of an alliance the NASW group had built with lobbyists from the powerful Associated Industries of Florida, which included in its membership the large supermarket chains operating in the state. The supergrocers wanted the sales income likely to be generated by food stamps. So lobbyists from opposite sides, allied for a temporary period, walked the halls together. The alliance worked.

Using the Media

Just as the leadership of a political party or the governor can create a positive or negative environment for a bill or a program, so have the Florida social workers as lobbyists been able to make adroit use of the press conference, the feature article, and the television interview to achieve legislative ends. This was particularly striking in the Florida lobbying unit's systematic attack on independent adoptions in the state, which culminated in a 1975 law that puts controls on such adoptions.

Care must be exercised in the use of the media. Social workers can produce case material more effectively than others, but they have to exercise caution in the use of numbers and predictions. They have to develop skill in the use of cost-benefit procedures or of statistical indicators in support of some forms of preventive intervention. They can, within reason, document the economic as well as the social costs of some current dysfunctional systems.

Collecting Professional Expertise

The "authority of expertise" is probably one of the most potent skills in the professional's arsenal. In the case of social workers, this skill derives naturally from direct knowledge of, and competence in assessing and dealing with, dysfunctions in society. The most common outlets for an informed viewpoint include position papers on matters of social policy, testimony before a legislative committee hearing, or privately offered recommendations on changes in service delivery systems. Expert witnesses among chapter members in the state were often brought in for consultation or to present testimony on various matters.

On several occasions the state lobby drew on the expertise of members of other professions. For example, assistance was received from Legal Aid lawyers on a landlord–tenant bill; from a member of the law faculty at one of the state universities on a mental health bill involving an issue of due process; from a mental health legal specialist with the Kennedy Foundation on a bill of rights for the retarded; from the state American Civil Liberties Union for material on a right to treatment bill; and from the Day Care and Child Development Council of America for help on interpreting the provisions of Title XX of the Social Security Act, which deals with child care services. The list could go on.

Despite anticipatory planning, occasions will arise when a spontaneous response is asked for at a legislative committee hearing. Without benefit of a prepared statement, it may be necessary to "wing it." This is a risk a social worker-lobbyist may have to take. An honest response is usually best if one simply does not have the answer to the question posed.

As the state lobby established its credibility and competence over time, staff members of the state legislature solicited background material in support of forthcoming legislation, requested NASW review of drafts of new legislation, or invited the association's testimony as expert witnesses either in support of or in opposition to major health and welfare bills.

Maintaining a Legislative Presence

Maintaining a legislative presence is a subtle yet consistently successful strategy. It was not simply a matter of the NASW lobbyist's being physically present during committee hearings. Rather, legislators became aware of the monitoring function being performed on behalf of a constituency that is usually ignored. All major committee meetings were monitored because it is at this juncture that political influence can be exercised. As the people's advocate, the lobbyist's legislative allies came to trust her contribution, and her adversaries came to resist her efforts. Some legislators were constrained by her participation—sometimes silent, sometimes vocal—being aware of her assignment to serve as a watchdog on their comments and action. Legislators, who out of personal conviction may take a public stand that is unpopular but favors the social workers' stand, need support and backup. The NASW lobbyist's testimony in their support leaves them less isolated and linked to a constituency to whom she represents the bridge.

Generating New Legislation

As the trust and confidence of friendly legislators and their staff is won, the lobby can propose or initiate major social legislation. For example, out of the state lobbyist's efforts, a bill for the establishment of a state commission on child advocacy and licensing for child care centers evolved. Also, a law that established a demonstration on community care for the impaired elderly as an alternative to institutionalization grew out of a state-commissioned social policy study undertaken by one of the chapter members.

In the process of bill development, the third objective of the state social work lobby (i.e., monitoring human services legislation or administrative procedures) frequently comes into play. This is one point where line workers, state administrative staff, the lobbyist, or any chapter member with sufficient evidence can make use of the state lobby to propose, and perhaps help to prepare, a bill that corrects a deficiency in human services legislation or administrative procedures. In most instances, such bills are introduced with the concurrence of key administrators in the state's human resources agency; in other instances, bills may be introduced as part of the advocacy role of the lobby on behalf of aggrieved clients in opposition to the state bureaucracy.

THE CASE FOR LEGISLATIVE LOBBYING BY STATE UNITS

The essential thesis of this paper can be stated simply: Lobbying as an instrument of advocacy for the poor and the powerless is a legitimate *professional* responsibility of social workers. The experiences of one state NASW unit has served as one model; undoubtedly there are others equally worthy of attention. A case can be made for state units of NASW to develop a consistent legislative effort to effect changes in state public social policy by coalescing their determination, resources, and skills.

State policy actions regarding the human services are increasingly vital because such actions are embodied in laws and public appropriations determined by state legislatures. Consider the combined effects of the New Federalism, of the new revenue-sharing procedures, and of state-level planning on traditional social services, on new social programs such as Supplementary Security Income, and on community development, housing, social transportation programs, land use, and similar significant aspects of social life. Federal grant programs to urban areas that revealed a federal-local nexus are slowly giving way to a three-way relationship among federal, state, and local political jurisdictions. In this new triumvirate, states are increasingly decisive, serving as the linchpin of the policy interpretation and implementation process. States are being literally forced into new policymaking roles, and it is reasonably certain that their role is on the increase.

No single organization can lay claim to exclusive candidacy for leadership of a state human services lobby. When properly motivated and equipped, however, state chapters of NASW possess the organizational skills necessary for representing the interests of the economically and socially deprived, and such interests are harmonious with the goals of social work. Because public policy is a matter of choice and influence, social workers must acquire lobbying skills to be influential in policy decisions, rather than find or train lobbyists to carry their message. As Mahaffey suggests, "It may well prove easier to train a social worker to be a lobbyist than to train a lobbyist to understand and represent social work goals." [17]

A decade ago Wilbur Cohen spoke out on the political nature of policy change and urged social workers to participate directly in the political system:

> Do not underestimate the fact that the political process increasingly involves important, well-financed, well-organized lobbies, directed toward pursuing the objectives of the group they represent. On the American scene, these organizations are becoming more important and more effective than ever before and, as a consequence, social workers also have to move into the political arena and get organized. Social workers too are just responding to the inevitable situation in America in which every interested group attempts to organize and to bombard the Congress. When social workers are doing that, they must realize that others are doing it too and with more money, more members, and more political influence than they can develop at any given moment in time. So if social workers want to achieve results, they must practice and demonstrate perseverance in order to achieve successful political action.[18]

Rose says that "the economic elite has its greatest success in influencing government when there are no counter pressures." [19] In light of the realization that public policy takes the direction given by prevailing forces, can social workers avoid getting into the influence business?

NOTES

1. *See* Daniel Thursz, "Social Action," *Encyclopedia of Social Work*, Vol. 2 (New York: National Association of Social Workers, 1971), pp. 1189–1195; Daniel Thursz, "The Arsenal of Social Action Strategies: Options for Social Workers," *Social Work*, 16 (January 1971), pp. 27–34; and Irwin Epstein, "Social Workers and Social Action: Attitudes Toward Social Action Strategies," *Social Work*, 13 (April 1968), pp. 101–108.

2. *See* Ad Hoc Committee on Advocacy, "The Social Worker as Advocate: Champion of Social Victims," *Social Work*, 14 (April 1969), pp. 16–22; Sherry Arnstein, "A Ladder of Citizen Participation," *Journal of the American Institute of Planners*, 35 (July 1969), pp. 216–224; George Brager, "Advocacy and Political Behavior," *Social Work*, 13 (April 1968), pp. 5–15; Paul Davidoff, "Advocacy and

Pluralism in Planning," *Journal of the American Institute of Planners*, 31 (November 1965), pp. 331–337; Charles F. Grosser and Edward V. Sparer, "Legal Services for the Poor: Social Work and Social Justice," *Social Work*, 11 (January 1966), pp. 81–87; Melvin Mogulof, "Coalition to Adversary: Citizen Participation in Three Federal Programs," *Journal of the American Institute of Planners*, 35 (July 1969), pp. 225–232; and Edward V. Sparer, Howard Thorkelson, and Jonathan Weiss, "The Lay Advocate," *University of Detroit Law Journal*, 43 (1966), p. 493.

3. Davidoff, op. cit.

4. *See* Wilbur J. Cohen, "What Every Social Worker Should Know about Political Action," *Social Work*, 11 (July 1966), pp. 3–11; Maryann Mahaffey, "Lobbying and Social Work," *Social Work*, 17 (January 1972), pp. 3–11; and Charles S. Prigmore, "Use of the Coalition in Legislative Action," *Social Work*, 19 (January 1974), pp. 96–102.

5. Cohen, op. cit.

6. Arnold Rose, *The Power Structure* (New York: Oxford University Press, 1967).

7. Jack Rothman, *Planning and Organizing for Social Change* (New York: Columbia University Press, 1974), p. 212.

8. Ibid., p. 200.

9. Ad Hoc Committee on Advocacy, op. cit.

10. Ibid.

11. Rothman, op. cit., pp. 95–96.

12. William Mansfield, "The Greening of the Legislature," *Miami Herald*, April 7, 1965.

13. Lobbying activities discussed in this paper spanned the period 1970–75. During that period the NASW chapter in Florida underwent reorganization, consolidating in 1974 some seven separate chapters into a single statewide chapter. The lobby actually began in the spring of 1970 under the aegis of the then State Council of Florida Chapters, NASW, which in 1974 was transformed into the Florida Chapter of NASW and continued the lobby without interruption.

14. Thursz, "Social Action," p. 1192.

15. Rothman, op. cit., p. 238.

16. William G. Bell, ed., *Proceedings of a Legislative Institute on the Health and Welfare Crisis in Florida* (Tallahassee: State Council of Florida Chapters, NASW, March 1972).

17. Mahaffey, op. cit., p. 11.

18. Cohen, op. cit., p. 7.

19. Rose, op. cit., p. 485.

Part III:

New Areas of Practice

Social Work and the Women's Movement

BETTY S. JOHNSON AND CAROL HOLTON

The basic tenets of social work are deeply rooted in humanistic, pluralistic values. Each individual is presumed to have the right to full development of his or her talents, capacities, and total human potential. Over the past fifteen years the social work profession has been bombarded by a series of shock waves calling into question the gap between rhetoric and practice. The poor, the young, the alienated, and the minorities confronted us in the 1960s.

Today, in the 1970s, the profession is being challenged to examine its values, its assumptions, its organization, its personnel, and its consumers of services in light of the unique role and place of women. In 1971 the National Association of Social Workers (NASW) established the elimination of racism and poverty as the two overriding priorities of the profession. In June 1975 Maryann Mahaffey, in her presidential address to the Delegate Assembly, added the elimination of sexism as a third priority and of equal magnitude.[1] A cursory review of social work literature confirms the impression that women's issues have barely begun to be recognized. Social workers must understand women's issues and be prepared to interpret, help, support, and educate women in their efforts to be and to become their best selves. Social workers must concern themselves with the status of women in the profession, with the status of women as clients, and with the status of women at large.

Social work education at all levels carries a heavy responsibility to prepare the present generation of social workers for nonsexist social work practice. And continuing education must see to it that those already in the field catch up and keep up.

WOMEN'S RIGHTS AND SOCIAL WELFARE

Many of the underlying assumptions of social welfare practice and organization, by their very nature, serve to perpetuate sex-role stereotyping. Although both men and women suffer from the stunting of human potential as a result of role stereotyping, psychological conflict and economic discrimination more obviously affect women. Thomas states that "societal notions and stereotypes of the female as being more feeling-oriented, and a domestic tension manager, are . . . reflected in the organization of social agencies." [2] Females tend to have horizontal job patterns, remaining at a worker level, closer to the approved "feminine" helping role. At this level, they continue lifelong patterns of being more closely supervised than men. The dearth of women in high-level positions keeps them at a disadvantage in salaries, status, power, and influence and reinforces stereotypes in a circular fashion, which affects both the female worker and the female client.[3]

As Epstein confirms, "For all occupations in all societies, as one approaches the top, the proportion of men increases and the proportion of women decreases." [4] Ironically, women in social work supposed that as men increasingly entered the field, male-related rewards—such as higher salary levels and a more prestigious professional image—would accrue to women. Instead, "Men remain dominant in their traditional occupations and invade women's occupations at the highest levels. Thus women are forced either to accept this situation or fight it at substantial personal and psychological costs." [5]

Given this institutional bias influencing the professional role and functioning of females in social welfare, their socialization into treating clients in like manner becomes obvious and inevitable. Women practitioners are not necessarily innocent of incorporating sexist values into their social work practice and perpetuating the oppression of women clients.

This oppression occurs in the form of diagnostic emphasis that focuses on personal incompetence rather than on external conditions over which the client has no control and/or on solutions that tend to preserve the social institution at the expense of the rights and welfare of the individual.[6] Professional women are subtly encouraged to behave according to the persisting mystique that it is unfeminine to succeed, to be capable, to achieve. This devastating cultural imperative is then filtered through professional training to emerge in the perpetuation of a welfare system that systematically discriminates against the women who are its victims. Just as social, economic, and educational institutions have systematically perpetuated the oppression of minorities, in parallel fashion these same institutions have oppressed women. With reference to the social welfare system, the issue of women's rights is indeed central to social welfare and racism because ". . . a latent function of welfare, reflecting the general social attitudes of society, is to enforce the female roles of economic and social dependence, while at the same time regulating the labor market . . . to prevent the uprisings of poor people." [7]

The welfare system controls the participation of poor women in the labor market by making AFDC (Aid to Families with Dependent Children) eligibility contingent on the recipient's acceptance of employment, without regard to minimum wage; by forcing the recipient to disclose the whereabouts of a father without consideration of family relationships and tensions; by restricting access to higher education; and by controlling the licensing and provision of day care services. Thus the welfare system does in fact control all those factors vital to the employment, survival, and autonomy of poor women.

Women and men will need to develop new personal, professional, and organizational skills. Women in the human services must take the initiative in learning to perceive themselves and their clients as individuals who can control their own destinies. They must, further, work together to bring into being an environment that makes possible, facilitates, and rewards women for self-determination and autonomy. For social workers, this means breaking out of traditionalist career patterns into policymaking, decision-making, money-making positions. For clients, it means a redefinition of status, away from an illness model. For both, a recognition of and support for experimentation with new life-styles and modes of family organization and an insistence on the development of child-rearing adjuncts will provide the societal underpinning necessary for such changes to occur.

WOMEN IN THE SOCIAL WORK PROFESSION

Despite a professional history replete with the vision, accomplishments, and contributions of extraordinary women, the following conditions exist.

1. Over a representative seven-year period, salaries for male social workers rose 85 percent, while salaries for female social workers rose 71 percent.

2. A comparison of average annual salaries of male and female workers employed full time, according to period of graduation, revealed that salaries for males ranged from 17 percent to 38 percent higher than salaries for females.

3. The average male supervisor salary is $1,600 higher than the average female supervisor salary.

4. Thirty-four percent of all males in social work are directors.

5. Seventy-eight percent of director positions are held by males.

6. Ninety percent of women cluster at the worker or first-line supervisor level.

7. Men hold more leadership positions in NASW and the Council on Social Work Education than women do.

8. Men get published more than women.

9. In the planning of NASW's Twentieth Anniversary Symposium, the underrepresentation of women as major presenters was a serious issue.

10. In social work education, men predominate heavily at the full professor and dean level, while women are far more likely to be at junior, nontenured faculty ranks.

11. There are three times as many men Ph.D.'s as women Ph.D.'s in the social welfare field.[8]

The role of schools of social work should be closely scrutinized. Data from a study of students undertaken at Columbia University indicate that "social workers segregate themselves according to sex into different practice specialties." [9] The predictable results: Women choose the more passive, female congruent, nurturing, lower-paid casework method. One is prompted to wonder about recruitment and advising influences as well as the factor of self-selection.

Racism has been identified as an institutional phenomenon, perpetuated despite the actions of any given individual, in any given organization. Discrimination on the basis of sex is likewise so built into the fabric of social systems that it, too, must be attacked and rooted out at the institutional level. The NASW Committee on Women's Issues can and should play a key role in seeing that nonsexist policies and practices are universally established within the profession. Through the national and chapter structure, NASW should seek to influence social agencies to examine and modify practices that discriminate against women workers and women clients. Agencies should be urged to have affirmative action programs with effective monitoring mechanisms, whether such programs are federally mandated or not. National standard-setting organizations, such as the Child Welfare League, the Family Service Association, and the American Public Welfare Association, should require nonsexist, nonracist practice as a condition of membership. United Way agencies are ideally situated to guide their funded agencies.

The Council on Social Work Education needs to attend to matters of sex discrimination at the faculty level and to the inclusion of women's content in curricula as part of its accrediting responsibility. Questions included on licensing examinations and examinations for the Academy of Certified Social Workers should be drafted to assess the individual practitioner's understanding of women's issues. Legal and professional regulation must be used as a tool to protect women clients as well as to certify competence—particularly in light of the growth of private practice, for which evaluative mechanisms may not exist.

The conventional wisdom of the 1960s taught that future employment prospects for social workers were virtually limitless. In 1965 the profession looked forward confidently to filling a 100,000-person graduate social worker gap.[10] A scant decade later that gap has not only disappeared, but has been replaced by a shortage of jobs. The ominous implications of this phenomenon have been little noted by women in the field. Scotch limns the future in bleak terms in an article that has received far too little attention.[11] He foresees a shortage of MSW jobs, especially in casework; continued discrimination against women in salaries and in upward mobility as women begin to be forced to compete directly with men for the available jobs; and a continued preference for men in higher-level positions.

Stripped of all other considerations, this stark economic discrimination projected into an insecure future should galvanize professional women into action. Individually, as agency employees, and as members of their profession, women are going to be forced to reexamine their career and life patterns if they are to fulfill their human and professional potential. The economics of the profession, as well as changing cultural patterns, point to such a reexamination. As Stevens points out: "The pace of our society today and the demand of jobs and professions are such that no one can successfully take ten years off to raise children. Ten years off means no seniority, atrophied skills, forgotten knowledge." [12]

WOMEN AS CLIENTS

Welfare as a Women's Issue

Welfare is a women's issue and a crucial economic issue for the women, white and nonwhite, and their children who depend on AFDC.[13] Welfare recipients in no other category of assistance have had to endure the same degree of infantilization, invasion of privacy, substandard levels of assistance, or general public opprobrium: "It has not occurred to the public that the sex lives or child care practices of social security, Medicare, workmen's compensation or oil depletion allowance recipients be investigated." [14] Over and beyond indignity, men have an undisputed advantage in referral priority and in having a wider range of jobs and higher salary levels in such programs as the Work Incentive Program (WIN) and the Vocational Rehabilitation Public Assistance programs, in which they are heavily enrolled.[15]

The deplorable fact is that female social workers help to perpetuate a welfare system that is degrading, inadequate, and discriminating. The magnitude of the task of revising present-day practice is formidable, but the time to begin is yesterday. Political and social action for public policy change is clearly one route toward enabling welfare recipients to have a chance to live productive, self-respecting lives. From the radical feminist orientation, it is the only productive route.[16]

Equally compelling, however, is the need for social workers to help recipients overcome the psychological impact of years of socialization in a sexist society. Providing individual counseling only will not achieve this end. For their own sake and for their clients, women social workers need to direct strenuous efforts toward preparing for and breaking into administrative and policymaking positions. They must recognize, come to terms with, and effectively combat their own subordinate position in the society and in their profession, as they also work for and with client groups. In addition, the options of alternative life-styles, more personal assertiveness, greater autonomy in decision-making, and rewards for giving up passive-dependent behavior must be supported.

Women in Treatment

Women in their middle years and women between 20 and 30 years of age stand out as specific groups whose self-concepts have been affected by the women's movement. A number of women have sought new self-understanding, new direction, and new information from attending continuing education programs designed to meet their needs.

In the middle years, the role of wife, mother, and homemaker becomes markedly less demanding; this is more of a situational than a chronological state, which for decades has presented women with an identity crisis. This crisis has been intensified in the past decade by developments in the women's movement. Women who are beginning to feel some lessening of their nurturing function are at the same time being bombarded by media programs and popular literature that question the legitimacy of the roles they have been performing for years. Social workers are called on for treatment of the resultant feelings of doubting self-worth, despondence, and anger.

Younger women, too, are being bombarded with exhortations and messages regarding the women's movement and the freedom to choose and to "be," but they are receiving these messages at the stage of their lives when they are making decisions about their immediate futures. They have been exposed to feminist thinking, but at the same time have had many years of exposure to traditional sex-role stereotyping. These women are now attempting to deal with the crises resulting from the double messages they continue to receive. The conflicts of the 20–30-year-old group can be outlined as follows:

1. The choice between career and marriage
2. The combination of career and marriage
3. The choice between career and family
4. The combination of career and family

To the cultural conflicts must be added the state of postindustrial technology. The future of many occupational areas is doubtful for both women and men, and the economic depression of the 1970s is a monumental complication.

These, then, are some of the sociocultural dilemmas faced by many women who seek therapy. Available evidence suggests that therapists are far from being prepared to consider these factors. Broverman, Broverman, and Clarkson document that clinicians are likely to attribute the characteristics of healthy adults to men more than to women. In essence, they found that therapists perceive health in women as different from health in men and, further, they tend to define women as having more neurotic traits.[17]

A study by Brown and Hellinger evaluated the psychological, sociological, and sexual attitudes toward women of a cross section of therapists; the attitudes were assessed as reflecting traditional and contemporary stands. Brown and Hellinger state that "fifty percent of all therapists questioned held a relatively traditional stance, with males obtaining significantly higher traditional scores than females."[18] Given the facts that over one-half of all therapists hold traditional attitudes toward women and that nearly 70 percent of their clients are women, and assuming that the results of the Brown and Hellinger study can be generalized, the need for reeducation and the development of new skills is clear.[19]

Hauptman et al. state that theoretical frameworks for approaching the problems of women must be examined and seen as a manifestation of basic societal problems rather than as illness. They "prescribe for social welfare professionals a heavy dosage of reading and contact with the women's movement and hope that the new premises and goals put forth by women's groups will influence our 'therapies.'"[20]

More specifically, staff development programs within agencies must be designed to bring about awareness and to confront traditional attitudes among male and female personnel at all levels. Agency staffs must be educated to the need for and intent of affirmative action. Programs that exist only on paper lead to statistical tokenism unless admission of the problem is made and commitment to the solution is secured.

New professional styles, such as peer supervision, have great potential for monitoring actual agency practice. Many a closet chauvinist has perpetuated sex-role stereotyping unbeknownst to anyone but his/her immediate supervisor, who may or may not be aware of and concerned about it. Peer supervision provides a mechanism for the exposure of negative attitudes and increases the possibility of heightening the level of consciousness.

Continuing education programs under university auspices must assume responsibility for providing new information and for bringing together practitioners from a variety of settings to examine and reevaluate traditional practice. Even if women's studies were systematically incorporated into every graduate school of social work tomorrow, the mass of practitioners would still not be reached. It is the responsibility of continuing education to be aware of what is being developed and to see that reeducation occurs.

WOMEN AT LARGE

Assuming that the status of women in the profession can be changed and that services to women clients can be altered, social work must examine its responsibility to the masses of women who will never come into contact with a social worker, a social welfare program, or a social service agency. The profession can play a significant leadership role in helping women to redefine themselves and their problems.

The term "consciousness raising" has come to mean many things to many people. Eastman incorporates many of the variations in her description of consciousness raising as a resocialization process that "becomes a way of reinterpreting the past to conform to the present reality: when resocialization occurs, the past is seen in new ways." [21] Consciousness raising as a resocialization process is helpful to many women, but others need an additional content framework in a somewhat more formalized setting.

Continuing education programs sponsored by the Center for Social Service (University of Wisconsin—Extension) have provided some of the benefits of consciousness raising. But an additional dimension is the educational focus in a guided group discussion, led by a highly skilled professional with skills in group dynamics, diagnostic sensitivity, knowledge about community resources, and newly developed content on the developmental stages of family and individual life cycles. The role of continuing educators should be to design and pilot programs such as this under university auspices. As these programs are tested and validated, agencies should be incorporating them into their ongoing services and should be providing family-life outreach programs, based on the need for preventive mental health services. In southeastern Wisconsin, such agencies as the Young Women's Christian Association and the Mental Health Association are adapting pilot programs to meet the needs of their own constituents.[22]

The social work profession must be strongly supportive of movements such as this, and social work educators must make their consultation available. The profession of social work can play a significant leadership role in helping women to redefine themselves and their problems. At the present time, the women identified as being in crisis have few resources other than psychotherapy. The programs being developed may well provide an alternative to therapy for many women by giving support and help but avoiding the illness model.

NOTES

1. Maryann Mahaffey, *NASW News,* 20 (July 1975), p. 8.

2. Cordell H. Thomas, "Women's Rights in Social Welfare Agencies," *The Social Welfare Forum, 1972* (New York: Columbia University Press, 1972), pp. 232–233.

3. Cited in C. Bernard Scotch, "Sex Status in Social Work: Grist for Women's Liberation," *Social Work,* 16 (July 1971), p. 7.

4. Cynthia Epstein, "Encountering the Male Establishment: Sex-Status Limits on Women's Careers in the Profession," *American Journal of Sociology,* 75 (May 1970), p. 965.

5. Janet Saltzman Chafetz, "Women in Social Work," *Social Work,* 17 (September 1972), p. 18.

6. Thomas, op. cit., pp. 228–231.

7. Leatrice Hauptman et al., "Women's Issues in Social Welfare," *The Social Welfare Forum, 1972* (New York: Columbia University Press, 1972), p. 219.

8. The figures cited were gleaned from the following sources: Aaron Rosenblatt et al., "Predominance of Male Authors in Social Work Publications," *Social Casework,* 51 (July 1970), pp. 426–429; Hauptman et al., op. cit., p. 215; Thomas, op. cit., p. 232; Scotch, op. cit., p. 6; and Martha William, Liz Ho, and Lucy Fielder, "Career Patterns: More Grist for Women's Liberation," *Social Work,* 19 July 1974), pp. 463–466.

9. George Brager and John A. Michael, "The Sex Distribution in Social Work: Causes and Consequences," *Social Casework,* 50 (December 1969), p. 601.

10. *Closing the Gap in Social Work Manpower,* report of the Task Force in Social Work Education and Manpower (Washington, D.C.: U.S. Government Printing Office, November 1965), p. 79.

11. Scotch, op. cit., pp. 9–10.

12. Barbara Stevens, "The Psychotherapist and Women's Liberation," *Social Work,* 16 (July 1971), p. 13.

13. Johnnie Tillman, "Welfare Is a Women's Issue," *MS. Magazine* (Spring 1972), pp. 111–116.

14. Betty Mandell, "Welfare and Totalitarianism: Part II. Tactical Guidelines," *Social Work*, 16 (April 1971), p. 92.

15. Hauptman et al., op. cit., p. 219.

16. Rosemary Chapin, Susan Jones, and Nancy Wilderman, "Sex Role Stereotyping: Implications for Human Services" (Minneapolis, Minn.: Minnesota Resource Center for Social Work Education, 1973) contains a discussion of the radical feminist viewpoint opposing individual treatment and favoring social action, *see* especially p. 89.

17. David Broverman, Inge Broverman, and Frank Clarkson, "Sex Role Stereotypes and Clinical Judgments of Mental Health," *Journal of Consulting and Clinical Psychology*, 34 (February 1970), pp. 1–7.

18. Caree Rosen Brown and Marilyn Levitt Hellinger, "Therapists' Attitudes Toward Women," *Social Work*, 20 (July 1975), pp. 266–270.

19. Thomas, op. cit., p. 230.

20. Hauptman et al., op. cit., p. 224.

21. Paula Costa Eastman, "Consciousness-Raising as a Resocialization Process for Women," *Smith College Studies in Social Work*, 42 (June 1973), pp. 155–156.

22. The authors have developed a variety of continuing education programs sponsored by the University of Wisconsin—Extension Center for Social Service. Descriptive material and training manuals are available on request.

Feminist Theory and Casework Practice

MARJORIE D. MOSKOL

This paper is based on the author's experiences in private casework practice in a feminist counseling service and as an active feminist. Professional Services for Women, Inc., was established as a private corporation in March 1973 by five feminists having a variety of professional backgrounds. They believed it important for women to provide services for other women, especially in the areas of casework, career counseling, job placement, information and referral, and legal services. The decision to incorporate privately stemmed from a desire to maintain complete autonomy and to work outside traditional male-controlled agencies and institutions. Hence fees are charged for services, and each woman functions as a private practitioner under the organizational umbrella.

Initially it was expected that the typical client would be experiencing marital stress, would be dealing with confusion and frustration around desired or imposed role changes, and would be between 35 and 50 years old. In fact, most women out of the seventy-seven seen from March 1973 to June 1975 have never been married, and more than half were between 21 and 30 years old. Most of these young women were college educated and almost all were employed. Feelings of depression and/or anxiety were presented by most. These data suggest that it is apt to be the well-educated, younger woman who is most likely to have a feminist consciousness and to seek out a feminist caseworker.

WHAT IS FEMINIST CASEWORK?

Feminist casework is more than casework practiced by a social worker who is a feminist because feminism is a complex ideology that has social, cultural, political, economic, and historical components.[1] In feminist theory, women are seen as having been systematically relegated to an inferior, disadvantaged status in which they are excluded from the enclaves of power and responsibility and are required to perform mostly sexual, reproductive, and related roles.[2] A feminist seeks to effect change by promoting the redistribution of power so that a proportionate share is in the hands of women as a whole. She also seeks to gain greater control and power over her own life.[3] The matter of role change has been overemphasized (mostly by those outside the women's movement) as a primary goal of the movement. In fact, the principal goals of feminists are the acquisition of greater power over society and the achievement of total control over themselves. Therefore the most significant goal of the feminist caseworker is to assist clients to gain this personal/social power.[4]

THEORY AND SKILLS COMMON TO SOCIAL WORK AND FEMINISM

An important tenet of social work is "self-determination"—the client's right to make her (his) own decisions about her (his) own life.[5] Closely related to this is the familiar concept of helping the client help herself (himself). Both these basic social work beliefs are consistent with the feminist belief in the right of women to control their own bodies, their own lives, and their own destinies. Social workers have always encouraged self-determination in their clients, and the awareness of the feminist caseworker that girls and women are deeply conditioned to think, feel, and behave in ways prescribed by others (mostly individual men and male-controlled institutions) brings an intensity and a new dimension to the application of the self-determination concept.[6]

For instance, many women are surprised to learn they have the right to conduct their lives the way they wish, not the way their parents, husbands, teachers, and others have told them they should. This right must be clearly, forcefully, and repeatedly conveyed to the client until it is transformed into useful behavior patterns. It cannot be assumed that casual references to self-determination will affect the therapeutic process. The worker and client examine instances in which the client has behaved according to demands not her own. The client is asked to consider whether those demands have helped her to help herself, that is, to gain control of her own life and to move toward her growth potential. In doing this the worker must maintain a fine balance between strong encouragement and support, without overestimating the client's capacity for change action and without imposing her own notions of what is good for the client.

Focusing on client strength and de-emphasizing pathology so as to encourage the self-confidence needed for growth is a familiar social work technique. For a feminist caseworker, there is the added significance of consistency with two important and related concepts current among feminists: (1) Sociocultural determinants of problems are more prevalent than intrapsychic ones.[7] (2) Some psychoanalytic theory regarding what women's emotional problems are and what causes them is erroneous, especially theory having to do with female sexuality and the concept of "penis envy." [8]

Most of the women seen in the counseling service feel they are to blame for causing their own problems and feel guilty and perverse if their roles and behavior are different from sociocultural expectations. Thus it is important to help clients understand the tremendous impact on them of factors external to themselves. The feminist caseworker often uses an educational technique to achieve this by pointing out how customs, attitudes, and practices are affecting the client in ways that are causing her distress and impeding her progress. The caseworker examines the origin of customs and attitudes to determine whether they are still relevant and essential to the client or if they can be discarded. When clients realize that much social injustice masquerades as universal truth, they can release energy tied up in self-hate and use it to achieve the goals of personal control and growth.

The social worker's knowledge of social structures and institutions (marriage, family, schools, welfare agencies, medical facilities, workplaces) is especially useful to the feminist caseworker in helping clients to understand the impact of external factors on emotional status and behavior. Examining how the client's schooling, for instance, prepared girls for subordinate-passive behavior and discouraged them from pursuing knowledge and opportunities that would lead to nontraditional activities helps the client understand and overcome feelings of frustration and discouragement.

Among the most basic social work skills is knowing and using community resources.[9] Because of the many limitations and barriers hindering women's control over and development of their lives and society, it is essential that women use all existing relevant resources and develop new ones to meet their unique needs. The feminist caseworker acquaints herself not only with the agencies that provide these services but also with the way they provide them, looking for those whose attitudes and orientation are consistent with the goals of personal control and growth. In the author's experience, the resources most often requested by women are those dealing with control of their bodies and their destinies: gynecological and abortion services; education for careers; legal services; job, housing, or credit discrimination recourse; and child care facilities. Uniquely feminist structures—for example, consciousness-raising groups, women's health collectives, and feminist action groups such as the National Organization for Women (NOW) and the Women's Political

Caucus—are important resources. They are important not only for the services and activities they provide, but also for the opportunities they offer to identify and take action with women having similar needs and goals.

The worker-client relationship, so highly valued in social work practice, is even more important in feminist practice because the concept of woman-to-woman sharing and problem-solving in a condition of equality is basic to personal and social change.[10] Identification with an ego ideal as an aid to self-actualization, another concept used in social work practice, is basic to feminist casework, in which there is the constant search for competent, independent female role models.[11] These two concepts merge into the most significant aspect of feminist casework: skill in relationship. The feminist worker is a caring, empathic person, but does not mother; she encourages, educates, supports, but does not control; she clarifies, even interprets, but de-emphasizes pathology; she is an object of identification so must share her ideas, opinions, and experiences with the client while still encouraging independence. Because girls and women are conditioned to be dependent, the worker must avoid nurturing and must seek every opportunity to encourage independent functioning.

To diminish the conditioned feelings of inferiority and dependence, the feminist casework relationship attempts to establish greater quality between client and worker than is often found in authoritarian treatment situations.[12] This means, for instance, that the worker shares and compares her experiences and opinions with the client, and sometimes both are involved in the same feminist organizational activities.[13]

The worker presents herself as a role model for professional autonomy and competence and conveys confidence in the ability of women to take charge of their lives and succeed at a variety of endeavors. The office setting itself is designed to promote female pride through the use of paintings and prints created by women artists (local ones wherever possible). Newsletters of local feminist organizations, annoucements of meetings and other activities, literature on educational and job opportunities, and national feminist publications are on display. The focus is on women as significant persons of actual and potential accomplishment so that pride in being a member of the female group is developed and, eventually, self-worth and self-confidence develop as well.

Another useful tool for developing self-confidence and independence is "adventure." Boys and men are encouraged to be adventurous and to engage in physical activities and sports. A boy learns to depend on his own resources and to take pride in his physical accomplishments; men know that these adventures make their minds and bodies strong and make them "their own man." Girls and women are discouraged, indeed denied, these "adventures."[14] They are not permitted to be "their own woman" because they must belong to someone else—father, husband, or employer.[15]

Today, more and more, women are beginning to seek activities in which they can test and increase their self-reliance and diminish their feelings of powerlessness. Such activities as camping, backpacking, self-defense, sailing, and traveling are encouraged by the caseworker when appropriate. The emphasis is on mastering skills in activities that have an element of survival and through which the body is strengthened, which helps overcome the damage done by the "weaker sex" myth.

CLIENTS' PROBLEMS

Depression is the symptom most commonly presented to caseworkers in the feminist counseling service. Anxiety is also widely experienced, as are feelings of frustration and general dissatisfaction with life situations (e.g., marital status and employment). Usually, clients are having difficulty in resolving a "transitional crisis." They are changing jobs or living arrangements, beginning or ending their education, or, often, ending a significant relationship. They are passing from one phase of their lives to another and experience this passage as stressful. Other clients feel stuck in unsatisfactory situations and sense the need to move on to new chapters in their lives, but are uncertain and fearful of their course of action. Young college women are dealing with sexuality, emancipation from parents, relationships with peers, and career preparation. Single heterosexual and lesbian women are having difficulty in establishing guilt-free and anxiety-free social and sexual relationships because society provides few acceptable social structures for women outside of marriage. Married women are attempting to change their attitudes, roles, and functions to reduce conflict and frustration. These transitional crises represent the stress resulting from dealing with the usual developmental processes plus the drive for self-actualization newly intensified by the women's movement.

Case Histories

LINDA, age 23, was new to our community, having moved here with her husband Jeff, so he could do graduate work at a local university. She was depressed, expressed dissatisfaction with her job as a high school teacher, and was experiencing marital stress and feelings of loneliness because of alienation from her husband and not having found friends in the community. She considered separating from her husband, but feared being overwhelmed by loneliness; she was unsure of her ability to establish a satisfactory life situation outside of marriage and was unable to break her and Jeff's mutual dependency. The first interview revealed that Linda was functioning well below capacity in terms of career development and social relationships. As an undergraduate, she had been an excellent student and had majored in physics, a field in which women are rare and hence in great demand by organizations required to fulfill affirmative action employment plans. She was now teaching physics, had a number of other interests and abilities, had a mature and pleasing personality, but had few friends or activities outside of work. Ironically, despite all her talent, she lacked feelings of self-worth. She had deliberately sought out a feminist caseworker because she sensed connections between her problems and the issues raised by the women's movement.

The worker focused on Linda's many abilities and accomplishments and pointed out the ways the traditional expectations of women, transmitted by her family and other social institutions, were hampering her use of these talents and contributing to her self-depreciation, frustration, and depression. Emerging opportunities in her field were discussed, and she was encouraged to make use of them. Linda was referred to a member of the local NOW chapter, who was also a physicist, to acquaint her with career opportunities and educational requirements. The worker, who also organized consciousness-raising groups for NOW, helped Linda to join a consciousness-raising group so she could share her concerns in a mutually supportive atmosphere.[16]

Linda and Jeff subsequently came for an interview together. They were able to express some of their concerns and feelings about each other and their marriage and to reach at least a temporary understanding on the status of their marriage.

Within their families, in schools, in jobs, or within their marriages, women receive almost no positive reinforcement for nonnurturing achievement. Linda's case demonstrates the integrated use of both feminist and traditional theory and practice, the use of feminist referral resources, as well as the rapid and positive response many women can make when their abilities are recognized and their potential is encouraged realistically.

ELLY, age 22, was ambivalent about her upcoming entrance into law school because of her fear of failing and anxiety about moving away from familiar surroundings to a distant city, where the law school was located. In addition, the rejection she was feeling because of the current loss of some important friends was intensifying her persistent feelings of abandonment caused by the death of her father when she was 14 and the chronic mental

illness of her mother. Her manner was pseudomature as a result of the responsibilities she had to assume for the care of her mother and younger
brothers and the financial deprivations she had endured since her father's
death. The lack of money and parental availability diminished her feelings
of self-worth as she compared herself to the more affluent students at her
Ivy League college.

Elly was told by her family that she should abandon her educational and
career plans to look after her mother and contribute to her support. When
these stresses became intense, she began to suspect that her friends and
brothers were disloyal to her. She would drift into fantasies, often of an
irrational nature, and would have suicidal thoughts. Despite all this, Elly
was an especially intelligent, talented young woman determined to pursue
a career that woud enable her to take action to achieve her high social and
political ideals. Her student employment in a law office convinced her that
law was an appropriate route. But at the same time, she was afraid that
studying law would hinder the development of good relationships with men
and prevent her from recapturing, through them, the satisfying, secure,
family life lost to her as a child.

Casework with Elly had the traditional aspects of helping her to sort
out the real from the unreal in regard to her fantasies, suicidal thoughts,
and inadequacies. It also clarified how her ambivalence about her future
partly reflected her identification with the quite different characteristics
of her mother on the one hand and her idealistic father and suffragist
grandmother on the other. Feminist theory was used to explain to her how
society expected her, not her brothers, to care for her mother and to give up
her career. She was able to understand that this pressure was consistent with
the servant roles assigned to women but did not represent a fair distribution
of responsibility or an appropriate use of her abilities. In addition, she
learned that the changing forms of human relationships, marriage, and
family life that women are now developing are designed to allow women
to have careers, not prohibit them; it was suggested that Elly might establish this sort of arrangement when the need arose. Alternate ways of caring
for Elly's mother were explored. The caseworker encouragd Elly to seek help
from a feminist therapist in the new city should severe stress occur again.

The following spring Elly returned for a visit, having completed the first
year of law school. She reported that she had made some new friends and
her mother was functioning well. Although she still had some anxiety about
her mother's health and her own capacity to cope with the pressures of law
school, she was planning to return for the second year and to work part-
time in a law firm.

SHEILA, age 37, had made a recent suicide gesture, which she readily
explained was meant to force her husband, Joe, to deal with dissatisfac-

tions she felt with their marriage but which he avoided. Although loyal, hardworking, and devoted to their four children, Joe had been uninvolved with her for a long time; he was focusing most of his time and energy on his job and the education he was acquiring for career development. Meanwhile, Sheila was left to deal with the often boring drudgery of household care and child rearing. Her self-worth diminished while her feelings of frustration and dissatisfaction rose.[17]

The worker and Sheila reviewed the factors in her life and in society that contributed to her present unhappy situation. For instance, her desire to become a teacher had been thwarted because her parents thought it more important to use their limited financial resources to send her brother to college. A job with the telephone company was the best she (and millions of other young women with high school education) could find. The boredom and dead-end nature of this job impelled her into marriage.

Sheila was reassured that she had valid reasons for her dissatisfaction, that these feelings were being experienced by millions of women in similar situations, and, most importantly, that they were not indicators of personal pathology. It was emphasized that she had a right and the ability to develop a different sort of life without feeling guilty and that she was not a failure as a wife and mother. She began to seek to improve her life through the resumption of her education and through changes in her relationship with Joe.

Sheila and Joe attended a religious retreat which so improved their relationship that she became pregnant. This posed a problem they both brought to the worker. Sheila did not want to have another child because of her fear of again having severe postpartum depression, because she had as many children as she wanted and could care for, and because having another child would delay her plans for new activities. Although Joe thought Sheila's reasons were valid, he was ambivalent about her wish to have an abortion; he feared they would somehow be punished for violating their religion's rules. Sheila insisted she had the right to decide what would happen to her body. The worker referred her to the local abortion clinic.

Later, Sheila reported that she had had the abortion, was sure she had made the right decision, and was optimistic about developing a more satisfying life. Their marriage appears to have been strengthened rather than undermined by Sheila's challenges to its status. It became a more equal relationship based on mutual respect rather than being held together through the coercion of tradition.

QUESTIONS FOR FURTHER STUDIES

Because most of the clients who come to Professional Services for Women, Inc., are young, well-educated, fee-paying, white women, the question might arise whether a feminist casework practice can be effective only with that limited segment of the population. A small number of clients having characteristics different from the majority—a few adolescents, men, black women, and some middle-aged women—do, however, come to the counseling service. This suggests that the approach can indeed have wide applicability.

Can a man be a feminist caseworker? Certainly men can apply feminist theory in their practices, but the important element of developing female pride would be diminished. More important, the critical factor of identification with the worker as a competent woman would be lost, as would other related aspects of relationship (e.g., trust), because the experiences of many women have given them reasons to distrust male professionals.

Can feminist casework be practiced within institutionalized casework settings, such as family service agencies, community mental health clinics, social welfare agencies? Basic theory and skills are consistent enough to permit this, but conflict might arise over feminist challenges to established social and religious beliefs regarding marriage, child rearing, role performance, and the like.[18] Also, a feminist is likely to have difficulty practicing in psychiatric settings that adhere to patriarchal psychiatric theory and patriarchal control of the management of the agency itself. In addition, the important element of female pride would be difficult to develop in traditional, male-dominated settings.

NOTES

1. Kate Millett, *Sexual Politics* (New York: Avon Books, 1971), pp. 23–58.

2. The Boston Women's Health Book Collective, Inc., *Our Bodies Ourselves* (New York: Simon & Schuster, 1973), p. 7.

3. Ibid.

4. Anica Vesel Mander and Anne Kent Rush, *Feminism as Therapy* (New York: Random House, and Berkeley, Calif.: The Bookworks, 1974), pp. 18–19.

5. Florence Hollis, *Casework: A Psychosocial Therapy* (New York: Random House, 1964), pp. 12–13.

6. Jo Freeman, "The Building of the Gilded Cage," in Anne Koedt et al., eds., *Notes from the Third Year: Women's Liberation* (New York: Notes from the Second Year, Inc., 1971), pp. 44–55.

7. Ibid., pp. 50–54.

8. Mander and Rush, op. cit., pp. 21–24, 39–43; and Phyllis Chesler, *Women and Madness* (Garden City, N.Y.: Doubleday & Co., 1972), pp. 58–113.

9. Gordon Hamilton, *Theory and Practice of Social Casework* (2d ed., rev.; New York and London: Columbia University Press, 1951), pp. 83–84.

10. Ibid., pp. 27–50; and Mander and Rush, op. cit., pp. 58–59.

11. Hollis, op. cit., p. 160.

12. Chesler, op. cit., pp. 106–108.

13. Mander and Rush, op. cit., p. 38.

14. Boston Women's Health Book Collective, op. cit., pp. 83–85.

15. Millett, op. cit.

16. *See* Pamela Allen, "Free Space," in Koedt et al., op. cit., pp. 93–98.

17. *See* Gabrielle Burton, *I'm Running Away from Home, But I'm Not Allowed to Cross the Street* (Pittsburgh: Know, Inc., 1972).

18. Freeman, op. cit., pp. 50–54.

Legal Skills for Social Workers

DONALD T. DICKSON

Social workers have traditionally used a variety of legal skills in their work. In direct service, they have used such legal skills as investigation, interviewing, interpretation of laws and regulations, and informal representation. Social workers in policy, planning, and administration have used a different order of legal skills, including legislative analysis, statutory and rule drafting and interpretation, and discretionary decision-making. In the last decade, however, both the range of legal skills needed and the opportunities for social workers to exercise them has increased dramatically. Through legislation and judicial action, due process protections and hearings have been extended to a number of individuals, many of them social welfare clients. Courts have showed an increasing willingness to intervene actively in the administration of human service organizations to insure that clients receive fair, humane, and adequate treatment. Individual rights and liberties, particularly when threatened by governmental or organizational action, are receiving increased protection.

Given these trends, social workers now and increasingly in the future will need to master legal skills if they are to provide effective service to clients. Moreover, in light of the social work code of professional ethics, mastery of these legal skills is more than desirable. It may be seen as a necessary part of social work education if social workers are to serve clients professionally.[1] The first provision of the Code of Ethics of the National Association of Social Workers requires social workers to regard the welfare of the individual or group served as their primary obligation; this includes taking action to improve social conditions. Other provisions call for a respect for the privacy of others, the mastery of professional knowledge and skill, support of professional education, and the responsibility for working toward the creation and maintenance of agency conditions that will facilitate the conduct of professional social work. These provisions, along with the requirement that social workers "master a body of knowledge and skill" for the "performance of a service with integrity and competence" can be seen as imposing an obligation on professional social workers to acquire a sufficient knowledge of law and a sufficient mastery of legal skills to perform service effectively.[2] To date, however, few attempts have been made to systematically develop, structure, and monitor social workers' use of legal skills—in spite of a longstanding recognition that a special relationship between law and social work exists.[3]

In this paper, some judicial and legislative trends through which law has substantially expanded its impact on social work and social welfare clientele are examined, with emphasis on the expansion of due process protections. Then the legal skills social workers need to develop are examined, and the implications of the development of legal skills for social work practice and human service organizations are discussed. Finally, the future of legal skills in social work are considered, and barriers to effective service and policy issues that must be resolved if these developments are to have lasting effect are discussed. It should be kept in mind that it is not argued that social workers should practice law or that only social workers can or should utilize legal skills in the settings described.

JUDICIAL AND LEGISLATIVE TRENDS

Through judicial and legislative action, the work of human service organizations and their relationship with social welfare clients have been altered substantially. Among areas now affected are clients' protection from arbitrary agency action, clients' right to have or not to have treatment, and the protection of individual rights. Courts and legislatures have been increasingly concerned with individual client rights, such as the right to privacy, the right of access to heretofore unavailable files, protection against self-incrimination, and the right to counsel at various stages of the criminal, juvenile, and mental health process. Awareness of and respect for these rights are particularly important for social workers who perform the conflicting roles of adviser, counselor, or therapist on the one hand and agent of the human service organization or the state on the other. For example, social workers in juvenile courts, probation offices, correctional and mental hospital facilities, and child abuse proceedings may be in conflicting roles because any information they receive or any conclusions they reach may become the basis for criminal charges or decisions to incarcerate or extend incarceration.

At the same time, there is increasing concern that human service organizations provide the services they purport to—particularly if the client is involuntarily confined—and that clients not be coerced into receiving them. To date, the U.S. Supreme Court has not decided whether a constitutional right to treatment exists, but a number of lower courts have reached this conclusion.[4] Equally important, under federal law prison and mental hospital officials may be held financially liable for punitive or compensatory damages resulting from violations of inmates' civil rights.[5] Issues regarding the right not to have treatment are less clear. The individual's right not to partake in group therapy, behavior modification programs, and psychosurgery, whatever the potential benefits, have been litigated.[6]

While social workers have an obligation to be informed of these legal issues and to provide advice, referrals, and action, perhaps the greatest need for social work education in law and for the effective use of legal skills lies in a third area: protection of the client from arbitrary action.

Through the Fifth and Fourteenth Amendments to the U.S. Constitution, individuals are entitled to "due process of law" before they can be deprived of life, liberty, or property by governmental action. In recent years, how much process is due and in what form have been extended by courts to a wide range of human service clients and organizations. Among the areas in which individuals are entitled to due process hearings and protections are the termination or reduction of welfare benefits, juvenile court proceedings, probation and parole revocations, prison disciplinary hearings, and high school suspension proceedings.[7] In addition, consumers facing repossession (in certain circumstances); public-housing tenants prior to a determination of ineligibility, eviction, or a raise in rent; and, in some jurisdictions, mental patients prior to involuntary commitment are all entitled to some form of due process hearings.[8]

Nor are the preceding the probable limits of due process proceedings. Among the cases now being litigated are those regarding the transfer of juveniles from open to maximum-security settings, the administrative transfer of state prisoners, the refusal to grant parole, the denial or reduction of social security or unemployment compensation, the denial of admission to a public hospital, and a patient's termination or transfer from a methadone maintenance program.[9] Thus due process protections have been expanded and probably will continue to be expanded. One significant limitation is that the deprivation of life, liberty, or property must result from governmental action. As a result, due process hearings have been denied in the termination of utility service and in private repossession actions against defaulting consumers.[10]

The Forms of Due Process

Three basic forms of due process proceedings have been required by courts. The choice of the form depends on a balancing of the potential injury or cost to the individual with the fiscal, administrative, or programmatic cost to the agency or state. Although variations exist, the three forms can be characterized as rudimentary, partial, and full due process proceedings.

Rudimentary due process proceedings provide minimal protection: an opportunity to know the charges and to be heard by an impartial body. A right to cross-examination and representation or assistance in case preparation may be allowed in special circumstances. Examples of this form are prison disciplinary hearings and high school suspension hearings, both of which are required because of recent Supreme Court decisions.[11]

Partial due process proceedings are administrative hearings. They may take place within an agency, but must be before an independent examiner. Proceedings are generally informal, with an opportunity for presentation of evidence and cross-examination and with representation by counsel or counsel-substitute permitted but not required. Welfare fair hearings, social security disability hearings, and parole revocation hearings are examples of this form.

Full due process hearings are essentially judicial hearings. They are more formal than the two other forms and are frequently held before a judge; counsel, appointed if necessary, represents the parties. Along with cross-examination and an opportunity to present evidence, there may be adherence to some rules of evidence and a right to a written opinion. Juvenile delinquency hearings and, in some jurisdictions, involuntary mental commitment hearings are examples.

LEGAL SKILLS SOCIAL WORKERS NEED

Social workers may have a role in any type of hearing and may represent clients or the agency or serve as impartial decision-makers. Along with a general knowledge of law, legal systems, and procedures, the legal skills social workers may need are investigation, interviewing, legal research, legal writing and preparation of case materials, informal and formal advocacy, and an understanding of discretionary decision-making.[12]

Perhaps the most difficult and sensitive skill areas are case preparation, advocacy, and discretionary decision-making because in these instances social workers and other human service workers are performing

essentially legal functions in agency settings. Complex issues, role conflicts, and ideological differences may increase the difficulties human
service workers face in these areas.

Case preparation may appear to be unexciting, but it is probably
among the most important of the skills mentioned. The combination of
gathering, winnowing, and ordering case materials (e.g., documents,
exhibits, testimony, and regulations) for formal or informal hearings is
a crucial legal skill. As in a legal brief, the case should be prepared so
that issues are clearly stated and explicated. Relevant statutes, rules, and
cases should be researched and evidence should be marshaled in support
of the client.

Advocacy may range from informal discussion or advice-giving to a
formal presentation of evidence, cross-examination of witnesses, and arguments based on law and fact in the client's, or the agency's, behalf.

Formal advocacy could include appearances with the client at welfare fair hearings, prison disciplinary hearings, or mental hospital commitment hearings, among others. In each, the social worker could take
an active role in arguing the client's case—either along with counsel or,
if counsel is not present, in lieu of counsel.

Discretion is the power to make individual judgments or decisions
that have not been predetermined by rules and regulations.[13] In formal
and informal hearings, there are two types of discretionary decisions:
those made by quasi-judicial officers (such as hearing examiners) and
those made by social workers representing the client or agency. Both
types of decisions require guidelines to limit the range of discretion;
monitoring to limit the abuse of discretion; protection from external or
agency influences; and knowledge of available alternatives and their consequences. In addition, quasi-judicial officers must be fair and impartial;
workers representing clients must be able to put the clients' interests ahead
of those of the worker or the agency.

Legal Skills in Human Service Organizations: Some Implications

The performance of representative, investigative, and quasi-judicial functions often results in a challenge to or review of agency actions. Whether
these take place within or outside of the agency, they have important
implications for the agency and for social work practice.

If the due process proceedings are to be effective, a more independent relationship between the client and the human service organization
will need to emerge—one in which the client no longer views himself as
powerless and subservient. Moreover, human service organizations will
have to establish rules and criteria governing the distribution of benefits

and services where none exist and will be forced to act less arbitrarily, more openly, and more speedily.

Several preconditions must be achieved, however, if proceedings are to be effective:

1. The social worker must be adequately trained and socialized in legal skills and thinking. If representing a client, he must be prepared to argue for the client and against the agency, even if he disagrees with the client's position. In magisterial roles, the social worker must make decisions independent of, and sometimes in conflict with, agency needs or policies. If representing the agency, the social workers must be prepared to argue the agency's case even if he agrees with the client.

2. The social worker's independence must be adequately protected and, when necessary, agency personnel must be socialized to tolerate dissent and challenge. Role-restructuring may be required to protect the social worker from external or agency influence and to facilitate effective performance.

3. Agencies must allocate sufficient personnel and financial and other resources to allow for effective proceedings. Agencies must encourage or provide necessary formal training in requisite legal skills.

4. Because past experience has shown that clients are often reluctant to challenge agency actions, agencies must take a more pro-active stance, searching for and encouraging meritorious cases. Active review of agency decisions—a legal skill in itself—is one possible approach.

5. Evaluation of effectiveness must be an ongoing process. This evaluation, perhaps through auditing case decisions, should encourage rather than deter experimentation in other forms of representation or other types of proceedings. To promote accountability, an adequate appeal system, possibly culminating in judicial review, should be established.

A LOOK TO THE FUTURE

Despite the many obvious benefits, the expanding legal impact on social welfare organizations and practitioners has costs and limitations. Attempts to protect individual rights are difficult to monitor and easy to subvert through discretionary behavior. The judicial review of agency programs tends to focus on measures of effort rather than effect. Due process hearings will not be effective unless cases meriting review are reviewed and unless there is adequate representation of client interests. Fundamental to all these concerns is the adequacy of training in legal skills, the structuring of situations to enhance their use, and the allocation of sufficient resources.

Finally, in that this paper has focused particularly on due process proceedings, it must be kept in mind that due process is not a panacea. It can insure a fair share of limited resources, treatment, or service, but it cannot increase or improve them. Moreover, the sheer potential volume of due process proceedings raises serious questions of their future effectiveness. In 1974 there were an estimated 59,000 welfare fair hearings and 94,000 requests for hearings. These included an estimated 38,000 Aid to Families with Dependent Children (AFDC) fair hearings, which comprised only 2 percent of the total 1.85 million unfavorable AFDC actions—reduction, termination, or denial of benefits—that could technically and, in many instances probably meritoriously be reviewed. In 1974 there were also 81,000 social security administrative hearings and 123,000 requests for hearings—a doubling in the number of hearings and a trebling in the number of requests within four years. In addition, as many as 10 percent of all high school students are suspended sometime during their career and, therefore, may qualify for a hearing.[14]

One outcome of these staggering statistics may be increased reliance on rudimentary hearings, making legal skill training for nonlawyers all the more important. Whether such mass justice is possible or desirable is a fundamental policy question, and the future will probably bring attempts at such other structures as ombudsmen or one-person informal tribunals. But whatever the changes may be, there is little doubt that social workers with legal skills will have an important role in them.

NOTES

1. A comparable point for psychiatrists is made by Saleem Shah in his foreword to Alan A. Stone, "Mental Health and Law: A System in Transition," *Crime and Delinquency Issues Monograph Series* (Rockville, Md.: National Institute of Mental Health, 1975). Prof. Paul Lerman of Rutgers University raised this issue with the author.

2. NASW Code of Ethics, adopted by the Delegate Assembly of the National Association of Social Workers, October 13, 1960, and amended April 11, 1967.

3. This relationship is discussed in detail in Charles I. Schottland, "The Law, the Courts and Social Policy," in the *Fifteenth Anniversary Conference Papers of the Florence Heller School*, Brandeis University, October 1974, pp. 13–26 (Mimeographed.) *See also* National Conference of Charities and Corrections, *Proceedings of the National Conference of Charities and Corrections, 1874–1880* (Boston: George H. Ellis); National Conference of Social Work, *Proceedings of the National Conference of Social Work, 1923–1933* (Chicago: University of Chicago);

and John Bradway, ed., "Law and Social Welfare," *Annals of the American Academy of Social and Political Science*, 145, Part 1 (1929), pp. 1–149.

4. In *O'Connor* v. *Donaldson*, 442 U.S. 563 (1975) the court sidestepped the right to treatment issue. Among important lower-court decisions are *Wyatt* v. *Stickney*, 344 F.Supp. 373 (1972), which held that there was such a right and set guidelines for the staffing, structure, and administration of a mental hospital system, and *Holt* v. *Sarver*, 309 F.Supp. 363 (1970), in which the court held the entire Arkansas prison system to be unconstitutional and mandated substantial change.

5. *See Sostre* v. *McGinnis*, 442 F.2d 178 (1971) and *O'Connor* v. *Donaldson*, op.cit.

6. *See Rouse* v. *Cameron*, 373 F.2d 461 (1966) (group therapy); and *Kaimowitz* v. *Dept. of Mental Health for the State of Michigan* (Cir. Ct. for Wayne County, Mich., 1973) (psychosurgery). *See also* Ralph K. Schwitzgebel, "Development and Regulation of Coercive Behavior Modification Techniques with Offenders," Crime and Delinquency Issues Monograph (Washington, D.C.: National Institutes of Mental Health, Center for Studies of Crime and Delinquency, 1971).

7. *See Goldberg* v. *Kelley*, 397 U.S. 254 (1970), regarding welfare; In Re Gault, 387 U.S. 1 (1967), regarding juvenile court; *Morrissey* v. *Brewer*, 408 U.S. 471 (1972), regarding probation; *Gagnon* v. *Scarpelli*, 411 U.S. 778 (1972), regarding parole; *Wolff* v. *McDonnell*, 94 S.Ct. 2963 (1974), regarding prison; and *Goss* v. *Lopez*, 42 L.Ed.2d 725 (1975), regarding high school.

8. *See* cases collected in Donald T. Dickson, "Law in Social Work: Impact of Due Process," *Social Work*, 21 (July 1976), pp. 274–278.

9. *See* ibid., especially those cases cited in n. 5.

10. *Jackson* v. *Metropolitan Edison*, U.S. Sup. Ct. (December 23, 1974); and *Mitchell* v. *W. T. Grant*, 42 U.S. *Law Weekly* 4671 (May 13, 1974).

11. *See Wolff* v. *McDonnell* and *Goss* v. *Lopez*, op. cit.

12. Some of these skills are discussed in detail in William Statsky, *Introduction to Paralegalism* (St. Paul, Minn.: West Publishing Co., 1974).

13. Generally, *see* Kenneth Culp Davis, *Discretionary Justice: A Preliminary Inquiry* (Urbana: University of Illinois Press, 1967).

14. *See* Social and Rehabilitation Service, National Center for Social Statistics, "Fair Hearings in Public Assistance" (Washington, D.C.: U.S. Department of Health, Education, and Welfare, January–June 1974; July–December 1974) (Mimeographed); and Henry J. Friendly, "Some Kind of Hearing," *University of Pennsylvania Law Review*, 123 (1975), n. 91.

Industrial Social Work

BRADLEY GOOGINS

Over the past several decades, a human service enterprise has begun to develop in a context somewhat outside the traditional field of social work. American business and industry have initiated a variety of human services—from alcoholism programs to employee assistance and counseling units. Although these programs are not usually found in large numbers or in a high priority within a company, they do represent a significant movement: industry's involvement in employee welfare.

This paper explores the challenge and opportunity for social work to apply its knowledge and skills in establishing and maintaining programs within the business and industrial sectors. The background against which it is written is the author's experience as project supervisor and instructor for the Industrial Alcoholism/Employee Assistance Training Program at the Boston College Graduate School of Social Work. Working with five businesses and industries in Massachusetts, the program is one of the first training programs in industrial social work in the country. It seeks to train graduate students in developing a solid base of experience and skills in establishing and delivering social services within the work environment. This program is intended to look ahead to the needs of companies over the next five to ten years.

In comparing social work in the work environment with social work in a more traditional setting, distinct differences emerge. Perhaps one of the more obvious, but relatively unexplored, differences is the emphasis on work. Freud refers to work as man's strongest tie to reality, and work itself provides basic social and economic satisfaction to individuals in most societies.[1] People spend more time at work and work-related activities than at any other single function, including sleep; without work serious emotional and social complications often develop. It is to this important facet of an individual's life that social work practice and theory need to relate.

Problems that occur within industry (e.g., alcoholism and marital, legal, financial, and emotional problems) are no different from those found in any social work agency. What is different is the nature of the presenting problem. In the work environment, the problem first appears as absenteeism, tardiness, inaccurate reports, an inability to work harmoniously with others, and so on. The job itself forms the environment for the problem, and the restoration to an acceptable level of job performance is the primary treatment goal. The underlying problem frequently involves marital difficulties, children in trouble, legal and financial difficulties, and other problems rooted outside the workplace. But their manifestation, or symptoms, can be detected in job performance. For successful resolution, the treatment choice must take into account both the work and the outside environment.

EMPLOYEE ASSISTANCE PROGRAM

One model of a social service program being utilized by business and industry is the Employee Assistance Program (EAP). It could be characterized as a program established to assist employees in the resolution of personal and social problems that have appeared as symptoms in deteriorating job performance. If an employee's problem surfaces through documented job deficiency, it falls within the realm of the EAP, whose sole criteria for identification, management, and treatment of the problem is job performance. The major assumptions underlying this concept are the following:

1. Unless job performance is impaired, a person's life or problem is his or her own.

2. Most human problems manifest themselves over time in job deterioration.

3. Because it is the role of supervisors within industry to monitor and evaluate job performance, they are able to identify deteriorating job performance without having to diagnose the nature of the underlying problem.

The EAP works with all levels of employees within a company to provide services that will assist troubled employees. The major components of the program are as follows:

1. A policy and set of procedures that outline the company's stance on managing and treating problems.

2. A training and education program for supervisors and employees on how problems should be managed, as well as an awareness of what the signs of problems are and what resources can be utilized, particularly the EAP itself.

3. An information and referral system that ties in community-based social services for the use of company employees.

4. An employee assistance unit that is responsible for carrying out and coordinating the above components as well as providing treatment to employees.

For the most part, EAPs are in an initial stage of development. The growing need for trained industrial social workers becomes apparent as one realizes that the majority of EAPs are staffed by personnel whose backgrounds lie in other fields. An example of this is the program of a large public utility; it is staffed by seven counselors, all of whom worked as repairmen before assuming the counseling roles. A recent publication of the U.S. Department of Health, Education, and Welfare addressed itself to the sets of occupational skills needed for such programs. After analyzing specific skills such as consulting, training, diagnosis and referral, and organizational skills, it concluded: "These skills are somewhat similar to those used in the specialty of industrial social work, a profession well recognized in Europe, but rarely included in professional social work training in the United States." [2]

SKILLS NEEDED

As the field of industrial social work emerges, the interplay between social work and industry sets the stage for a new set of skills. Transferring casework, group work, and organizing and planning skills from the traditional social welfare system into the workplace has not proved sufficient for developing effective programs. This does not negate the need for good practice skills, but recognizes that certain other skills must be used to build linkages between the needs of the troubled employee and any systematic assistance. As the industrial social work practitioner moves within the work environment, several skills must be called on, which are manifested in the roles of translator, outreach, negotiator, and consultant.

Translator

In the industrial and business world, human problems manifested through unsatisfactory job performance are often seen and dealt with within the disciplinary framework. The industrial social worker in the role of translator has the opportunity to assist others in looking at problems in a wider perspective. These efforts at translation bring the world of social work to the workplace in a way that benefits the employee.

The establishment of social services within a company offers an alternative to problem-solving, one that has its own concepts, assumptions, values, and ways of operating. This alternative has to be translated in many different ways if it is to be understood, accepted, and used. An employee who has had repeated absences and long periods of tardiness, for example, presents a distinct problem. Several alternatives can be constructed for dealing with this problem: It can be ignored, it can be disciplined, it can be dealt with as a symptom of an underlying cause, or it can be dealt with by a variety of the preceding alternatives.

For the EAP to become an effective mechanism, employees, supervisors, union stewards, and personnel staff have to understand and accept the approach and the program. The task of the industrial social worker is to effect this through a series of translations. How does the union steward, working with a union member manifesting problems on the job, recognize and operationalize the goals of the EAP? A supervisor who often finds an employee in fights with fellow employees seeks an appropriate solution. Does he fire the individual or does he see the problem as a symptom of underlying causes? An employee has a difficult time concentrating on her job and consequently, reports are not being done on time; her mind is on her daughter, who has a serious drug problem. Can she see the EAP as a resource for dealing with both her daughter's problem and her own anxiety?

The industrial social worker has to design translations of program policy, procedure, and philosophy to fit the range of employees if the EAP is to meet its objectives successfully. Much of this is done through training and education throughout the company on a regular basis. Another way is through being available at staff or department meetings. One more method is through the one-to-one relationship established over time, whereby the translation is concretized around a particular case or employee.

Outreach

Unlike a traditional social service agency within a community, the EAP is relatively new and is established within an entirely different type of community. Because the concept, the service, and the role of the social worker are not institutionalized, an aggressive outreach must be established to form both formal and informal lines between the program and the community. The role of outreach has several functions:

1. As in any community, the social worker must utilize his set of skills in understanding the community. This is particularly true in the community of the workplace, where the roles, patterns of behavior, values, and relationships are quite different from those in the geographic community. The social worker has to become familiar with what people do; how labor and management roles interact; what the formal and informal systems of authority and power are; and how problems are defined, perceived, and treated within the work environment.

2. Another function of outreach is that of selling the program. The

role of the salesman is not one usually found within the social work profession and is usually seen as crass and unprofessional. Perhaps by looking from another perspective, this role can be justified. Establishing a program is in a sense developing a product. The EAP's product is a set of skills that can be utilized in human problem-solving. How to get the client group aware of this product is the role of the salesman. He has something to offer (sell), and the client group (customer) may well have use (purchase) for this service (product).

3. The EAP is usually seen as a support service within the company, and thus its visibility is limited. The function of outreach is to sustain a high visibility so that the client population will be aware of its presence, its personnel, and its purpose. Many excellent social service programs have withered and died because potential recipients of the service were either unaware of its existence or misinformed as to its purpose.

The three functions just discussed are the primary rationale for a strong outreach role. The specific skills needed in implementing this role vary. Whereas "hanging around" may be an appropriate tool in the field of community organization, it becomes quite difficult to hang around in the workplace. The social worker, however, must take an active role in moving within the workplace, listening, finding out what employees do on the job, what problems they encounter, and how they presently deal with them. In addition, a visible effort to be seen at work sites, having coffee in the employee cafeteria, and asking supervisors or managers to lunch creates a positive relationship of trust and confidence. A systematic plan of outreach that permeates all levels of personnel will make utilization of the program more likely and at the same time will give the social worker a better picture of the dynamics of the work environment.

Negotiator

It is perhaps not surprising that negotiating is a needed skill for social workers within industry. The labor-management relationship existing within most work environments produces a natural series of contentions, and negotiating is a necessary skill. The social worker negotiates between union and management and between the management of the problem and the treatment of the problem. Because most EAP programs attempt to bring assistance to all levels of employees, the social worker attempts to maintain neutrality between labor and management. The realities of the workplace, however, frequently do involve the politics of labor-management affairs. Attempts to treat an employee with problems can get entangled in disciplinary procedures or action. Negotiation on the part of the social worker involves working with management and labor in clarifying the nature of the problem, that is, what is properly within the realm of disciplinary action and what is within the realm of treatment.

In examining a human problem within industry, a clear distinction must be made between the management and the treatment of the problem. The management relates to the supervisory function of monitoring and evaluating job performance. For example, a person who is consistently absent presents a problem to the supervisor, who in turn is responsible for managing this problem. In this case absenteeism must improve or additional management actions, such as warnings or termination, will follow.

The treatment of the problem addresses itself to the causes of the problem. For example, the person who is frequently absent may have an alcoholic spouse who is creating unbearable family problems. The social worker's role is primarily in the area of treatment: working with the employee manifesting job performance problems to get at the underlying factors that have brought about those problems. (In the example given, both the alcoholic spouse and the nonalcoholic spouse would be brought into a treatment plan.)

Because the management and treatment functions are not unrelated, the social worker often must intervene with both supervisors and unions to help negotiate a treatment perspective. In some instances supervisors, through frustration, push toward disciplinary action without offering treatment, thus treating the symptoms rather than the causes. In other situations union officials, in an attempt to protect their members and carry out their union roles, get caught up in arguing and pursuing job performance issues with management, ignoring the need for treatment. The social worker must work skillfully with both to insure a proper resolution that does not ignore the disciplinary actions but guarantees a treatment path for the employee.

Consultant

The social worker in industry should allocate a large amount of time for consulting with supervisors on how to deal with troubled employees. In consultation, the social worker helps the supervisor outline a course of action for an employee with problems. Together they decide whether job problems are symptoms of underlying problems that will keep occurring unless treatment is initiated. The social worker helps the supervisor understand the limits of his own intervention and insures support for him by higher level supervisors.

Supervisors play a critical role in any industrial program. They form a first-line detection system, where problems are usually first observed.

Supervisors are also in a position to refer troubled employees to the social worker because of their day-to-day relationship with and observation of employees. Any program that does not have good relationships with supervisors will not be able to effect a successful penetration of the troubled employee population.

The social work skills involved in the role of consultant are often a blend of knowing how the work environment operates and giving the right amount of support and encouragement to the supervisor in his difficult task. Consultation also establishes relationships with supervisors, thereby forming an important link to the treatment resources of the program. The social worker should actively market his availability in this role so that the first link in getting help to the employee can be realized. Another benefit lies in the nebulous area of prevention. Supervisors, through their consultation relationship with the social worker, will achieve a quicker referral to the EAP, thereby getting assistance to the troubled employee at an earlier stage. Through this process supervisors become "educated" to detect symptoms in other situations, thereby preventing problems from developing into crises.

IMPLICATIONS FOR SOCIAL WORK

Industrial social work represents a small part of social work practice. Over the past ten years, only scattered programs have been developed and there is little feedback on them to the profession.[3] An examination of recent experiences within business and industry reveals a definite role and challenge for the profession. The American Manufacturing Association estimates that some 2,000 companies have begun to establish some type of alcoholism program or EAP over recent years. Thus, while businesses are beginning to address themselves to human problems, social work has remained on the periphery of the movement. Although they possess the skills and knowledge needed to develop and operate effective programs, social workers for the most part have remained on the sidelines, viewing the challenge as either unrelated or unethical.[4]

Nevertheless, small beginnings are being made. And, as social work reaches out to employees in their environment through the development of programs and the linkage of social services, several implications for the profession become clear.

New Field of Practice

The working population represents a group relatively unserviced by the social work profession. The history of social work reveals only minor incursions into the industrial sector.[5] Models of practice are few, leaving a largely uncharted journey for the field. Unquestionably, the working population and the work environment constitute a need for service. As a field of practice, the challenge lies in developing appropriate sanctions and effective programs. Bridging the gap between the workplace and social services marks the overall objective for the industrial social worker.

New Set of Skills

A direct challenge to the profession is the "how" in establishing industrial programs. Although many social workers concur on the need and desirability of such programs, little has been done to pave the way. Because of the uniqueness of the work environment, social workers cannot simply rely on basic casework principles. Although these are greatly needed, they are but one facet in an overall program. Several of these skills have been addressed in this paper, but much more exploration and testing must occur. Basic questions have yet to be answered. How is a company or union best approached? Where should the program be located? How can social services outside the company be best utilized? What functions, in addition to counseling, can be performed? How can the service gap between management and unions be bridged? What kind of training is best suited for the social worker in industry?

Just as the profession has carved out practice areas in schools, corrections, and hospitals, so too must it face the challenge of the work environment by developing services and programs and the skills needed to become an effective resource within business and industry.

Linkages with the Existing Social Service System

If social work is going to make a significant step into the industrial world, it must consider more than its resources within the company. The range of problems found within any company will parallel those found in the community. Direct ties should be developed between the company program and the social services found in the community. This linkage between the functional community of the industry and the geographic community of social services allows for a comprehensive system of services. Many employees have problems not amenable to treatment at the work site. Others prefer to receive assistance in their own community rather than where they work. Well-developed lines between the industry and the social service system insure that the employee and the industry will receive the benefits of comprehensive quality care within the resources available.

Training Practitioners

A final implication for social work is that of training and education. If social work practice is to move into the industrial setting, an accompanying set of knowledge and skills must be developed and transmitted. Presently, only a few schools of social work throughout the country have courses and field placements where appropriate training can occur. Until these are developed, the profession risks the danger of moving into a field unprepared and with insufficient skills.

Training programs in the schools and through continuing education programs must be developed. At Boston College, for example, a course called "The Management and Treatment of Human Problems in Industry" has been developed within the Graduate School of Social Work. Such issues as labor-management roles, establishing sanctions and programs in the work environment, developing skills, and training the troubled employee are explored.

The promise for progress in industry is bright. But, as in any new undertaking, new methods of intervention must be developed. The opportunity lies with social workers and social work educators to translate this opportunity into programs and services for the employed population.

NOTES

1. *Civilization and Its Discontents* (London: Hogarth Press, 1953).

2. U.S. Department of Health, Education, and Welfare, Washington, D.C., *Alcohol and Health: New Knowledge*, preprint edition (Washington, D.C.: U.S. Government Printing Office, 1974), pp. 173–174.

3. Two of the more developed programs are those at the Polaroid Corporation in Cambridge, Massachusetts, and the Insight Program at Kennicott Copper Corporation in Salt Lake City, Utah.

4. Robert Jacobson, "Industrial Social Work in Context," *Social Work*, 19 (November 1974), pp. 655–656.

5. For a good review of this point, *see* Hyman Weiner et al., *The World of Work and Social Welfare Policy* (New York: Industrial Social Welfare Center, Columbia University School of Social Work, 1971).

Social Work in the Doctor's Office

BARBARA S. BROCKWAY, JUDITH WERKING,

KATHLEEN FITZGIBBONS, AND

WILLIAM BUTTERFIELD

Despite the profession's commitment to health-related issues, an analysis of the health care delivery system suggests that social workers are not operating where the bulk of health care is delivered—in the office-based practice of physicians.[1] The coverage of outpatient services by third-party payers has contributed to a shift in emphasis from hospital-based care to outpatient-based diagnosis, treatment, and preventive medicine. The growth of Health Maintenance Organizations in the private sector and the eminence of national health insurance reflect a potentially "healthy" trend toward comprehensive care, orchestrated by primary-care personnel, and away from fragmented care provided by various specialists.[2]

Conversely, most social workers who deliver health-related services appear to be institution- rather than office-(clinic) based.[3] An exception is the group of mental health professionals who provide ambulatory services. They are not usually located near the other health care agencies that provide services to the patient. A recent study estimated that only 10 percent of group medical practices in the country, including Health Maintenance Organizations, offer social services provided primarily by social workers.[4]

This paper describes the author's experience in instituting a problem-oriented, empirically based practice model for social work in three clinics attached to the University of Wisconsin and one private clinic. Social work services were already established at one university clinic, but not fully utilized; at the private clinic, the incorporation of social work services had been tried and abandoned. The experience highlighted the factors that may inhibit the movement of social work into the primary-care arena.

MOVING INTO PRIMARY CARE

Part of the failure to move into primary care is related to social workers' almost total reliance on skills grounded in psychodynamic theory. Although a legitimate theoretical framework, it is restrictive and inadequate for meeting the demands of practice in primary care.[5] Both physicians and patients at the clinics complained that this approach took too long to show measurable results. Physicians complained that it was too expensive and was broad based rather than problem oriented. Furthermore, they felt that the approach intimated pathology and suggested mental illness; it was therefore stigmatizing and, as such, an inappropriate construct for dealing with normal developmental problems in the population.

The second set of inhibiting factors was accountability and economics, a theme familiar to social workers and verbalized as "We don't know what you do and, whatever it is, it costs too much." To increase utilization and sell the program, the authors felt it imperative to (1) redefine the social worker's role as problem-solver, (2) educate the staff to accept a new social work model of practice, and (3) become economically self-supporting. The following are strategies that were used to implement these goals.

Role redefinition rested on the application of new intervention strategies developed in the last decade. As a demonstration to the staff, the authors sought out problems they knew could be resolved in a short time with a high probability of success, such as temper tantrums and psychogenic pain in children. Coincidentally, those same problems were complained about at high frequencies by patients and often frustrated the intervention efforts of the staff. Managing to effect rapid change in previously recalcitrant problems was a most effective strategy.

A less well-defined but essential factor in the role redefinition was the "professionalization" of the social worker's position. Physicians and nurses complained about workers who treated their position as "merely a job," meaning that they participated little in the problems of the clinic, stuck to 9:00 A.M. to 5:00 P.M. hours, and accepted no on-call responsibilities. Consequently, the authors tried to be highly visible and available to the staff, educating themselves about clinic problems and offering to help with resolutions. They arranged to see employed clients after regular office hours and placed themselves on night and weekend call. Finally, they recorded directly in the patient chart, using the problem-oriented approach adopted by the clinic.[6]

Such record-keeping, as it turned out, was a significant factor in shaping staff attitudes and in educating staff. Social workers, like psychiatrists, have traditionally kept separate process notes, which were unavailable to other medical staff. The problem-oriented record provided an excellent teaching tool because theoretical considerations could be outlined clearly and skills could be demonstrated through outcome data. As the staff saw demonstrable change, their interest in the authors' work increased. The authors took advantage of the interest to offer formal teaching seminars, supervise staff who wished to apply the strategies, and assist staff members in setting up treatment programs for themselves or their families.

The third strategy, to become self-supporting by charging fees, was not difficult to implement; but it takes about two years. It necessitates either that the clinic provide a base salary (independent of the number of patients seen or fees generated) or a willingness by the worker to endure one lean year. Because the worker is dependent on referrals, a planned demonstration/education phase is essential. In such a phase or trial period, the worker charges low or no fees, with the stipulation that the clinic provide a base salary after an initial demonstration of effectiveness. As referral rates rose, the fees rose accordingly until they were compatible with other health care charges. To remain viable, social work services eventually had to produce sufficient income to cover at least the worker's salary and fringe benefits.

SELECTION OF TREATMENT METHODS

Criteria for selecting treatment or intervention strategies were established. They had to demonstrate effectiveness, incur low delivery costs for the clinic and patients, be of limited duration, and be compatible with principles of scientific analysis.

The language of science is descriptive and operational, generating hypotheses that can be tested empirically. The data of science are observable, measurable, and ultimately manipulable. These characteristics combine to produce a systematic evaluation procedure for problem-solving: the process of hypothesis-testing. Through this process, presenting problems are conceptualized as dependent variables, with specified treatment techniques constituting the independent variables. The scientist sets an acceptable outcome level in advance, predicts which treatment will produce the desired effect, and then measures the results. Hypotheses themselves are assumptions intended to explain behavior and its controlling factors. This entire process is self-corrective. Unpredicted results force a reexamination of data and a reformulation of hypotheses; it also forces a reevaluation of the theory upon which the selected treatments were based.

When hypothesis-testing constitutes the social worker's evaluation procedure, there is a built-in guarantee that treatment methods will not persist simply because they are traditionally practiced. Rather, they will persist because they produce demonstrated effectiveness. In a sense, this process exposed accumulated practice wisdom to the light of scientific analysis.

Because of its conformity with the established selection criteria, treatment methods based on social learning theory (such as systematic desensitization, contingency contracting, behavioral rehearsal, and token economy) were ultimately chosen. Comparative research already completed on these methods strongly documents that effective outcomes can be achieved in relatively short periods, producing lasting gains with little or no iatrogenic effects.[7] Social learning holds that human behavior can be understood and explained by analyzing the current environmental factors that surround it. These include events that precede the behavior (antecedents), those that accompany it (parallels), and those that follow it (consequents); past events are important only as clues to similar present events. This is a radical departure from psychodynamic theory, which searches for the ultimate explanation of current behavior in past events.

Behavior itself is any human event that is observable and/or measurable. Covert events such as thoughts and emotions can be observed or measured through verbal statements (self-reports) or such physiological responses as pulse rate and galvanic skin response readings. Overt events such as crying can be seen and described by observers. Whether public or private, events are defined as behavior because they have a common denominator; each event is capable of operational description and empirical measurement. This characteristic exposes the event to the rigors of scientific analysis and hypothesis-testing.

BEHAVIOR ASSESSMENT

The behavior problem referred to the social worker is analyzed in two distinct but integrated testing phases. In the first phase, hypotheses concerning the nature of the disturbance (i.e., those environmental factors that currently maintain it) are tested. Data from this phase operationally describe the problem and indicate how it is under environmental control. In the second phase, the worker tests hypotheses about the most adequate treatment given data from phase one. The worker wants to know what treatment, given x problem with y environmental controllers, will be most effective in achieving a "cure."

The two phases correspond, respectively, to the processes of behavior assessment and treatment. Unlike psychiatric diagnosis, which generates differential pathologic labels that do not necessarily lead to differential treatment techniques, a behavioral assessment indicates specific interventions compatible and effective with specific problems.[8] Treatment plans, not psychiatric classifications, become the end product of the assessment process. As the key to treatment planning, accurate and comprehensive assessment is crucial to effective outcome. It is imperative that the worker approach assessment with scientific rigor.

Operationalizing Problem Behaviors

The assessment process begins by specifying the problem behavior in descriptive operational language. The term "depression," for example, is not a description. It is an abstract construct that summarizes a wide range of possible dysfunctions, including decreased sexual interest, suicidal wishes, indecisiveness, and loss of appetite.[9] The label "depression" gives the worker no specific information about a particular client's depressed behaviors. Describing depression in operational language may resemble the following: The client sits in his living room for extended periods, crying and refusing to participate in family activities; he is unable to sleep without medication; his conversations include high-frequency statements of self-blame and hopelessness.

Operationalizing abstract constructs like "depression," "anxiety," "social withdrawal," "sexual perversion," and "psychotic episodes" to expose their behavioral components has several advantages:

1. It individualizes the problem to the client. The term "depression" does not give any relevant information about the problems a *particular* client is experiencing. It only gives a range of possible problems that any client labeled "depressed" might experience.

2. It offers the first clue about who or what should be treated. A problem behavior is often a problem of labeling. Consider parents who label their son's creative attempts at dancing and dramatics as "homosexual." The reformulation of a problem into observable and measurable descriptions is essential to a decision about whether the person with the labeled problem or the labeler should be considered the client.

3. It supplies the data base for treatment. The worker can measure events that constitute the operational definition on several parameters. The most common are *duration, intensity, frequency,* or *situational appropriateness* of the problem behavior. How much time does Mr. Jones spend sitting alone? In how many different family activities does he participate? Where does he verbalize self-deprecatory statements? At home alone or in the middle of a busy downtown intersection? Each of these questions results in measurable data whose change in direction or location can be noted over the course of treatment.

4. It suggests possible treatment goals. The operationalized problem description is usually stated in negative terms. It suggests that opposite behavior is preferred. Mr. Jones probably wants to cry less, sleep without medication, and enjoy time spent with his family. An operational description, then, is the first step toward goal-setting between the worker and client.

5. It specifies the criteria of evaluation. Successful treatment will eventually be measured by how well the worker succeeds in helping the client increase, decrease, or eliminate the measured behaviors and/or acquire those specified as goal or target behaviors. "How well" in this context means data changes in the predicted direction.

Identifying Controlling Factors

Once the problem behaviors are operationalized, the worker begins to search through the range of antecedents and parallel and consequent events to identify controlling factors. Not all antecedent events will function as controlling stimuli; only those that tend to be consistently present prior to the behavior will. The latter can be conceptualized as environmental cues that set the stage for certain patterns of response. When they are present, the probability of the client performing the maladaptive behavior is high; when absent, the probability is low. Thoughts about difficult work assignments, criticism from a spouse, the death of a parent, or a sudden shift in life-style may trigger response patterns labeled "depressive." Similarly, drinking a cup of coffee, finishing a meal, picking up a telephone, or experiencing a sudden elevation in anxiety may elicit cigarette-smoking.

Manipulating Antecedent and Subsequent Events

The subsequent behavior can be affected by manipulating the antecedent events. It can also be changed by manipulating consequent events—those that follow the behavior. Again, by searching through the range of environmental events that follow the behavior, the worker can identify the controllers. They will appear with some consistency and will have one of two effects: Their presence will increase and strengthen the behavior or decrease and weaken it. For example, whenever John begins to cry and discuss his helpless feeling, his wife responds with empathy and physical affection; when Sally, age 4, has a temper tantrum, her dad usually spanks her. If John's crying and self-deprecatory statements increase or Sally's temper tantrums become more frequent, the worker assumes that the attention from wife as well as the spanks from father are functioning to reinforce the behavior. If they had the opposite effect, namely, if the crying and temper tantrums decreased after attention and spanking occurred, these consequent events would be labeled "punisher."

The importance of accurate, inference-free environmental observation is particularly striking during the assessment phase. The worker may be misled if possible reinforcers or punishers are identified by assumed qualitative characteristics. Despite the observed quality of pleasure (empathic attention) or pain (spanking), if the event increases the behavior, it is a reinforcer; if it decreases the behavior, it is a punisher. The reinforcing or punishing quality of the events can be determined only by noting their effect on the behavior. It is an unfortunate irony that clients often reinforce the very behaviors they wish to eliminate.[10]

The search for controlling variables is conducted jointly by the social worker and client. Information is collected by watching the client respond in a variety of settings, ranging from direct interview to simulated and natural-environment observations.[11] The client or a representative is taught to collect similar environmental information by periodically monitoring or counting the occurrences of the problem behavior and logging coterminous events.

CHOOSING AN INTERVENTION STRATEGY

It is in the assessment process that the client is first introduced to the social worker as teacher in a training context rather than therapist in a traditional treatment process. Once conceptualized in the form of response patterns, the problem and subsequent goal behavior are labeled as *skills* that must be learned or unlearned. They are not diagnosed as symptoms of unconscious conflicts. During assessment, the factors that inhibit or facilitate the client's learning process emerge. In a real sense, the task of the worker is to determine a client's prerequisites for learning and to adapt them to subsequent individualized teaching strategies. The intervention strategies of social learning theory are similar to instructional strategies used in classroom teaching.

Intervention strategies fall into four general areas:

1. Those that establish a new behavior pattern
2. Those that increase or strengthen an established behavior
3. Those that reduce or weaken an established behavior
4. Those that eliminate a behavior

Data from the assessment determine which one or which combination of strategies should be used. The specific strategies attached to each area have been described adequately elsewhere. Each has been well researched and documented for effectiveness.[12]

In their professional concern to alleviate personal, family, or social distress, practitioners all too frequently hurry to use procedures without thorough assessment. This rush to provide cures often blinds them to the real pursuit of a clinical scientist: the search for causes and explanations of individual and social behavior. Once discovered, these usually point toward effective curative procedures. The most difficult task of a social worker following a social learning theory model of practice is to develop an accurate and comprehensive assessment of the environmental events that control the problem behavior. Because assessment is such an important aspect of professional efforts, the authors chose to emphasize it in this discussion rather than treatment strategies. Treatment strategies are only as effective as the assessment is accurate.

In their combined practices, the authors have treated presenting problems ranging from the more common, like thumb-sucking, eating disorders, temper tantrums, marital conflicts, and sexual dysfunctioning, to the exotic, like femeral anteversion (forward turning of the thigh bone), torticollis (muscle spasm in the neck), and anorexia nervosa (refusal to eat food); the last three are conditions we hardly knew existed during our graduate training days, much less were told we could treat.[13] While most of our treatment directly helps the client, some also directly aids the physicians. For example, some patients fear needles or do not take prescribed medication consistently. Adequate medical treatment may depend on the social worker's ability to rearrange environmental contingencies to produce the behaviors more compatible with effective patient care.

VIABILITY OF THE PRACTICE MODEL

Although all our cases do not end in outstanding success, the majority do. In one clinic—the Counseling Unit of the University of Wisconsin Family Health Service—the following outcome data were recorded for the seven-month period ending June 1975: Out of the forty-four cases reported, 85 percent were treated successfully as measured by achievement of the targeted goals; the remaining 15 percent were labeled failures. Only 5 percent of the failures, however, were attributed to ineffective treatment strategies; 10 percent of the clients had not implemented their treatment programs as designed.

It has been implied that social work services in the physician's office can be self-supporting. The authors have found that the income derived from fees can be substantial. For example, a six-week examination of the income and expenses of the social work service at one of the clinics yielded the following annual income projections:

Income:	$30,028.00	Based on 27.2 patient contact hours per week times $24 times 46 weeks
Expenses:	$12,800.00	Social Worker's Salary
	1,920.00	Fringe Benefits
	2,000.00	Overhead Costs
	$16,720.00	Subtotal
Net Profit:	$13,308.00	

As Hookey points out, the income generated by a social worker does not compare favorably with income generated by a physician occupying the same office space.[14] Adding another physician to a practice might give all the physicians more time to offer comprehensive care, including intervention in psychosocial problems, or the patient might merely get more of the same treatment. Unless a physician is specially trained, he or she does not have the skills comparable to those of a well-trained social worker and is probably unable to do more than offer support and give advice regarding psychosocial problems.

The utilization of the authors' practice model provides evidence of viability. Of the four clinics, only one (the Dean Clinic, a private group practice) had a medical staff large enough and stable enough to warrant a comparison of initial levels of utilization with levels two years later. In that clinic the program began with two pediatricians referring. Two years later, all the pediatricians (eight), as well as ear, nose, and throat specialists, internists, and neurologists, were referring. Referrals from other clinic staff (dietician and nurses), referrals from patients, and referrals from community agencies and practitioners were being received at high rates. In the third year of practice, a part-time social worker was added to the staff to handle the increase.

The programs in all four clinics have persisted and grown, even when the originators left. This is strong evidence that the success of the programs is not dependent on personal relationships; rather, it depends on the value of the programs to primary-care practitioners. The crucial factors have been that patients value the social work service and are willing to pay for it and that the physicians are willing to refer and assist in development. The physicians have been instrumental in negotiations with third-party payers, including the major insurer in the state and a Blue Cross-sponsored Health Maintenance Organization, both of whom now cover the social work services.

Replication lends further evidence of the practice model's viability. Three physicians in private practice are actively developing similar services in their practices. Other have indicated an interest if suitable workers can be hired.

PREREQUISITES AND STRATEGIES
FOR REPLICATION

For the social worker who wishes to replicate the practice model, several prerequisites and strategies can be recommended. The significance of assessment and treatment skills should be apparent. But the necessity for grounding them on empirical data, whatever the theoretical orientation, must be reemphasized. The social worker as solo practitioner operates without supervision, often in isolation from peers who can act as consultants.[15] This necessitates a capacity for self-education in medicine as well as social work practice. In a primary-care setting, the team concept may exist only as a group of professionals serving the same patient, each providing input in respective areas of expertise. Previously untreated problems are certain to arise, and the theoretical framework becomes the only basis for accurate assessment and treatment. It, in effect, functions as the supervisor.

Once armed with the prerequisites, three strategies can be suggested. First, survey the community to identify receptive physicians. Family practitioners, pediatricians, and general internists are usually the most likely candidates. Pediatricians, for example, point out that 60–80 percent of their practice is well-child care, which includes a significant incidence of nonmedical problems. Second, establish credibility. This can be done in the following ways:

1. Present a problem or set of problems at grand rounds in a local hospital or at a clinic meeting that has high priority for the physicians. Document with data the ability to treat problems of high nuisance value or social concern.

2. Submit a written proposal of the model to possibly interested physicians.

3. Seek out a well-respected member of the medical community who might act as an advocate.

Third, build a support system to prevent professional isolation. The social worker employed at the private clinic, for example, accomplished this by establishing a social work field unit. She also served as an in-service trainer for various community agencies and university programs.

Health care is the largest service sector in the United States and is certainly an area of great concern. A planned intervention at the grass-roots level can have a strong impact on the health care system, and in health care the grass is rooted in the physician's office or clinic. Social workers who have the skills outlined in this paper can function as influential advocates for the delivery of comprehensive health care services. Their influence can be exerted by virtue of their documented

success as practitioners. Few schools of social work, however, have programs that provide students with the skills needed to initiate this style
of practice. If social work is to make a major impact in health delivery,
schools of social work must begin to train social workers in a problem-
oriented, empirically based practice model.

NOTES

1. According to the American Medical Association, the major professional
activity of 292,302 physicians is patient care. Of that number, 201,302 are in
office-based practice and 49,931 are in hospital-based practice; 47,931 of those
in office-based practice (excluding general practitioners) are in medical specialties—24,954 in internal medicine and 11,433 in pediatrics. Obstetrics/gynecology,
which is considered a surgical specialty, claimed 14,735 members in office practice.
See G. A. Roback, ed., *Distribution of Physicians in the United States: 1972,* Vol.
1 (Chicago: American Medical Association Center for Health Service Research
and Development, 1973), p. 21. These data and the authors' experience indicate
that general practitioners, pediatricians, general internists, and obstetricians/
gynecologists deliver the bulk of primary care. *The Supply of Health Manpower:
1970 Profiles and Projections to 1990* (Washington, D.C.: U.S. Government Printing Office, December 1974), p. 27, reports that the direct care of patients was
the primary activity of 90 percent of the active physicians; two-thirds were in
office-based practice, and slightly less than one-third were in hospital-based practice.

2. Marc F. Hansen, "An Educational Program for Primary Care: Definitions
and Hypotheses," *Journal of Medical Education,* 45 (December 1970), pp. 1001–
1015, presents a good description of a health care system and defines its component parts and its terminology. The conceptual model of the primary-care practice
the authors helped to develop is also described. Richard M. Magraw, "Trends in
Medical Education and Health Services: Implications for a Career in Family
Medicine," *New England Journal of Medicine,* 285 (December 16, 1971), pp.
1407–1413, points up trends toward primary care and factors influencing development or inhibition. Magraw concludes that programs require strong advocacy.
Hans O. Mauksch, "A Social Science Basis for Conceptualizing Family Health,"
Social Science and Medicine, 8 (September 1974), pp. 521–528, gives a good
description of the developing "nonorgan/nondisease"-related medical specialty
that incorporates field theory instead of relying on a cause–effect model. Sidney R.
Garfield, "Prevention of Dissipation of Health Services Resources," *Journal of
Public Health,* 61 (August 1971), pp. 1499–1506, discusses the Kaiser-Permanente
prepaid group plan and model of regulating the flow of patients into primary-care
services so that resources are used appropriately.

3. Few meaningful statistics that estimate the number of social workers employed in nonpsychiatric medical settings exists, which is good evidence for this point. The February 1975 statistics from the Manpower Data Bank of the National Association of Social Workers (NASW) list 16.1 percent of its membership as being in "health," 14.4 percent in "mental health"; there is no breakdown on ambulatory versus institutional setting. Biomedical Technology Information Service, *Health Care Statistics Report*, 2 (February 28, 1975), p. 8, lists 29,500 social workers and 4,300 social work assistants practicing in medical and psychiatric settings. Neil F. Bracht, "Health Care: The Largest Human Service System," *Social Work*, 19 (September 1975), p. 338, reports on NASW statistics which show that nearly one-third of its members practice in the health field. Bracht questions whether social workers who charge professional fees and cover their costs can be employed in ambulatory settings. U.S. Department of Health, Education, and Welfare, Health Resources Administration, *Health Resources Statistics: Health Manpower and Health Facilities* (Rockville, Md.: National Center for Health Statistics), p. 238, reports that 190,000 social workers were employed in social welfare settings in 1972. Of these 29,500 were in health and related programs, with 20,000 in psychiatric settings and 9,500 in medical settings.

4. P. G. Hookey, "Quantitative and Economic Aspects of Social Work in Primary Health Care Settings." Paper presented at the annual meeting of the Society of Teachers of Family Medicine, Washington, D.C., November 1975. *See also* Caroline J. Hobson and W. Grayburn Davis, "Social Work in Group Medical Practice," *Group Practice*, 18 (June 1969), p. 25: ". . . at least 14 multispecialty medical clinics . . . have social workers on their staffs." This article describes one such clinic.

5. *See* Bess Dana, "Social Work in the University Medical System," *Johns Hopkins Medical Journal*, 124 (May 1969), pp. 277–282, for a discussion of changing needs and changing roles, with suggestions for program conceptualization. *See also* Bernice Harper, "Social Work in Health Programs: A Look Ahead," in Laura Bertino and Robert C. Jackson, eds., *Social Workers as Trainers in Public Health Programs* (Berkeley: University of California, Program in Public Health Social Work, 1972), pp. 1–11. Harper contends that social workers need a more thorough grounding in the relationship between the host environment and the resultant development or exacerbation of disease; she proposes that an organization to promote and study community-based medical care be established. For discussion of interteam problems, *see* Bess Dana and Kurt W. Deuschle, "An Agenda for the Future of Interprofessionalism," pp. 77–88; Alfred J. Kahn, "Institutional Constraints in Interprofessional Practice," pp. 14–25; and Jeanette Regensberg, "A Venture in Interprofessional Discussion," pp. 35–73, in Helen Rehr, ed., *Medicine and Social Work: An Exploration in Interprofessionalism* (New York: Prodist for Mt. Sinai Medical Center, 1974).

6. *See* Lawrence L. Weed, *Medical Records, Medical Education and Patient Care* (Cleveland, Ohio: Case Western Reserve University Press, 1971) ; and

Rosalie A. Kane, "Look to the Record," *Social Work*, 19 (June 1974), pp. 412–419.

7. Richard B. Stuart, *Trick or Treatment: How and When Psychotherapy Fails* (Champaign, Ill.: Research Press, 1970).

8. P. Meehl, "Some Ruminations on the Validation of Clinical Procedures," *Canadian Journal of Psychology*, 13 (1959), pp. 102–128.

9. Aaron Beck, *The Diagnosis and Management of Depression* (Philadelphia: University of Pennsylvania Press, 1973).

10. For a more extensive discussion of social learning theory, *see* Albert Bandura, *Principles of Behavior Modification* (New York: Holt, Rinehart & Winston, 1969); William Butterfield, "Behavior Modification: 1. Counterconditioning Techniques" and "Behavior Modification: 2. Changing Behavior by Modifying Its Consequences," *Update International* (February and March 1974), pp. 91–93, 167–170; L. Keith Miller, *Principles of Everyday Behavior Analysis* (Monterey, Calif.: Wadsworth Publishing Co., 1975); and D. L. Whaley and R. W. Malott, *Elementary Principles of Behavior* (New York: Meredith Press, 1971).

11. Paul McReynolds, ed., *Advances in Psychological Assessment*, Vol. 3 (San Francisco: Jossey-Bass, 1973).

12. Michael J. Mahoney and Carl E. Thoresen, *Self-Control: Power to the Person* (Monterey, Calif.: Wadsworth Publishing Co., 1974); K. D. O'Leary and G. T. Wilson, *Behavior Therapy: Application and Outcome* (Englewood Cliffs, N.J.: Prentice-Hall, 1975); and D. C. Rimm and J. C. Masters, *Behavior Therapy: Techniques and Experimental Findings* (New York: Academic Press, 1974). Although treatment strategies in this paper have focused on casework, social learning theory and its corresponding intervention strategies can serve as a model for practice in all areas of social work. *See* Edwin J. Thomas, ed., *The Socio-Behavioral Approach and Applications to Social Work* (New York: Council on Social Work Education, 1967); and John Kunkel, *Behavior, Social Problems and Change: A Social Learning Approach* (Englewood Cliffs, N.J.: Prentice-Hall, 1975).

13. In regard to eating disorders, *see* William Butterfield and Ronald R. Parsons, "Modeling and Shaping by Parents to Develop Chewing Behavior in Their Retarded Child," *Journal of Behavior Therapy & Experimental Psychiatry*, 4 (September 1973), pp. 285–287; in regard to temper tantrums, *see* Barbara Brockway, *Training in Child Management: A Family Approach* (Dubuque, Iowa: Kendall/Hunt Publishing Co., 1974); *see also* Judi Werking and Marc Hansen, "Clinical Applications of Learning Theory: Femoral Anteversion." Paper presented at the fiftieth annual meeting of the Ambulatory Pediatric Association, Toronto, Canada, June 1975.

14. P. G. Hookey, "The Economic Viability of Social Work in Group Medical Practice." Paper presented before the Conference on Social Workers in Family Medical Settings, Rochester, N.Y., October 1974.

15. *See* Laura Epstein, "Is Autonomous Practice Possible?" *Social Work*, 18 (March 1973), pp. 5–12, for a discussion of models of supervision.

Group Work and Peer Counseling in the Gay Community

MICHAEL B. SCHWARTZ

Social work and the other mental health professions are in the midst of a revolutionary change in perspective regarding the treatment of homosexuals. The view that homosexuality is symptomatic of pathological processes is being challenged and, with it, the view that homosexuals should be "treated" to alter their sexual preference. Instead, prevailing professional opinion seems to be moving toward the view that homosexuals, like heterosexuals, constitute a mixed group of both well and poorly adjusted individuals of whom only a minority require psychotherapy. In fact, a significant proportion of the mental suffering of homosexuals is now believed by many to be attributable to the prevailing public attitude of revulsion and hostility toward them, which is codified in criminal law and institutionalized in discriminatory practices in employment, housing, law enforcements, and other areas. Indeed, it may be argued that proponents of the pathological view may well have been contributing to the suffering of those they were attempting to help by providing the lay public with an easy rationalization for their discrimination against and rejection of homosexuals.

This new perspective seems to be giving rise to a new philosophy in the treatment of homosexuals. The homosexual patient is being helped to make a better adjustment *within* his sexual preference. The recognition that the proportion of disturbed homosexuals may not be greater than the proportion of disturbed individuals in the general population and that homosexuals have certain problems in common arising from their status as a rejected minority is stimulating considerable experimentation. The Homosexual Community Counseling Center and the Institute for Human Identity, both in New York City, are two novel programs that have evolved. These programs attempt to provide competent psychotherapeutic service without heterosexual bias to members of the gay community.

ORIGINS OF THE GAY PROGRAMS

The Gay Peer Counseling and Gay Rap Group programs represent an attempt to meet some of the developmental and social needs of a small group of homosexuals through use of the social group work method developed within the social work profession. The programs were developed under the auspices of the University Counseling Center (UCC) at Florida State University in Tallahassee, Florida (population 100,000). Before describing these programs, it is helpful to list the key elements that distinguish social group work from group psychotherapy:

1. In addition to addressing itself to the psychological maturation of the individual, social group work also attempts to engender *social* maturity by educating the individual to function democratically within a group and within the community.

2. Social group work provides a mechanism by which individuals may combine to help themselves by changing their environment.

3. Social group work is not confined to work with individuals suffering from mental or emotional problems.

4. Since its inception in the 1920s, social group work has given the same importance to the ultimate goal of attaining a more democratic society through teaching people to function democratically within the small group that the mental health professions in general have given to the goal of mental health.

These principles of social group work seem to be especially well suited to social work within the homosexual community, where mental health is no longer the major concern, where there is considerable need for peer support and mutual assistance, and where basic human rights in a democratic society are a major issue.

The Gay Peer Counseling and Gay Rap Group programs were stimulated in part by a small group of students who were members of the Gay Liberation Front. Approximately one year prior to the beginning of the gay programs in October 1973, several of these students initiated a series of meetings with the staff of the UCC. At the meetings, they presented a number of pointed questions regarding the treatment of gay students who applied for counseling. Some of these questions involved the willingness of counselors to accept homosexual clients who wanted help on their own terms in functioning better as homosexuals. Others involved counseling that might be given to a "closet case," an individual who had not acknowledged either to himself or others the real nature of his sexual preferences. In general, the students communicated to the UCC staff the sincere interest of the organized gay community in modifying existing programs and creating new ones to meet their specific needs; no specific proposals were made, however.

For the ensuing year, there was little action on this matter by the UCC and some loss of momentum on the part of the Gay Liberation Front. The author reestablished contact between the UCC and the gay community by joining with an anthropology instructor and a doctoral candidate who were leading a gay discussion group on the campus of Florida University. Eventually, this group formed the nucleus of the new gay rap group and a group of gay peer counselors.

STRUCTURE OF THE GAY PROGRAMS

The structure of the gay programs has evolved from the dual initial interests of its members in maintaining both a gay rap group and a gay peer counseling service. The program is open to all members of the community—not just university students and faculty. An individual may refer himself or herself after hearing about the program through local radio or television interviews or through advertisements in the "personal" column of the university newspaper. Or, he or she may be referred by community mental health professionals. The program coordinator (the author, originally) generally interviews each applicant briefly to determine needs and to assign the applicant to one or more roles within the program. One of the important reasons for this initial professional screening is the reluctance of peer counselors and Gay Rap Group members thus far to have contact with individuals whose needs and interests have not first been evaluated professionally.

In the screening session, the individual is given a choice to participate in any one or more of three roles: (1) recipient of one-to-one gay peer counseling, (2) member of the Gay Rap Group, or (3) gay peer counselor-intraining. Each of these roles is explained, and the individual is given the opportunity to choose and discuss his choice of role. In general, this self-selection process has worked well; it has not yet been necessary to suggest that anyone has made an inappropriate decision.

Initially, the Gay Peer Counseling training meeting and the Gay Rap Group were combined in a 2½-hour weekly meeting. It seemed consistent with the democratic philosophy of the program that the counselor-counselee roles be interchangeable. A number of the Gay Rap Group members who were not also gay peer counselors felt, however, that too much of the group's time was spent discussing the individual cases of the gay peer counselors and that confidentiality (a complex problem in any such program) was being compromised. Therefore it was decided to hold the Gay Peer Counseling training meeting just prior to the Gay Rap Group, in which all the gay peer counselors also participate.

In the first twelve months of the program, fifteen individuals participated in training as gay peer counselors. About two-thirds of that number have continued long enough in their training (at least six weeks) to be assigned counselees. Fifty individuals have received counseling so far. Approximately two hundred individuals have attended Gay Rap Group sessions.

THE GAY RAP GROUP

The Gay Rap Group has been conducted on the basis of giving maximum responsibility for its direction to the group members themselves, with interventions aimed primarily at encouraging the process of democratic decision-making. Thus the group has had relatively little structure imposed by its coordinator and has evolved through several critical periods.

There have been periods of intense longing on the part of many group members for greater intimacy and sharing of deep-seated feelings and concerns. These periods have provided an opportunity for many group members to express their sense of alienation and isolation from the straight world and some of their frustration at the failure of the local gay community to provide an adequate alternative. For example, glowing accounts have been given of the complexity and sophistication of the gay subculture in large cities.

A period of intense longing is often followed by a period in which there is considerable expression of feelings and open accounts of some of the relationship problems of individual members. When these problems are related to the member's relative inexperience within the gay subculture, the group often gives considerable support and helpful advice. When the nature of the problem is common to most homosexuals, however, the trend of the discussion is often toward intellectualization. Topics that tend to recur in the Gay Rap Group are these:

1. The relative paucity of social life in the local gay community
2. The possibilities of long-term homosexual relationships being successful
3. Homosexual promiscuity
4. Problems regarding parents' and relatives' knowledge of one's homosexuality
5. Whether it is possible for someone to be truly bisexual and suspicion of bisexuals by exclusive homosexuals
6. Problems related to selecting a career and finding and keeping a job
7. Discrimination against homosexuals by the dominant culture.

When these and similar concerns are raised, the group often enters into a discussion of the possibility (versus the futility) of various courses of social action it could take. Such a dialogue often brings to the surface much of the deep-seated fear, resignation, and fatalism that many, especially the older, homosexuals feel toward the prospects for effective collective social action in a small southern city. Nevertheless, the group has been able to participate in various efforts at social action, for example, planning and conducting a number of social events, planning and participating in a local television interview program that devoted forty minutes to homosexuality and the gay programs, and attempting to integrate a straight lounge.

Alternating with periods of sharing deep feelings and of making self-disclosures have been periods of relative superficiality. During these periods, members discuss less emotionally laden material (e.g., films, literature, and research findings involving homosexuality), exchange mutually useful information, and tell humorous stories. These periods of mutual supportiveness have facilitated cohesiveness in the group.

The Gay Rap Group has served a number of functions within the small local homosexual community, not all of them anticipated. Partly because it has always accepted new members, it has served as a point of socialization within the gay community. For example, individuals from out of town occasionally use the group as their first point of contact with the gay community. The group has also been used as a vehicle for communication, as when individuals wish to make known the beginning or ending of relationships or when an individual seeking a roommate with a similar sexual orientation (though not for sex itself). It is also quite likely that several individuals who become sexually involved first met through the Gay Rap Group.

One problem has developed out of the fact that the group has always remained open to new members. Many newcomers have not remained with the group for more than a few sessions, which has tended to create a schism between the "regulars," many of whom have been with the group since its inception, and the newer members. The regulars have tended to feel somewhat inhibited in being open and making self-disclosures in the presence of a shifting membership. They have partially resolved this problem by impressing on newer members the confidentiality that is expected of them.

All in all, it is believed that the experience of mutually sharing has strengthened the group's and its members' abilities to function socially. The Gay Rap Group has provided a kind of refuge for homosexuals from the stresses of the straight world and, incidentally, of the small homosexual community itself.

GAY PEER COUNSELING

The gay peer counselors comprise a subgroup of individuals who both attend the Gay Rap Group regularly and make themselves available for consultation. They are available to individuals who seek to learn more about homosexuality, to university classes in the social sciences, and to various community groups. The philosophy underlying the Gay Peer Counseling program is based on the recognition that much of the stress which homosexuals encounter is related to their membership in a rejected subculture. Rather than providing psychotherapeutically oriented counseling, the gay peer counselor shares the kind of subculture-specific social skills and knowledge that are required to be able to function within an occult and outcast social group. Some of the specific issues and questions with which the peer counselors have been dealing —in both their counseling and consultation roles—are the following:

1. How one comes to decide that he is homosexual. This is an extremely complex issue, and the answer is probably different for different individuals. The peer counselor is probably able to be of greatest help by sharing his own experiences and those of other homosexuals he has known well.

2. How one can look more deeply into the nature and origins of one's sexual orientation. The program emphasizes that it does not attempt to provide a substitute for professional counseling and psychotherapy in this area.

3. How one establishes contact with other homosexuals. Although the program does not attempt to provide social contacts, the peer counselor describes as candidly as possible how other homosexuals go about making contact with each other.

4. Whether the peer counselor is available for sex with the counselee. Surprisingly, this a recurrent question and is probably based on the naive assumption made by those unfamiliar with the gay subculture that any avowed homosexual is always available for sex with anyone. Counselor-counselee sex is not permitted.

5. Whether, if the individual has engaged in a small number of homosexual contacts, he is destined to become exclusively homosexual if he fails to suppress his homosexual impulses.

6. How homosexuals can prudently control the flow of public information about their sexual orientation. This relates to the whole question of coming out, or sharing knowledge of one's homosexuality with other homosexuals, close friends who are straight, relatives, business associates, and so forth.

7. Which factors determine how successful and popular one will be within the homosexual community.

8. What the various cliques are within the homosexual community. Many of these questions call for the kind of information best supplied by an individual who has had personal experience.

Training

The gay peer counselors meet weekly with the program coordinator for training and discussion of cases. The training has been a two-way process. The peer counselors contribute to the program coordinator's knowledge of the homosexual community, while he attempts to provide rudimentary training in principles of interviewing, establishing a helping relationship, and making effective referrals. Because of the relatively small number of counselors in the group, it has been possible to gear training to the individual needs of each. Because of the familiarity of the counselors with the homosexual community, it has been possible to involve them fairly promptly in direct work with clients; it has also been possible to use their reports of this work as a basis for further training rather than present them with a long, formal course which attempts to anticipate situations that could arise.

This *in vivo* training has several other advantages. It provides for continuous feedback to the coordinator of information about the needs of the target population. It reduces the anxiety of the trainees by providing early successful experience in a previously unfamiliar activity. The reality of the clients' needs and of the helping relationship seems to make a more lasting impact on the trainee. The coordinator is afforded the opportunity to individualize each client–counselor relationship, while also using it to illustrate various principles to the group.

Clients

The types of clients who have availed themselves of the Gay Peer Counseling Services are easily divided into two major categories. The first group is comprised of individuals who have sought counseling in relation to some aspect of the coming-out process. This ranges from individuals who are in conflict about even giving serious consideration to adopting a bisexual or homosexual identity to those individuals who have decided to do so and require only the means to become assimilated. Of those individuals who have been undecided about their sexual identity, approximately half have decided in the course of their counseling *not* to come out. Among the half who have come out to some extent, their decisions seem to be the result of a lengthy process that has lasted several years and culminates in their counseling experience.

The peer counselors are cautious not to proselytize for the homosexual life-style but, instead, to present a candid, balanced picture of its burdens as well as its pleasures. Nevertheless, even if the peer counselors were to be somewhat biased in favor of homosexuality, their influence could only be minute in view of the predominantly proheterosexual and antihomosexual conditioning of the dominant culture that is the experience of most individuals.

The second major group is comprised of individuals who have already chosen a primarily homosexual adjustment and have already established some identification with the gay subculture but are having difficulty functioning in some major social role (e.g., career or family). Some of these individuals have had a long history of institutional psychiatric management and/or have been withdrawn and isolated, not only from the straight world but also from the functioning homosexual world. Casual homosexual contacts may constitute the closest affectional ties that they possess the strength to tolerate. In such cases, the ongoing relationship with the gay peer counselor can serve as a link with reality and as a source of real acceptance in the face of the individual's double stigma as homosexual and mental patient. In these cases, the peer counselor works with the program coordinator to make appropriate referrals to the Gay Peer Group, to the UCC for psychotherapy, or to agencies outside the university.

It became evident in the course of individual peer interviews, as well as in discussions held by the Gay Rap Group, that of the approximately 250 individuals who had contact with both elements of the program, only a small minority (10 percent is a rough estimate) had any history of psychiatric treatment, including outpatient psychotherapy, by other mental health practitioners. Therefore it appears that the gay program was able to establish contact with a group of individuals who, for a variety of reasons (perhaps including lack of need or fear of rejection), would not otherwise have had exposure to any professional help with social or emotional problems.

A recurrent theme is evidenced in discussions with the gay peer counselors of their reasons for volunteering for involvement in this kind of work. This theme seems to sum up the philosophy of both the Gay Peer Counseling and the Gay Rap Group programs: These individuals have in their lives undergone long periods of inner conflict and turmoil, both in the course of and as the price of their decisions to become identified with a feared and outcast subculture. It is their purpose and, through them, the purpose of the gay program to do everything possible to alleviate this unnecessary suffering.

The Case Manager Function in the Delivery of Social Services

ROBERT M. RYAN

Case manager job descriptions are as varied as the organizations in which this position can be found. The degree to which persons filling this position have been successful in improving the quality of care is equally varied. At least four factors help in understanding the diversity of the case manager position in human services organizations. First, the case manager was originally conceptualized as a new position in a different organizational arrangement of public social welfare service delivery systems. Second, this different organizational arrangement, which would combine a number of programs within a single structure, did not call for a change in administrative or management styles. Third, the functions of a case manager were never clearly specified or operationalized. Finally, neither the staff who were to become case managers nor the staff who were to work with this new breed of workers were prepared for the shift in service delivery patterns. While there are doubtless myriad other intervening factors, these four appear to be common to most agencies that have attempted to implement the position of case manager.[1]

The author's own observations, in working with various social welfare organizations, have revealed no less than five general patterns of implementation of the case manager position. On the one extreme is a person who "manages" cases by assigning them to various members of a particular unit within an organization as the result of being the unit supervisor; in other words, the agency has renamed the supervisory position "case manager." The other extreme is represented by a relatively large urban agency that has renamed its intake workers "case managers." The management of a case, in this instance, involves the intake worker's decision concerning the selection of an appropriate worker to *carry* the case. Within the limits of these two extremes are persons assigned as case managers who may be the liaisons between intake and service delivery workers and those who may be responsible for the liaison among agencies; finally, in one agency, all direct service practitioners are defined as case managers.

THEORETICAL MODELS OF CASE MANAGERS

The preceding observations illustrate the marked differences in responsibilities assigned to case managers throughout the country. When these positions are examined in relation to descriptions such as those found in publications of the American Public Welfare Assocation (APWA), the Social and Rehabilitation Service (SRS), and the Southern Regional Education Board (SREB), major discrepancies are immediately apparent.

Client Programmer

Bloedorn et al., in an APWA publication, talk of a *client programmer* who is a high-powered diagnostician. Operating at the point of intake, the programmer helps the client articulate unmet needs; assesses the available resources; and arrives, with the client, at a case prescription.

> . . . after the prescription is formulated, the primary function of the programmer reverts to "case management" which consists of review solely as indicated by the prescription and modification or termination thereof with the client. Thus case management stands in contradistinction to classical case-carrying by eliminating the latter's provision of counseling at regular intervals.[2]

Although the meaning of the preceding statement is not entirely clear, to have the most highly qualified members of agency staff act as client programmers can certainly be questioned. In spite of the need for and value of highly competent diagnosticians, they are not necessarily the "best" practitioners. The requisite skills of a good diagnostician are different from the requisite skills of a good therapist. The two may go together in some instances, but in at least as many instances they do not.

Service Manager

An SRS publication, *Building the Community Service Center*, like the APWA document, begins with a proposal for a comprehensive human services delivery system. This document identifies the *service manager*, whose primary responsibility is "working with the consumer to identify and clarify the nature of his difficulty and the kind of assistance he requires," as the key person in any given unit.[3] This document is much more specific than the APWA material in explicating the activities of a case manager.

The GSW/SM [generalist social worker/service manager] must be fully informed about the full range and quality of services available within the center through functional service units and service resources. On the basis of this knowledge, the GSW/SM makes a plan with the consumer for his use of the agency's services. In accordance with the plan, the GSW/SM gives immediate information and referral or other short-term service and arranges for the appropriate functional service unit, or units, to know what the plan is, to initiate work promptly, and to carry out the plan on schedule. The GSW/SM who makes the plan is kept informed of progress or lack of progress and of suggestions for change in the service plan; he coordinates the activities of the functional units when more than one unit is serving a consumer. Changes in service plans are made by the GSW/SM with the consumer. The consumer understands that the GSW/SM (and supporting staff) is his ally, supporter, and advocate and that he may rely on the GSW/SM for reconsideration of his situation and for replanning at any time. The GSW/SM may use case staffing or any other feasible method to draw in the experience and advice of the functional service units and service resources in replanning for more effective performance. Such changes are shared with and concurred in by the consumer.[4]

Generalist

Teare and McPheeters, in a monograph published by the SREB, focus on worker roles and tasks. They begin, not with an emphasis on service delivery systems, but on human need. They proceed to identify those factors that keep people from satisfying their basic needs. On the basis of this identification, criteria are formulated for developing service delivery systems and. for establishing jobs within those systems. The central figure in their formulation is the *generalist:* "the person who plays whatever roles and does whatever activities are necessary for his client at the time the client needs them. His primary assignment or concern is the client, not specific tasks or techniques." [5]

This formulation, illustrated in Figure 1, employs a two-dimensional matrix with "level of task" representing one dimension and "roles" the other dimension. Levels of worker tasks can be differentiated on the basis of three major intrinsic characteristics:

FIG. 1.   A HUMAN SERVICES TASK MATRIX

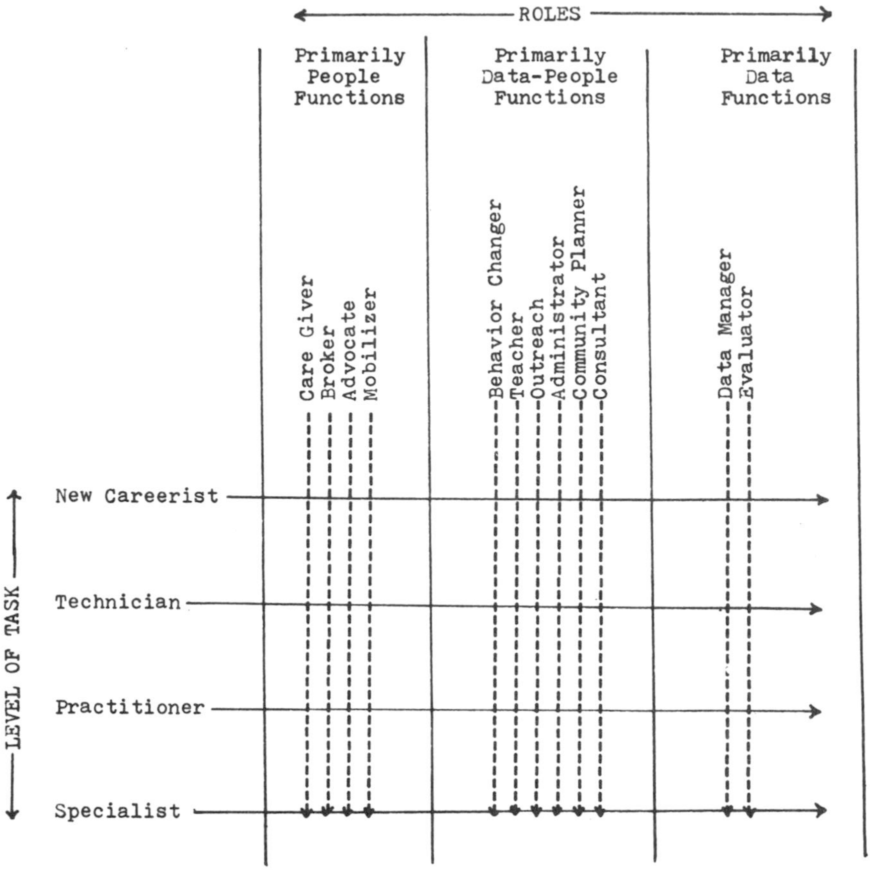

1. Complexity of the problem being dealt with by the worker
2. Difficulty of the task (in terms of technical skills and knowledge)
3. Risk (in terms of vulnerability of the client) if the work is poorly performed.[6]

Each dimension of this matrix (see Figure 1) is conceptualized as a continuum. The *level of task* dimension represents a worker's level of skill based on education and/or work experience. A Technician level practitioner, for instance, would be expected to have a higher level of skill than that expected of a New Careerist level worker, but would not be as competent as the Practitioner level worker. A Specialist represents the highest level of skill—however defined and however achieved.

The *roles* dimension illustrates a means for defining the activities, the work if you will, in which human services workers engage. Roles are subdivided into three groupings here, each reflecting a work emphasis, with each grouping, or combination of groupings or roles, intended to outline a given worker's job. Thus, one who engaged in all of these roles—some roles more than others, and with a higher level of skill in some roles than in others—would be called a generalist. A worker who was almost entirely engaged in the *data manager* and *evaluator* roles, for example, might be a researcher, i.e., specialist.

In brief, the intersecting dimensions of this matrix illustrate the view that workers engage in a variety of roles, or work activities, dependent on the work expectations. Level of education and amount of work experience are additional intervening variables in any consideration of definition of the work of human services workers. The interaction of these three variables, i.e., work expectations, level of education and amount of work experience, in relation to client need and agency purpose should define work expectations—not one or two of these factors (i.e., education and agency requirements) alone. Worker roles, as described below, are intended to present a general thrust pertaining to what workers do. Each of the roles incorporates all four levels of tasks, with the combination of all twelve roles representing the work of a generalist.

Human Service Worker Roles

Outreach

Implies an active reaching out into the community to detect people with problems and help them find help and to follow up to assure that they continue toward as full as possible fulfillment of their needs.

Broker

Involves helping a person or family get to the needed services. It includes assessing the situation, knowing the alternative resources, preparing and counseling the person, contacting the appropriate service, and assuring that the client gets to it and is served.

Advocate

This has two major aspects:

1. Pleading and fighting for services for a single client whom the service system would otherwise reject (because of regulations, policies, practices, etc.).

2. Pleading or fighting for changes in laws, rules, regulations, policies, practices, and so on, for *all* clients who would otherwise be rejected.

Evaluator

Involves gathering information, assessing client or community problems, weighing alternatives and priorities, and making decisions for action.

Teacher

Includes a range of teaching from simple teaching (i.e., how to dress, how to plan a meal) to teaching courses in budgeting or home management to teaching staff development programs; the teaching aims to increase people's knowledge and skills.

Behavior Changer

Includes a range of activities directed toward changing people's behavior rather precisely. Among them are simple coaching, counseling, behavior modification, and psychotherapy.

Mobilizer

Involves working to develop new facilities, resources, and programs or to make them available to persons who are not being served.

Consultant

Involves working with other persons or agencies to help them increase their skills and help them in solving their clients' social welfare problems.

Community Planner

Involves participating and assisting in planning—with neighborhood groups, agencies, community agents, or governments—for the development of community programs to assure that the human services needs of the community are represented and met to the greatest extent possible.

Care Giver

Involves giving supportive services to people who are not able to fully resolve their problems and meet their own needs, such as supportive counseling, fiscal support, protective services, day care and twenty-four-hour care.

Data Manager

Includes all kinds of data-gathering, tabulating, analysis, and synthesis for making decisions and taking action. It ranges from simple case data-gathering to preparing statistical reports of program activities to evaluation and sophisticated research.

Administrator

Includes all the activities directed toward planning and carrying out a program, such as planning, personnel, budgeting and fiscal operations, supervising, directing, and controlling.

Teare and McPheeters recognize that a given worker may not actually perform all these roles all the time, that the nature of a given worker's job will be such that level of skill will be higher in some areas than others, and that the thrust of the role statements is on what a worker does—not on his interactions with a client. Consequently, there is little discussion of client concerns in the role statements. These are spelled out in more detail in a subsequent document written by McPheeters and Ryan.[7]

Case Manager in Human Services Delivery System

The final theoretical model to be considered is incorporated in a document titled *The Human Services Organization: A Proposed Model.*[8] Originally written as part of an SRS-funded demonstration grant proposal, the case manager described in this monograph draws on selected concepts from each of the three preceding formulations. The case manager is described in the context of a *human services delivery system*, the design of which was strongly influenced by SREB notions concerning human need. The case manager functions as the central figure in this system, following the SRS formulation, with the APWA notion of a high level of skill in diagnosis and evaluation being central to the worker's activities.

Unlike the other three models, worker activities are conceptualized in terms of a human services generalist who carries both diagnostic and service delivery responsibilities. More specifically, as illustrated in Figure 2, the case manager is seen as one who is a diagnostician having special knowledge regarding the eligibility requirements of programs within a given service delivery system, as well as special skill in obtaining services from resources external to the system when necessary and appropriate.

Referring to Figure 1, the case manager would be expected to spend most of his time engaging in those roles labeled "Primarily People Functions"—*care giver, broker, advocate,* and *mobilizer*—and, from the "Primarily Data Functions" column, *evaluator.* A secondary set of roles are found in the "Primarily Data and People Functions" column: *behavior changer, teacher,* and *outreach.* These roles are client oriented,

Fig. 2. FLOWCHART FOR SERVICE DELIVERY

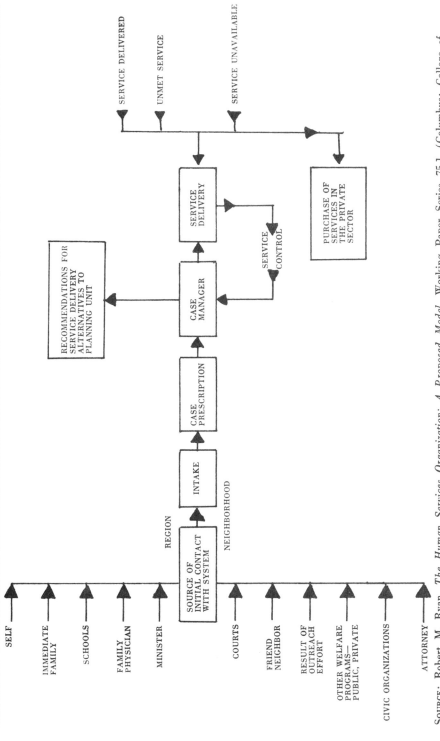

SOURCE: Robert M. Ryan, *The Human Services Organization: A Proposed Model,* Working Paper Series 75-1 (Columbus: College of Administrative Science, Ohio State University, 1975), p. 36.

tend to emphasize direct interaction with clients, and call for the case manager to work with both the client and the system. The nature of the work, coupled with the responsibilities of this worker, require the manager's interactions with the client to focus on the more concrete, tangible, and synthesizing activities necessary to "pull it all together" with the client.[9]

A third set of roles is geared toward the organization in which the case manager is employed. These roles, found in the "Data and People" and "Data Functions" columns, include *community planner, consultant, administrator, evaluator,* and *data manager.* There is an implicit recognition in these roles that a case manager—functioning in the manner described here—is in an ideal position to provide valuable information to the administrative and planning units concerning the quality of services available to consumers. In many respects, case managers may be in a better position than clients to evaluate programs and practitioners.

THE PROJECT MANAGER

Each of the four models falls short in several respects. The focus of each tends to be on the worker and/or worker interactions with a client. Each model presupposes a rearrangement of existing service delivery patterns, with new structures incorporating either a variety of existing programs or an alternative form of service delivery pattern. In no instance is consideration given to alternative managerial arrangements.

Social welfare organizations have tended to function on a vertical basis, with a strong emphasis on superior/subordinate relationships. These vertical relationships have been rationalized on the basis of professionalism and bureaucratic accountability issues; little apparent consideration has been given to client responsiveness. This appears to be true even though many of the proposed alternative service delivery patterns have been rationalized on the basis of improved service delivery.

If it is true that centralized human services delivery systems were conceptualized for the express purpose of improving the delivery of services to clients, and if it is true that the case manager was perceived as that worker in the system who is charged with responsibility for assuring that a client receives the services which are needed and wanted, then it seems to follow that a vehicle must be found for providing a case manager with the means to accomplish those responsibilities. A vehicle that seems to offer considerable promise is *project management.* This managerial style was originally conceived as a means for coordinating the efforts of a number of different units in the space program of the National Aeronautics and Space Administration. It has become widespread in industry, especially in research and developmental units. The central issue to which this form of management addresses itself is coordination:

> A project may be defined as an ad hoc team of human and nonhuman resources pulled together in some authority and responsibility relationships to accomplish an end purpose. In today's complex society an organization typically faces a "stream of projects" that provide the basic work opportunity for the members of the organization. The management of those projects requires a different approach to the delegation of authority and the exacting of responsibility from what is traditional in management thought.[10]

The promise to be offered by project management in human services agencies is one of coordination of personnel from various programs who are providing services to a given client. This management style would permit the various programs (e.g., vocational rehabilitation, public welfare, child welfare) to maintain their functional autonomy while permitting individual workers from these programs to come together on an ad hoc basis with respect to a given client. In such an instance, the case manager would be responsible for coordinating the efforts of these personnel around the unmet needs of a given client.[11]

Operationally, the case manager would function in a manner similar to that presented in Figure 2. Specialized services, if required, would be obtained from specialists assigned to various functional programs within and external to the agency. For the duration of a given program specialist's involvement with a given client, the specialist would be accountable to the case manager working with that client. If a client required one hour of family therapy per week for a year, for example, the family therapist would be accountable to the case manager for that fifty-two hours of work. The same would be true for other program specialists. Accountability to the case manager relates to service provided to a client. Professional accountability for the quality of that service, professional supervisory responsibility if you will, would remain with the unit to which that program specialist was permanently assigned.[12]

The case manager's responsibilities would include conducting case conferences with various program specialists, working with the client around implementation of recommendations, maintaining supportive involvement with the client, and *doing whatever necessary for and with the client at the time it needs to be done.*

This brief, oversimplified description of the case manager's functions is similar to that outlined in the service manager and human services delivery system models. It differs in that a greater emphasis is placed on the coordination function and a specific theory which offers definite promise for the implementation of such a model is identified.

CONCLUSION

Unlike an intake worker position, the case manager position is marked by diversity and confusion in its implementation. The case manager is conceptualized as a high-powered diagnostician having some service responsibilities. The position requires a practitioner who is prepared educationally as a human services generalist, preferably at the baccalaureate level. Implementation of this position places a high priority on coordination as well as diagnostic functions.

Project management, which is based on a matrix organizational structure, is proposed as a model having considerable promise. Social welfare organizations have usually been viewed as having only vertical relationships, but unmet client needs call for an organizational structure that is horizontal in operation; this need provides a strong rationale for the matrix structure. Human services organizations in particular would seem to benefit from the matrix model. Those social welfare agencies that purchase services from outside their own organizations, particularly when the case manager position is used to insure client receipt of necessary and appropriate services, would also benefit.

NOTES

1. *Integration of Human Services in HEW*, Vol. 1 (Washington, D.C.: Social and Rehabilitation Services, 1973).

2. Jack C. Bloedorn et al., *Designing Social Service Systems* (Chicago: American Public Welfare Association, 1970), p. 22.

3. *Building the Community Service Center* (Washington, D.C.: Social and Rehabilitation Services, 1970), p. 8.

4. Ibid., pp. 8–9.

5. Robert J. Teare and Harold L. McPheeters, *Manpower Utilization in Social Welfare* (Atlanta, Ga.: Southern Regional Education Board, 1970), pp. 23–24.

6. Ibid., p. 25.

7. *A Core of Competence for Baccalaureate Social Welfare and Curricular Implications*, by Harold L. McPheeters and Robert M. Ryan (Atlanta, Ga.: Southern Regional Education Board, 1971), expands on the manpower utilization material

by identifying the specific knowledge, skills, and values that should be expected of a Level III generalist. The work of Sid Pine with the Upjohn Institute in Washington, D.C., is also of interest in this regard.

8. Robert M. Ryan, *The Human Services Organization: A Proposed Model*, Working Paper Series 75-1 (Columbus: College of Administrative Science, Ohio State University, 1975).

9. Major textbooks that purport to address the skills and philosophy appropriate to this model include Robert W. Klenk and Robert M. Ryan, *The Practice of Social Work* (2d ed.; Belmont, Calif.: Wadsworth Publishing Co., 1974); Allen Pincus and Anne Minahan, *Social Work Practice: Model and Method* (Itasca, Ill.: P. E. Peacock Publishers, 1973); William J. Reid and Laura Epstein, *Task-Centered Casework* (New York: Columbia University Press, 1972); Max Siporin, *Introduction to Social Work Practice* (New York: Macmillan Publishing Co., 1975); and James K. Whittaker, *Social Treatment* (Chicago: Aldine Publishing Co., 1974).

10. David I. Cleland and William R. King, *Management: A Systems Approach* (New York: McGraw-Hill Book Co., 1972), p. 71.

11. John W. Stewart, "The Promise of Project Management," in Roland Mann, ed., *The Arts of Top Management* (New York: McGraw-Hill Book Co., 1971), pp. 326–338.

12. Keith Davis, "The Role of Project Management in Scientific Manufacturing," in David I. Cleland and William R. King, eds., *Systems, Organizations, Analysis, Management: A Book of Readings* (New York: McGraw-Hill Book Co., 1969), pp. 308–314.

Practice by Objectives

JOHN M. DALEY

Social work is being challenged to prove the effectiveness of its professional interventions. The call for professional accountability is viewed alternately as a threat or a challenge, depending on the practitioner's perspective and possibly the nature and source of the demand.[1] The current "crisis of accountability" has changed the complexion of the issue of accountability. In summary, the crisis refers to increasing pressure from *funding sources* to evaluate *systematically* the *outcomes* of professional interventions. Implicit in these demands by funding sources is at least the possibility that interventions or programs that are unable or unwilling to document the successful accomplishment of desired outcomes may suffer a reduction in their required resources.[2]

Given the inevitability of systematic evaluations of intervention outcomes on the demand of funding sources, this paper proposes Practice by Objectives (PBO) as a tool to assist social workers in the development of intervention objectives and strategies consistent with the needs of an outcome accountability model. PBO applies Management by Objectives (MBO) concepts and principles to a model of social work intervention that lends itself to the development of generic skills. PBO suggests the application of MBO not only to administrative functions of practice (e.g., personnel evaluation and development), but also to agency or program planning and evaluation, to community organizing, and to the planned interventions of direct practice workers with client systems.

Before introducing the PBO model, a few caveats seem appropriate: (1) Properly used, PBO can assist social workers to make better choices among interventions and programs competing for needed, but scarce, resources. It will not, however, make the hard decisions for them. (2) PBO can be used to support their claims for additional needed resources, based on the proved effectiveness and efficiency of their interventions. ("Effectiveness" refers to the accomplishment of desired results; "efficiency" is the ratio of resource input to desired result output.) It will not, however, directly create additional resources. (3) PBO cannot compensate for many of the problems that arise from deficiencies in social work's theoretical base or in its interventive skills themselves. These important issues must be addressed elsewhere. (4) Concern for setting and achieving objectives should not preclude active concern for the process of problem-solving. Social workers must be ever willing to monitor and question not only the attainment of objectives, but also the important issues of *why* and *how* they succeed, or do not succeed, in helping to solve problems.

The opening section of this paper reviews factors contributing to the need for a model such as PBO. Then a PBO model is elaborated, examples of the use of PBO are given, and the resistance to and advantages of PBO are discussed.

THE NEED FOR PBO

Historically, social workers have not had to account for the effectiveness of their professional interventions. Serious flaws persist in efforts to make professionals accountable to the consumers of services, either directly or through agency mechanisms.[3] The systematic evaluation of outcomes of professional intervention runs contrary to much of social work's heritage. Social workers' interest in program and intervention inputs (educational levels and numbers of practitioners) and process far exceeds their concern over outputs. As Newman and Turem note: "It is virtually in the nature of the social work profession to try to assist an individual who lays claim to assistance, regardless of whether anything can actually be done to help." [4]

The following factors, among others, have contributed to the emphasis on inputs and process: First, input and process models are virtually failure-proof. Lack of goal accomplishment can be viewed as supporting the need for more intervention or as a failure on the part of the client system. Second, broadly stated goals and limited resources may program failure into social interventions. Third, although much is known about specific social problems, less is known about the social conditions that contribute to or support problems or about reasonable intervention objectives and strategies given current resource levels. In summary, social workers may avoid facing "no-win" situations by emphasizing inputs and process; playing under no-win conditions, no one keeps score.

THE MODEL

Raia notes that MBO is a philosophy of management and

> a *process* consisting of a series of interdependent and interrelated steps:
> (1) the formulation of clear, concise statements of objectives; (2) the development of realistic action plans for their attainment; (3) the systematic

monitoring and measurement of performance and achievement; and (4) the taking of the corrective actions necessary to achieve the planned results.[5]

PBO is, similarly, both a philosophy of practice and a process of professional intervention. The logic of the models is similar, as is the basic premise that the steps in each model are interdependent.

Social intervention may be viewed as a problem-solving process in which a client system interacts with a change agent around mutually identified problem areas.[6] In each problem-solving episode, if intervention effectiveness is to be determined, the professional must (1) develop a set of negotiated objectives, based on an initial evaluation of the situation; (2) plan a strategy of intervention; (3) establish an information system to monitor the dynamics of the situation during intervention; (4) implement the change plan; (5) periodically compare the emerging situation, the objectives, and the results; and (6) based on these comparisons, as needed, develop further objectives, strategies, information, and evaluations.

Phase I: Situation

Analysis of the intervention situation requires of the professional the ability to process information inputs within a systematic framework that, at the minimum, includes data on the following factors: characteristics of client system(s), problem(s) characteristics, characteristics of service system(s), resources (needed and available), possible goals and objectives, target system(s), and strategies and tactics available.

Social policy goal statements are frequently statements of values phrased in broad, imprecise language and open to a variety of interpretations, some mutually incompatible.[7] PBO requires the translation of social policy goal statements into intervention objectives. Definitions of two key terms may clarify this discussion.

A *goal* is a descriptive statement of a desired future state. Goals are long-range, broad statements intended to provide a general direction for efforts. The statement may be in quantitative or qualitative terms. Goals may or may not be attainable.[8] Examples of goal statements are "to enhance family functioning," "to improve intra-agency or interagency coordination," and "to improve the health levels of all citizens."

In contrast, *objectives* are statements of desired results to be achieved. Objectives are shorter term and include an explicit time frame. As far as possible, they are expressed in quantitative, observable, measurable, concrete terms.[9] Examples of objectives are "to raise John's school grades to a B average by next semester," "to implement a central records system for x agencies by January next year," and "to reduce the infant mortality rate for x population by y percent by next year." Objectives should, at a minimum, meet Raia's criteria: An objective should present a challenge, be attainable, be measurable, and be relevant to the key elements of the professional's job. Objectives should specify actions and results within a specified time and resource framework, but need not address why or how actions are to be taken or results achieved.[10]

In PBO, objective-setting forms the basis for the operation of the model. Without specific statements of the desired outcomes of intervention, subsequent steps in the process are flawed.

It would probably be impossible and unwise to operationalize objectives for all elements of a social worker's job. In recognition of this, PBO emphasizes the identification of key areas relevant to overall performance. In each key area of performance, a limited number of objective statements are developed.[11] The selection of key areas and key objective statements within each area is important to insure the relevancy of the PBO systems to the major thrust of the professional intervention. While objective-setting itself will not insure success, PBO cannot rise above poorly stated or poorly selected objectives.[12]

Input constituencies (e.g., sanctioning or funding bodies) provide the resources needed by the practitioner and generally influence the development of the goals of intervention. Output constituencies (e.g., client system elements) also tend to influence the objectives of interventions.[13] PBO formalizes the process by which these constituencies influence intervention objectives.

PBO takes the value stance that whereas the practitioner should initiate objectives, input and output constituencies should participate in the negotiated development of mutually agreed upon objectives. The PBO model requires the mutual analysis of the proposed intervention situation and, based on common areas of concern for and appreciation of the situation, the negotiation of mutual objectives. Social work practice models currently being utilized (e.g., task-centered casework and the use of contracts in professional practice) appear congruent with the requirements of mutual objective-setting.[14]

Objective-setting negotiations serve a linkage function among the policymaking, administrative, supervisory, and direct service personnel of service systems.[15] The dynamic effects of the tensions generated by these negotiations help insure that in PBO objectives are mutually agreed on; this avoids the twin problems of the imposition of objectives from above and the laissez-faire situation of lower-echelon personnel pursuing personal objectives unrelated to or in conflict with program purposes.

The negotiated translation of goals into objectives has important implications for practice. Objectives will probably direct interventions at fewer and narrower targets of change. In specific intervention programs, the scope of the purpose may be more limited than at present. Some critics will see such a notion as unwise in that it leaves areas of client need unaddressed; others will interpret a narrower focus as further fragmenting service delivery systems; others will fear the loss of professional turf or resources in that the focus would be on fewer and narrower change targets. Each of these concerns has a degree of validity and deserves careful consideration. Professional discussion of these issues must include, however, a consideration of the alternatives. The continued adherence to interventions and programs without specification of objectives in a PBO-like model may condemn social work to a continuation of defending unproved and perhaps unprovable claims of intervention effectiveness.[16]

Phase II: Strategic Plan of Intervention

The preliminary situation analysis, problem definition, and negotiated objectives reflect a consideration of possible strategies. In PBO, the desirability of an outcome is a necessary but not sufficient precondition for acceptance of an objective. The objective must also be feasible.[17] Social workers' preoccupation with the desirability of their objectives and relative lack of concern for the feasibility have contributed to the profession's image of softheaded idealism. Armed with good intentions, they have accepted goals far out of proportion to available resources.[18]

The action plan, although initially an approximation to be used flexibly, requires the professional to explicate intervention steps and to ask whether the proposed activities, if successful, will probably lead to the attainment of the intended outcomes.[19] If this connection cannot be made, the feasibility factor requires reconsideration of the problem, objectives, resources, and strategies.[20]

Raia proposes one model of an action plan: (1) specify objectives, (2) define major activities necessary to achieve objectives, (3) identify and coordinate critical relationships among major activities, (4) establish appropriate structural and procedural elements necessary to attain desired outcomes, (5) establish time frames and benchmarks, (6) analyze resource needs and obtain additional resources if needed, and (7) review the process and modify the action plan if necessary.[21] Situational factors might require modifications of this planning model; however, the important point is that PBO demands a systematic, logical approach to action planning, including feasibility adjustments among the problem, objectives, resources, and strategy factors.

During the phase of preliminary plan development, benchmarks are identified and acceptable performance criteria and standards are speci-

fied. Single "hard" measures of performance are probably not immediately available for many social intervention objectives. Social workers
must, therefore, proceed with caution to insure that the objectives and
the performance criteria and standards address key performance areas.[22]

Phase III: Practice-Focused Information System

Social workers probably record more information and get less use from
their recording efforts than any other professionals. Current practice
models may or may not specify the uses of recording information on interventions. Recording serves a function in the supervision and education
of fledgling professionals and has administrative uses. Also, elements of
recordings are useful in monitoring the progress of intervention efforts,
including outcomes. Much of what is recorded, however, has little relevance to the professional's subsequent practice. It is, and perhaps should
be, lost. It is perceived by the professional to be an archaic ritual to be
endured as a necessary evil, perhaps an offering to the god of accountability.

Based on a preliminary set of negotiated objectives and on a tentative
plan that specifies intervention activities, however, the information system can form a logical link with efforts to evaluate and improve the effectiveness of interventions. Information used to form the preliminary analysis of the situation is used as baseline data within the information system.
Some materials currently recorded might be eliminated, and PBO would
require the gathering, analysis, and use of new information. As Weiss has
noted concerning accountability systems, few current data systems include, in their array of information, adequate explication of objectives,
plans, and outcomes needed for systematic evaluations of intervention
outcomes.[23]

The professionals directly involved must initiate such an information
system in negotiation with both input and output constituencies. The decisions about which data are to be collected must be based on the priority
information needs of the principal users, including the practitioner. This
direct benefit to the practitioner may lessen the perception that recording-
information systems are administrative burdens unrelated to "real" practice.[24]

The information system should be designed to provide feedback to
the professional at regular intervals during the intervention process. Research on MBO indicates that objective-setting and appropriate feedback
increase the quantity and quality of task performance. Appropriate feedback should be specific, relevant to the task, and timely to the actor so it
will support adjustments during the intervention process.[25]

Phase IV: Implementation of the Change Plan

A crucial element of the implementation phase of PBO is the systematic use of appropriate feedback to the practitioner as a stimulus to reworking problem definition, objectives, and action strategies. During the implementation phase, the objectives and planned intervention are scrutinized in light of feedback from the information system. Instead of "before and after" evaluations, this constitutes a "during, during, during" process of feedback, which not only facilitates the monitoring of progress in relation to previously established interim benchmarks and performance standards, but also allows midcourse adjustments of objectives, resource mixtures, and strategies.[26] Scheduling and control techniques provide professional tools during this phase. The principles of the Program Evaluation and Review Technique (PERT) may be applied not only to program evaluations, but also to microintervention situations.[27]

Phase V: Comparison of Emerging Situation, Objectives, and Results

Phase VI: Development of Further Objectives, Strategies, Information, and Evaluations

In a sense, the early specification of problem definition, objectives, strategies, and so on is intended not as a master plan, but as a working document to be adjusted in response to new information.[28] The orientation during these phases departs radically from traditional study, diagnosis, and treatment linear models wherein evaluation is addressed at the conclusion of the process, if at all. A fitting analogy to the PBO approach is the pharmacological model, wherein ingredient mixtures are adjusted during intervention to achieve desired outcomes. In the PBO approach, the evaluation of interventions or programs is less a success-failure dichotomy and more a disciplined process of expected adjustments to achieve a desired result.

EXAMPLES

Professionals need only reflect on their own experiences in fulfilling various roles (counselor, supervisor, administrator, planner, organizer, consultant) to appreciate the importance of these skills for each professional role. The following examples serve to illustrate the use of PBO:

    1. The administrator of a Community Action Program might be

wrestling with the consequences of a prior acceptance by the agency of the global, goal-like objective "to eliminate poverty." A counselor in the program might, in another room, be struggling with how to go about helping a welfare mother "improve her social functioning." Both, obviously, could benefit from a practice framework, such as PBO, that specified objectives, based on an evaluation of the client situation and negotiated with the client.

2. If a direct service practitioner would substitute for the goal-like objective "improve family functioning," the objective "by June, Mrs. G. should be able to tell Mr. G. when she disagrees with him about a common decision they must make" (e.g., how to spend their annual vacation), PBO could provide a framework of directed social intervention. This framework would include situation-analysis (what causes/contributes to the present unhappy situation?), negotiated objective-setting (what does the client seek to achieve?), and monitoring (in this example the client should participate fully in reviewing the progress of the intervention).

RESISTANCE TO AND ADVANTAGES OF PBO

PBO can identify interventions and programs that have failed to achieve their desired outcomes. This is not psychologically, politically, or economically attractive to any of the people involved. The professional himself must be considered a major barrier to a PBO accountability model.[29] Furthermore, PBO may challenge professional styles (as MBO challenges traditional management styles). PBO requires additional planning time, especially while—during its implementation—professionals are learning its required skills, including the documentation of PBO processes.[30]

PBO offers advantages similar to those of MBO, including improved planning and evaluation. PBO integrates task and humanistic needs of the organization and its members.[31] It offers additional advantages to social work: (1) By providing a practice model stressing generic skills, PBO may provide social workers with a skill core that will have applicability to a number of different roles/positions which they may play during the course of their careers. (2) It can provide a mechanism of accountability that helps fulfill a moral obligation of the profession to provide effectiveness feedback to its constituencies.

SUMMARY AND IMPLICATIONS

In summary, PBO is a practice model that emphasizes generic, interdependent skills. The first four phases of PBO form the skill core, and

Phases V and VI are formalized adjustment cycles, in a pharmacological frame of reference. PBO provides both a philosophy of practice that values evaluation of intervention outcomes and a single process which, it is contended, can be applied profitably to interventions at the micro-levels and macrolevels.

PBO necessitates the development of specific skills appropriate to each step of the problem-solving episode. A brief list of skills required by PBO includes the following: situation analysis, decision-making, objective-setting, negotiation, strategy-planning, information systems development, and intervention evaluation. More important, PBO stresses that weakness in any skill component materially affects the utility of the total model.

A brief review of specific skills necessary for one phase of PBO may illustrate the manner in which PBO lends itself to generic skill development. In Phase I, the skills required draw heavily on both the analytic and the interpersonal powers of the professional, specifically, situation analysis, negotiation, and objective-setting. A professional, whether administrator or direct service worker, must be able systematically to analyze situations, negotiate with constituencies, and set objectives for his own practice.

NOTES

1. *See,* for example, George Hoshino, "Social Services: The Problem of Accountability," *Social Service Review,* 47 (September 1973), pp. 373–383; Edward Newman and Jerry Turem, "The Crisis of Accountability," *Social Work,* 19 (January 1974), pp. 5–16; Marvin L. Rosenberg and Ralph Brody, "The Threat or Challenge of Accountability," *Social Work,* 19 (May 1974), pp. 344–350; and Reed Henderson and Barbara K. Shore, "Accountability for What? and to Whom?" *Social Work,* 19 (July 1974), pp. 387–388, 507.

2. Melvin Mogulof, "Future Funding of Social Services," *Social Work,* 19 (September 1974), pp. 608–613.

3. *See* Newman and Turem, op. cit., pp. 12–13; and Hoshino, op. cit., p. 375.

4. Newman and Turem, op. cit., p. 11. *See also* James G. Coke and John E. Hanson, "Political Context of Evaluation," in William C. Sze and Jane G. Hopps, eds., *Evaluation and Accountability in Human Service Programs* (Cambridge, Mass.: Schenkman, 1974), p. 43; Rosenberg and Brody, op. cit., pp. 344–346; and Hoshino, op. cit., pp. 376–378.

5. Anthony P. Raia, *Managing by Objectives* (Glenview, Ill.: Scott, Foresman & Co., 1974), p. 11. *See also* Peter F. Drucker, *The Practice of Management* (New York: Harper & Row, 1954) ; Douglas McGregor, *The Human Side of Enterprise*

(New York: McGraw-Hill Book Co., 1960); and George Odiorne, *Management by Objectives: A System of Managerial Leadership* (New York: Pitman Publishing Corp., 1965).

6. Ronald Lippett, Jeanne Watson, and Bruce Westley, *The Dynamics of Planned Change* (New York: Harcourt, Brace & World, 1958).

7. Hoshino, op. cit., pp. 376–378.

8. *See* Rosenberg and Brody, op. cit., p. 346; and Raia, op. cit., p. 23.

9. Raia, op. cit., p. 24; Stephen J. Carroll, Jr., and Henry L. Tosi, Jr., *Management by Objectives* (New York: Macmillan Co., 1973), chap. 4; George L. Morrisey, *Management by Objectives and Results* (Reading, Mass.: Addison-Wesley Press, 1970), pp. 52–63, chap. 5.

10. Raia, op. cit., pp. 57, 64.

11. Ibid., pp. 37, 46–47.

12. Carroll and Tosi, op. cit., p. 12.

13. Roland Warren, *Love, Truth and Social Change* (Chicago: Rand-McNally & Co., 1971), pp. 173–174.

14. *See* William J. Reid and Laura Epstein, *Task-Centered Casework* (New York: Columbia University Press, 1972), especially pp. 20–22, 94–106, 194; William J. Reid, "A Test of a Task-Centered Approach," *Social Work*, 20 (January 1975) pp. 3–9; and Anthony A. Maluccio and Wilma D. Marlow, "The Case for the Contract," *Social Work*, 19 (January 1974), pp. 28–37.

15. This multilevel linkage concept is drawn from James D. Thompson, "Common and Uncommon Elements of Administration," in Harry A. Schatz, ed., *Social Work Administration: A Resource Book* (New York: Council on Social Work Education, 1970), pp. 30–42.

16. Sydney E. Bernard, "Why Service Delivery Programs Fail," *Social Work*, 20 (May 1975), p. 210. Note the lively discussion on casework effectiveness engendered by Joel Fischer's article, "Is Casework Effective? A Review," *Social Work*, 18 (January 1973), pp. 5–21; "Points and Viewpoints," *Social Work*, 18 (July 1973), pp. 3–4, 104–110; and, from the macrointervention field, "The Future of Practice," in Robert Perlman and Arnold Gurin, *Community Organization and Social Planning* (New York: John Wiley & Sons and the Council for Social Work Education, 1972), pp. 269–277; and Newman and Turem, op. cit., pp. 14–15.

17. *See* Reid and Epstein, op. cit.; and Robert Morris and Robert H. Binstock, *Feasible Planning for Social Change* (New York: Columbia University Press, 1966).

18. *See* Fischer, op. cit.; and Roland L. Warren, "The Model Cities Program," *The Social Welfare Forum, 1971* (New York: Columbia University Press, 1971), pp. 140–158.

19. *See* Morrisey, op. cit., chap. 6, especially p. 75; and Carroll and Tosi, op. cit., pp. 80–82.

20. *See* Peter W. Chommie and Joe Hudson, "Evaluation of Outcome and Process," *Social Work*, 19 (November 1974), pp. 684–685; Raia, op. cit., p. 149;

George Hoshino and Thomas P. McDonald, "Agencies in the Computer Age, *Social Work*, 20 (January 1975), p. 12; Maluccio and Marlow, op. cit., p. 34; Walter S. Wikstrom, "Management by Objectives or Appraisal by Results," in Arthur C. Beck, Jr., and Ellis D. Hillman, eds., *A Practical Approach to Organizational Development Through MBO* (Reading, Mass.: Addison-Wesley Press, 1972), pp. 303–308.

21. Raia, op. cit., pp. 68–75.

22. *See* ibid., pp. 56–57; Murray B. Meld, "The Politics of Evaluation of Social Programs," *Social Work*, 19 (July 1974), p. 454; Carroll and Tosi, op. cit., pp. 83–86; and Morrisey, op. cit., pp. 108–130.

23. Carol H. Weiss, "Alternative Models of Program Evaluation," *Social Work*, 19 (November 1974), pp. 679–680; and Hoshino and McDonald, op. cit., pp. 12–14.

24. Weiss, op. cit., pp. 675–680. *See also*, for specific applications, Rosalie A. Kane, "Look to the Record," *Social Work*, 19 (July 1974), pp. 412–419; and Martha L. Urbanowski, "Recording to Measure Effectiveness," *Social Casework*, 55 (November 1974), pp. 546–553.

25. Carroll and Tosi, op. cit., pp. 5, 42.

26. Edward A. Suchman, "Action for What? A Critique of Evaluative Research," in Carol H. Weiss, ed., *Evaluating Action Programs* (Boston: Allyn & Bacon, 1972), pp. 56, 64, 80–81.

27. *See* Federal Electric Corporation, *A Programmed Introduction to PERT* (New York: John Wiley & Sons, 1963); and Morrisey, op. cit., pp. 81–87; and, for comments on specific corrective actions, pp. 132–136.

28. Charles E. Lindblom, "The Science of Muddling Through," *Public Administration Review*, 19 (Spring 1959), pp. 79–88.

29. *See* Carroll and Tosi, op. cit., pp. 51–52; and Rosenberg and Brody, op. cit., pp. 348–349.

30. Carroll and Tosi, op. cit., pp. 48–52.

31. Ibid., pp. 121–123, 129–139.

Supervision by Objectives

JOYCE S. WANDO

Current in-service training for first-line supervisors is being focused in large part on management skills. Too frequently, training sessions and teaching aids are a duplication or slightly revised version of training packages prepared for business and industry. Supervisory training needs to be relevant to social work, with content and teaching aids specifically related to it. Supervision by objectives can provide a management content base for developing relevant and creative approaches to social work supervision and, ultimately, service delivery.

The concept of setting measurable objectives at both the supervisory and practitioner levels has been resisted by some social workers. But measurable objectives are important guides for structuring and facilitating the delivery of services. Methodologies and strategies for accomplishing objectives, as well as the intangible aspects of supervision and practice, are appropriate concerns for supervisory counseling and consultation. Measurable objectives are also important as an accountability base for social workers, supervisors, and administrators in the interest of providing clients with relevant services delivered effectively and efficiently.

Definitions of management usually have a common theme—the accomplishment of organizational goals or objectives. The definitions differ in the emphasis on the process by which the goals or objectives are to be achieved. Management definitions culled from a variety of sources stress three processes:

1. Management involves planning, organizing, guiding, and controlling the organization's operations so that objectives can be met efficiently.

2. Management is the allocation and utilization of resources to achieve organizational goals.

3. Management is a social process: a process because it entails a series of activities that lead to the achievement of the organization's objectives and social because these activities are primarily interpersonal.[1]

A more accurate definition would probably include all three concepts. Management is a social process involving the acquisition and utilization of resources through planning, organizing, guiding, and controlling to achieve organizational goals and objectives.

The central thrust of the management process is setting objectives and getting results. The process is composed of four basic, interdependent functions: planning, organizing, directing, and controlling. Planning consists of the determination in advance of what should be done; organizing is the determination of the structure, resources, and activities necessary to carry out the organization's objectives; directing is the mobilization of the human activity required to meet the organization's objectives; and controlling assures the effective accomplishment of these objectives.

SETTING OBJECTIVES

A definition of terms may be useful to differentiate among purpose, goals, and objectives. Purpose may be considered simply as an organization's raison d'être. Goals and objectives may be viewed in two ways. In the first way, a distinction is made between them. Goals are considered general statements of intent derived from the organization's purpose, and objectives are considered specific, clearly defined statements that indicate the end toward which some action is directed; objectives, then, would be derivatives of goals. In the second way, no distinction is made between goals and objectives, and the terms are used interchangeably. The former view is used here.

Objectives are statements of results to be achieved. As ends toward which some action is directed, a commitment to action is essential in the formulation of objectives. They usually begin with the preposition "to," followed by an action verb. In addition, an objective should do the following:

1. Describe one basic result to be achieved.
2. State a target date for achievement.
3. Be as measurable as possible.
4. Fall within the scope of duties and responsibilities of the writer(s).
5. State what is to be achieved and when, avoiding why and how.
6. Contain simple language.
7. Be realistic, but challenging.

Examples

A. To provide educational leave, not exceeding one calendar year, for 12 percent of the paraprofessional staff over a three-year period.

B. To reduce the number of children over 8 years of age awaiting adoption by at least x percent within one year.

The wisdom of setting objectives is rarely questioned. But some social workers vigorously question the validity of attempting to set measurable objectives. The argument is advanced that social services involve intangibles (interpersonal relationships, counseling) as well as tangibles (shelter, clothing, food). Questions frequently asked are, "How do you measure intangible aspects of service?" and "How do you measure quality?" One approach to setting measurable objectives is for the supervisor to list the results to be achieved, select those that can be clearly measured, and write measurable objectives for them. The remaining items can be reserved for counseling and consultation between supervisor and practitioner. As more experience is gained in writing objectives, supervisors will find that most of their results to be achieved are measurable.

Results to be achieved by a first-line supervisor could include the following:

1. Audit of caseloads
2. Reduction in pending dictation
3. Assessment of workers' ability to form in-depth, goal-directed client/worker relationships

Measurable objectives can easily be set for 1 and 2: to select two cases per month from each caseload for supervisory audit and to reduce pending dictation by 50 percent within three months. The third result to be achieved can be accomplished through supervisory counseling and consultation.

Measurable objectives, unfortunately, can become a numbers game, that is, attention may be fixed on the quantitative element rather than the result to be achieved. In objective B cited earlier, the basic result to be achieved is a reduction in the number of children over 8 years of age awaiting adoption. The quantitative element x percent within a year is merely an indicant by which to gauge the accomplishment of the result to be achieved. A numbers game is played when attention is fixed on the x percent and it is seen as having to be reached at all costs. The single-minded pursuit of an objective means that the supervisor has learned the name of the game, not the spirit of it.

When objective B is stated in measurable terms, according to the criteria mentioned previously, it seems to disregard the intangible elements of service in its accomplishment. The process by which the result is to be achieved, as well as the intangible aspects of the service, are appropriate concerns for counseling and consultation between supervisor and practitioner.

Unit Objectives and Individual Objectives

A set of objectives for an organizational unit is the basis that determines its activities. These are the activities performed by all members of the unit—supervisor and staff. For example, three objectives for a foster care unit of a child welfare agency could be stated as follows:

1. To complete x hours of orientation training for all foster parents no later than one week prior to their receiving their first placement.

2. To evaluate all active foster homes twice a year.

3. To increase the number of foster homes by x percent within y years.

A set of objectives for an individual determines the job to be performed and can be thought of as a different way to formulate a job description. Individual objectives actually represent a single person's expected contribution toward accomplishing the objectives of the unit and, ultimately, the fulfillment of the organization's purpose. Both supervisor and supervisee have individual objectives.

Unquestionably, supervisors must make the final determination of the individual objectives of supervisees. For the supervisor to prepare a list of arbitrary individual objectives for a supervisee is self-defeating, however. First, it is extremely difficult for people to develop a sense of commitment to accomplishing a list of directives. Second, the response to arbitrary individual objectives is likely to be resistance, both covert and overt. Third, setting arbitrary objectives deprives the supervisor of the knowledge and experience of those who perform the unit's work. Finally, arbitrary individual objectives can be causal factors in low staff morale, supervisor/supervisee communication difficulties, and failure to accomplish the unit's objectives.

Setting individual objectives should be a cooperative venture between supervisor and supervisee that meshes the need to accomplish the unit's objectives with the needs, goals, and skills of the staff person. A set of individual objectives for a first-line supervisor might include the following:

1. To conduct a quarterly performance conference with all unit staff.

2. To conduct a supervisory audit of x percent of the cases in each caseload every month.

3. To hold unit meetings at least twice a month.

4. To submit monthly progress/statistical reports no later than three working days after the end of each month.

5. To submit a written unit plan of proposed special activities for the next month by the last working day of each month.

After objectives have been set, plans of action for implementing them are necessary. A plan of action is a proposal to convert a present condition into some future condition (the objective). It is a statement of the activity required to accomplish the objective.

Example

Unit objective: to reduce pending dictation by 50 percent within three months.

Plan of action for supervisor:

1. List cases with pending dictation.

2. Confer with clerical supervisor regarding expected increase in dictation by unit.

3. Schedule additional time for use of dictating machine.

4. Confer with individual workers regarding their plans to reduce pending dictation.

CONTROLLING

The controlling function of management assures the effective accomplishment of the organization's objectives. It consists of three interrelated activities: establishing performance standards, measuring performance against those standards, and taking corrective action. Standards are predetermined criteria against which performance is measured; familiar standards are school grades, civil service exams, and governmental housing codes. Performance standards are guides for evaluating progress toward achieving objectives. The term "performance standards" may be used in reference to the performance of an individual, a unit of workers, a department, an office, or a product such as an airplane, a shoe, or a typewriter; each can have predetermined criteria against which its actual performance is measured. Performance standards as used by supervisors of social services most often refer to predetermined criteria for measuring individual employee work results.

Setting Performance Standards

For illustrative purposes, setting performance standards will be discussed in relation to casework, but the concepts presented are applicable to all phases of social services. Standards are a means of evaluating individual performance for the purpose of employee development, promotion, work assignment, compensation, and disciplinary action. They may also serve as a means of self-evaluation. Establishing standards involves two steps: determining what is to be measured and determining what constitutes acceptable performance. Setting standards for casework that measure both the quantitative and qualitative aspects of service is not easy. Assessment of the quality of service in the context of predetermined service objectives seems an appropriate concern for customary counseling and consultation. The focus here will be measurable aspects of service delivery.

Actually, the aspects of casework that lend themselves to some form of measurement are numerous. The following list of measurable aspects of service delivery is by no means complete and is offered merely as a thought stimulant:

Client contacts, complaints, referrals
Cases opened and/or closed, completeness of records, number of cases
Agency-sponsored client activities (information meetings, trips for children and the elderly)
Caseworker community involvement
Case conferences (with outside agencies)
Period of client service
Waiting lists (adoptions, residential placement, nursing home placement)
Current dictation
Staff turnover
Percent of overtime
Accuracy in completion of forms
Goal-directed client/caseworker relationships

Some of the areas mentioned are clearly subjective, and others suggest varying degrees of objectivity-subjectivity. Yet, each can serve as an indicant of successful performance.

After identifying measurable performance, what constitutes acceptable performance must be determined. Measurement is usually expressed in terms of numbers, percentages, time, completion points, and money. Each of the measurable aspects of casework in the preceding list can be related to one or more of the measuring devices:

Numbers

Cases opened and closed, client contacts, referrals, waiting lists
Agency-sponsored activities
Number of cases

Percentages

Staff turnover, overtime, current dictation
Client contact (home, office, phone)
Accuracy in completion of forms
Client complaints
Caseworker community involvement—percent of time

Time

Period of client service
Follow-through on client/caseworker goals (time lapse)
Caseworker community involvement—percent of time

Completion Points

Referrals—follow-up on outgoing requests for service
Dictation—transcribed and in record
Case records—contain necessary information and documents

What is being measured and what constitutes acceptable performance are italicized in the following list of standards:

1. *Dictation* will be kept current for at least *90 percent* of the caseload.

2. Caseworkers will provide *service* for *forty-five active* cases.

3. *Disposition* of protective service referrals are to occur within *forty-five* days of acceptance.

4. Intake studies are complete when *all questions* are answered and the *required documents are part of the record.*

Established performance standards help supervisors focus on the work to be accomplished. Thus less attention needs to be devoted to more nebulous issues, such as attitudes, attire, neatness, and work habits. These may indeed be important issues and if they are factors in the acceptable performance of the work, they will be related to the specific aspects of the assigned tasks that they affect.

Measuring Performance

The periodic written performance appraisal that is part of the employee's official work record is most commonly associated with measuring performance. Performance measurement, however, is a continuous activity, although it is not necessarily labeled as such. The day-to-day guidance provided by the supervisor is done in the context of both standards and objectives. Personal observation, supervisory conference, and review of case records, monthly reports, and work plans are used by supervisors in an ongoing activity of weighing planned performance against actual performance. Once a performance discrepancy is perceived, corrective action may be required.

Taking Corrective Action

It is not always necessary or desirable to take corrective action every time a performance discrepancy, or gap, is perceived. Discrepancies can be relatively minor or of temporary duration. A performance gap may exist because (1) there are obstacles to performing, (2) desired performance is punishing, (3) nonperformance is rewarding, (4) desired performance does not seem important, or (5) a skill deficiency exists. Uppermost in the supervisor's mind should be the question: Why does a performance gap exist? The answer to that question forms the basis for determining what corrective action, if any, is indicated.

Measuring actual performance against planned performance is a feedback mechanism for improving individual performance. The action required to correct individual performance gaps is an aspect of mobilizing human activity for the accomplishment of organizational objectives, the guiding function of management.

EXAMPLE OF SUPERVISION BY OBJECTIVES

In the following example, a format is given for supervision by objectives. In practice, however, a number of goals would be derived from the purpose, each with a set of objectives and performance standards.

Agency Purpose

To provide a wide range of services designed to assure that every child accepted for service develops and matures in a protected environment and has the opportunity for having wholesome interpersonal relationships.

Goal

To evaluate and act on every report of child neglect, abuse, or exploitation received by the agency.

Unit Objective

To determine the validity of reports within x day(s) of receipt.
Performance Standards:
> During review period, (1) x percent of determinations were made within the specified time, and (2) x percent of determinations were consistent with prevailing agency policy.

Individual Objectives

Caseworker:

To complete investigation on assigned cases within x weeks.
Performance Standards:
> 1. Complaints from field contacts do not exceed x percent per month.
> 2. X percent of investigations occur within specified time.

Supervisor:

To conduct audit of 2 percent of the cases in each caseload every month.

NOTES

1. Lewis Benton, *Supervision and Management* (New York: McGraw-Hill Book Co., 1972); Fremont Kast and James Rosenzweig, *Organization and Management: A Systems Approach* (New York: McGraw-Hill Book Co., 1970); and William H. Newman, Charles E. Sumner, and E. Kirby Warren, *The Process of Management* (4th ed.; Englewood Cliffs, N.J.: Prentice-Hall, 1976).

Developing a Rural New Town

SHIMON S. GOTTSCHALK

Is it fair to assert that increasing numbers of social workers are becoming disenchanted with grass-roots community organization practice? The disappointing experiences of the 1960s appear to have left their mark. On the one hand, there is greater sensitivity to the threat and fact of "welfare colonialism"; social workers in general and community organizers in particular have become more explicitly aware of their role as agents of social control. On the other hand, community organizers are often disillusioned by the apparent futility of political activism at the grass-roots level. This society is one in which those decisions that most importantly shape people's lives seem to be ever more distantly removed from people's ability to influence them.

There probably is no way to counter this pessimism and skepticism head-on. Arguments and exhortations to the contrary will be to no avail. The response is most appropriately located in practice. It is not that the critics and skeptics are entirely wrong, but rather that community organization practice must adapt to the new politics and ideologies of the times. The author's experience suggests that community organizers should learn to become less dependent on governmental support and should place ever greater emphasis on local and ethnic autonomy. They need to reexamine their traditional role, perhaps departing even further from the client/worker, implicitly therapeutic, model.[1] Finally, the significance and impact of community organization might be greatly enhanced if the substance of practice were to extend beyond the familiar social service strategy into economic development.

New Communities, Inc. (NCI), a social and economic development project now in its seventh year, constitutes an attempt to create an attractive, feasible alternative to urbanization for marginal, rural families. The significance of such an effort, especially in the light of the massive rural-urban migration of the last two decades, need not be emphasized. Suffice it to say that, despite this large migration, the aggregate number of poor families remaining in rural areas has remained constant.[2]

Located in Lee County, Georgia, NCI is in nominal possession of some six thousand acres of heavily mortgaged farmland and woodland. It lays claim to being the largest landholding controlled by a black community group anywhere in America. Its annual operating budget exceeds half a million dollars. Some thirty-five families are currently earning their livelihood from NCI, though most of these families do not physically live on the land. The major operation is agriculture—growing peanuts, corn, soybeans, cattle, hogs, and some vegetables. NCI also operates a roadside farmers' market/grocery store and a day care and remedial education program and, in its alliance with the Southwest Georgia Project, conducts a variety of community organizing efforts, cultural events, and the like.[3]

ORIGINS

The concept of a rural new town has distinctly ideological origins. In 1967–68, while liberal forces in the nation were beginning to disengage themselves from the euphoria of "We shall overcome," and while the forces of opposition to the war in Vietnam were beginning to gather force, a small group (including the author), representing a variety of academic and professional disciplines, began to gather in Exeter, New Hampshire, under the leadership of 80-year-old Ralph Borsodi. Borsodi had been active in the back-to-the-land movement during the Great Depression.[4] He and others in the group were influenced by the economic theories of Henry George.[5] Another ideological strain that contributed to the thinking of the group was the Gandhian notion of "constructive program."[6] Gandhi taught that *satyagraha* (a word he translated from the Sanskrit as "truth-force") is to be given expression not only as a method of protest by means of nonviolent resistance, but also in constructive work, by creating new, liberating institutional alternatives. The idealism and practice wisdom of social work community organization served as a further source of inspiration. Above all, this mixed group of economists, sociologists, social workers, and political activists was united in its commitment to the ideal of social justice, to be achieved through experimentation with the establishment of institutions embodying economic justice; these institutions were to be created and sustained by the people themselves from the grass roots up.

Gradually the idea of a rural new town—built on New Deal precedents, the Mexican *ejido*, and the experience of Israeli *moshav*—emerged.[7] The central idea was to acquire a large tract of land, most of which was to be developed collectively, while small plots for houses and private gardens were to be leased to the residents. The development would be not only agricultural but also industrial and commercial, organized as a community-owned enterprise, a Community Development Corporation (CDC). The necessary social, political, and educational institutions would evolve primarily out of the needs and demands of the residents.[8]

These concepts and plans were originally developed for possible application overseas, in India, Latin America, and the Philippines. Only gradually did the Exeter group move toward a recognition of their applicability to underdeveloped areas in the United States. The first practical move in this direction came in the summer of 1968, when a trip to Israel by six southern black leaders was sponsored jointly by the Exeter group and the National Sharecroppers Fund, with the financial support of the Norman Fund, a charitable foundation. These travelers, greatly impressed by their experience, served as the nucleus of the organization, eventually called NCI, that began to be formed in Atlanta, Georgia, in the fall of that year. In early 1969 a large tract of land costing over $1 million was located in Lee County, Georgia, and an option was taken on it. After a frantic year of fund raising among church groups and private foundations, the sale was consummated in January 1970.[9]

NCI has survived, since that eventful day nearly six years ago, seemingly struggling from problem to problem and from crisis to crisis:

1. The annual mortgage payments and taxes of over $100,000 have been a constant threat to survival. But even without considering these annual obligations, the farm operation has, to date, not yet turned an economic profit. The total operation has suffered from a chronic shortage of investment capital.

2. NCI has often suffered from inept, inexperienced management. Inadequate economic planning, poor bookkeeping, unclear lines of authority, and inadequate concern for public relations are some of the many problems attributable to a lack of management skills.

3. An initial Title I-D (community development) planning grant from the Office of Economic Opportunity (OEO) for nearly $100,000 was approved in 1970. It was never followed up by additional OEO funds primarily, though not only, because of political opposition on the local and state levels.

4. For several years, the vegetable crops were harvested annually by college student volunteers (a practice now discontinued). The conflicts between local people and volunteers on the one hand and between black and white college students on the other served as a major and dismaying source of disruption.[10]

5. A major conflict arose between "management" and "workers" in 1974. The workers began to seek affiliation with the United Farm Workers and to demand higher pay and better working conditions. Meanwhile, those in management positions and most board members countered with the argument that in a community enterprise such as this, all are one: there is no place for labor-management distinctions in the traditional sense.

6. A social survey conducted in 1969 among a sampling of ninety-two rural black families in and near Lee County indicated that, more than anything else, they hoped that NCI might be able to provide them with better houses (not jobs, money, social services, and so on). To date, NCI has been unable to move toward meeting this popular demand. There is no estimate of how many prospective residents have become disenchanted by this time.

7. The deep-seated racism indigenous to the rural South has been a source of potential or real threat throughout the history of NCI. When fires broke out in the woodlands, arson was suspected. When commercial dealings with local merchants were undertaken, the prices offered were suspect. When a local ordinance was enforced or a permit sought, the exercise of racial bias was to be assumed.

Yet, despite these seemingly endless crises and perennial problems, and many others too embarrassing and petty to mention, NCI continues to live. *Problems and crises are not solved; they are outlived.* The discussion that follows makes no pretense of explaining how this process works. The more modest aim is to identify, based on NCI experience to date, some of the key issues encountered and insights gained that are likely to have relevance for others who are similarly engaged in contemporary community organization/economic development practice. The discussion centers on the role of the social worker, the dilemma of CDCs, and the social planning process.

THE ROLE OF THE SOCIAL WORKER

From the time of his earliest involvement, the author's primary role has been that of idea man, adviser, friend, and occasional publicist, fund raiser, grant writer, mediator, and social researcher. He has been a member of the board of directors of NCI from the time of its inception but has never been a formal employee of NCI and has never asked, nor received payment, for his services. The author resides in Florida, some one hundred miles from Lee County. Although he has never denied nor consciously hidden his professional identity, in the minds of NCI members he has never been viewed primarily as a social worker. To these people the term "social worker" has a distinctly "public welfare" connotation and has little to do with agricultural and economic development. Perhaps it has been a mistake, but the author has not chosen to devote himself to the effort of attempting to change this narrow image of the social worker. There have been other, more pressing issues.

The leaders of NCI have a generalized mistrust of "experts," an intuitive sense that experts, even when well intentioned, tend to exploit, misunderstand, and impose their own values in a manner which does violence to the ideals of NCI. The young clergyman who is chairman of the board and president of NCI and has served as the major leadership force over the past six years has consistently insisted on a policy of radical self-determination. According to this view, the people must learn from doing—often from doing and failing and then trying again—with minimal interference and advice from the outside. Thus, if decisions are made by the board and not acted on, it is because there has been insufficient popular readiness for action. The success of NCI is to be measured, not in terms of monetary profits or other easily measurable accomplishments, but rather in terms of personal growth in the sense of self-confidence and dignity of the people.

Much of the preceding may sound like rhetoric, but there is ample evidence that NCI has conducted much of its business in the shadow of these principles. The success of NCI, in the traditional sense of the word, has been severely constricted because of this approach. More than once this policy has cost heavily in financial terms and has alienated well-intentioned but impatient friends.

Within the context of the quasi-caste system that continues to characterize most of the rural South, the word of the "man" (the white man) is experienced by most poor black as the expression of an absolute; that is, the "man's" word and the power that is implicit within it is experienced as a fact rather than an expression of opinion or of an idea. In NCI the presence and the words of the author, one of the few white persons on the board of directors, have been received inevitably within the light of this experience. In theory, the danger rests at both extremes: either to accept the word of the white man uncritically or to reject it out of hand. Whereas all members of NCI have consistently behaved in relation to each other (though not to the external world) as if this cross-racial issue had been fully resolved, in effect, it remains only a few inches beneath the surface. For each individual, depending on his particular experiences, background, and personality, it continues as a somewhat different, unspoken problem.[11]

The author began his association with NCI with a view of himself as a moderately experienced social administrator, social planner, and community organizer. He somewhat naively produced endless pages of plans, organizational models, and programmatic suggestions, hoping that one or another of these might take root or serve as the stimulus for new ideas or alternative approaches. Perhaps in some small sense that has happened. Yet, over the years, he has learned to assume an ever less assertive role, volunteering only specific, circumscribed skills, such as in proposal writing or in public relations. In meetings, his approach has been less one of submitting suggestions and plans than of aiming to remain alert to the opportunity to lend support to initiatives taken by others and of raising pertinent, but overlooked, questions.

THE DILEMMAS OF CDCs

The early plans have begun to gather dust, but NCI survives, and changes, and grows. Slowly but firmly a rural CDC is taking root. A CDC has been defined as an organization "created and controlled by the people living in impoverished areas for the purpose of planning, stimulating, financing, and when necessary, owning and operating businesses that will provide employment, income, and a better life for the residents of these areas." [12] CDCs are business corporations having primary social welfare objectives. As businesses, they need to remain economically solvent and, ideally, show a profit. In the service of their social welfare goals, they must remain maximally democratic and responsive to the demands of their local constituencies.

Unfortunately, these two goals—business success and community responsiveness—are frequently in conflict. For example, when the good, kind, friendly, but somewhat incompetent farm manager at NCI had to be dismissed, it became a difficult, drawn-out ordeal for the leadership group. At other times, when new personnel were hired, there were occasional charges of favoritism, or even nepotism. And yet, one might justly ask, "Is this wrong?" Most NCI members agree that friends and relatives need and deserve the jobs more than others who, though they may be more highly qualified, come from distant places and are not a part of the community.

At the annual meeting of NCI that took place in the winter of 1974, members were invited by the chairman to give expression to their dreams for the future of NCI. One of the people arose and courageously suggested that, hopefully, one day a big factory—perhaps an automobile assembly plant—might be established on NCI land. There would be jobs and prosperity for all. Many enthusiastic heads nodded in agreement. A beautiful dream, they thought. But no, warned the much more cautious and suspicious chairman. If NCI stands for anything, it stands for self-determination and community control. Prosperity at the price of a return to slavery is the paradise of fools . . . The chairman won the day.

In the long run NCI must achieve economic independence. The major donor foundations and church groups are impatiently awaiting this event. From their point of view, this is a costly experiment. It may well be wondered how long they will be prepared to give their support while the people at NCI search for and find appropriate expression for their true souls.

THE SOCIAL PLANNING PROCESS

To the extent that social planning has reference to the design of future reality, it has little relevance to what has occurred at NCI. At best, the plans and ideas projected by the Exeter and Atlanta groups served to provide an initial source of inspiration. They specified an abstract communal idea that continues to serve as a symbolic rallying point, but rarely as a practical guide for decision or action.

But planning is more than designing; it is also doing. Social planning is not simply planning for people; it is planning with people, involving them maximally in every step of the action. This has been the explicit planning strategy from the very beginning of NCI. Thus all meetings of all groups and committees have been open to all interested individuals, and broad participation has been encouraged, often at a severe cost to efficiency and order. Especially in the early days, this process often left the author with a sense of utter confusion. What had been decided? Indeed, what had been discussed? Over the years board meetings became better organized and the author's ear more finely attuned. Today these meetings are more regularly in the control of the more experienced, more skilled members of the group. But when decisions are made, even now one never knows whether they will be acted on. The decision-making process remains largely a learning/teaching experience. In effect, the real operational decisions are made in living and doing. Beyond this, the key decisions affecting the life and death of NCI are made either completely externally (e.g., in the offices of the large donor foundations) or by members of a small executive group.[13]

The familiar planning paradigm leading from problem definition to selection from among alternative solutions, to implementation, and then to the evaluation of results has rarely applied to NCI.[14] In large part, long-range planning and careful decision-making have been forced to give way to the frequently recurring need to respond to crises. There have often been no real options, only imperatives that forced decisions. At other times, some of the most important decisions seemed to be made more in the light of faith than of knowledge. Thus, when six years ago the board of NCI agreed to the purchase of six thousand acres in Lee County, thereby undertaking a financial obligation of more than $1 million, little attempt was made to think ahead and determine how the annual payments might be met. On all traditionally rational grounds, it was a foolhardy decision. And yet, it has turned out to be one of the most crucial and best decisions NCI has made. In view of the present political climate in America, which New York bank or which large insurance company would dare to foreclose on the mortgage to the largest black landholding in the country? Given the very size of NCI, how can the largest charitable foundations in America dare let it fall?

The short-range effect of the social planning process is one of precariously keeping NCI afloat while providing exceptional opportunities for what Friedmann would call "mutual learning," which in this case benefits a relatively small number of rural people and black community leaders and a few stray sheep (such as the author) within a unique experimental setting.[15] But who knows? One day soon the whole undertaking may really take off and become a model for a much-needed rural renaissance in America.

CONCLUSIONS

Whether NCI has to date been a success or a failure is, of course, a matter of individual judgment. For the author, it has served as a marvelous learning experience. The following list serves as a simplified set of randomly organized, tentative conclusions:

1. In grass-roots community organizing, the social worker must genuinely think and act in a manner which betrays his sincere conviction that he has at least as much to learn as to teach.

2. The community organizer must never allow himself to forget that what may be just another project for him is life itself for the people involved.

3. Noncoercive, planned social change is a long, tiresome process requiring great patience. One of the reasons governmental funding for this kind of undertaking is inappropriate is that the usual annual measures of progress and output are irrelevant if not disconcerting.

4. In community organization efforts of this type, survival itself—not specific outputs—becomes the major measure of success. Out of survival over time may come the kind of individual and collective growth that gives meaning to the entire effort. The net result is likely to be one that is quite different from the one originally intended.

5. The community organizer must have faith and trust in the people. This trust must exceed even the trust in his own expertise. Poor people especially have a phenomenal capacity to cope in the face of adversity, a capacity that far exceeds in importance the professional worker's ability to help, advise, or enable.

In the spring of 1975, a commercial farm management firm was engaged by some of the donor friends of NCI to conduct a comprehensive business evaluation of current conditions and future prospects. The summary of the firm's recommendations concludes with the following paragraph:

> From our point of view, NCI defies all laws of economic survival. It should not be in existence because it is highly financed at 8½–9 percent interest, directed by committees, managed by a preacher and a former Extension agent, and operated by a group of poor individuals, some of whom are illiterate. There is no way such a combination can survive; but it has, it is, and it will survive because these people want to succeed.[16]

NOTES

1. *See* Ronald Lippitt, Jeanne Watson, and Bruce Westley, *The Dynamics of Planned Change* (New York: Harcourt Brace, 1958).

2. U.S. Department of Agriculture, Economic Research Service, *The Economic Conditions of Rural America in the 1970s* (Washington, D.C.: U.S. Government Printing Office, 1971).

3. The Southwest Georgia Project is an offshoot of the Student Nonviolent Coordinating Committee. It predates NCI in southwest Georgia and has, on the whole, a somewhat more politically activist orientation. NCI was built, in large part, on the social and political foundations created by the Southwest Georgia Project.

4. *See* Ralph Borsodi, *Flight from the City* (New York: Harper & Bros., 1935).

5. *See* Henry George, *Progress and Poverty* (New York: Random House, 1880).

6. M. K. Gandhi, *Non-Violent Resistance* (New York: Schocken Books, 1961), pp. 68, 100.

7. The Mexican *ejido* and the Israeli *moshav* are two types of rural, agricultural collective. For a fuller discussion, *see* Raanan Weitz, *From Peasant to Farmer, A Revolutionary Strategy for Development* (New York: Columbia University Press, 1971).

8. *See* Shimon S. Gottschalk, *Rural New Towns: Toward a National Policy* (Cambridge, Mass.: Center for Community Economic Development, 1971).

9. For a more complete history of the early years of NCI, *see* Shimon S. Gottschalk and Robert Swann, "Planning a Rural New Town in Southwest Georgia," *Arête*, 1 (Fall 1970).

10. A black African participant observer, because of his marginal role was in a unique position to report in writing on these interactions: Harrison O. Akingbade, *Community Relations Aspects of Featherfield Farm.* Unpublished manuscript, Cambridge, Mass., Goddard Graduate School of Social Change, 1972.

11. This paragraph reflects, in part, the insights of Dr. James A. Goodman, who joined in the discussion of this paper at NASW's Twentieth Anniversary Professional Symposium.

12. Geoffrey Faux, *CDC's: New Hope for the Inner City* (New York: Twentieth Century Fund, 1971), p. 29.

13. *See* Peter Bachrach and Morton Baratz, "The Power of Non-Decision-Making," in Edward Banfield, ed., *Urban Government* (New York: Free Press, 1969), pp. 454–464.

14. *See* Lippitt, Watson, and Westley, op. cit., p. 123. *See also,* Arnold Gurin and Robert Perlman, *Community Organization and Social Planning* (New York: John Wiley & Sons, 1972), p. 62.

15. John Friedmann, *Retracking America: A Theory of Transactive Planning* (New York: Doubleday & Co., 1973), pp. 183–185.

16. Max W. Evans, Vice-President, Nortrust Farm Management, Inc., ᵐphis, Tenn., in cover letter to *New Communities, Inc., Report,* February 13, ʼ. 3.